A CURE
WORSE THAN
THE DISEASE

Fighting Discrimination Through
Government Control

A CURE
WORSE THAN
THE DISEASE

Fighting Discrimination Through Government Control

by

M. Lester O'Shea

Foreword by

Walter E. Williams

HALLBERG PUBLISHING CORPORATION
Nonfiction Book Publishers – ISBN 0-87319
Tampa, Florida 33623

ISBN Number 0-87319-048-3

Copyright © 1999 by M. Lester O'Shea

All Rights Reserved

No part of this book may be reproduced without
written permission of the publisher.

Cover design and typography by Michael X Marecek.

Printed in the USA. First printing October 1999.

For information concerning Rights & Permissions or other
questions contact:

HALLBERG PUBLISHING CORPORATION

P.O. Box 23985 • Tampa, Florida 33623
Phone 1-800-633-7627 • Fax 1-800-253-7323

4 3734828

To the Memory of my Parents

CONTENTS

FOREWORD

Blacks and whites who fought the struggles that yielded *Brown v. Board of Education* and culminated in the Civil Rights Act of 1964 had every reasonable expectation that our nation's racial problems would have been long solved by today some four decades later. Indeed, there has been unprecedented progress. It is not an exaggeration to say that black people, as a group, have made the greatest progress, over some of the highest hurdles, in the shortest span of time of any racial group in mankind's history. If we were to add up black income, and think of black Americans as a nation, black Americans would be the 14th richest nation coming in just behind Switzerland. Black Americans are, and have been, chief executives of some of the world's largest and richest cities. A black American, in the person of Colin Powell, headed the world's mightiest military. There are a few black Americans who are among the world's highest income earners, not to mention the many black Americans who are some of the world's most famous personalities.

Neither a slave nor a slave owner would have believed these achievements possible in the space of a mere century or so, if ever. As such these achievements speak well of the moral character and the intestinal fortitude of a people. But just as importantly they speak well of a nation in which these achievements were possible. These and other advances would have been impossible anywhere, except in America.

Despite the tremendous progress, racial discrimination remains an issue today. Racial discrimination might have died a well-deserved death but it has been constantly resuscitated in the name of fighting discrimination. Our government mandates activities that foster racial antagonism where it otherwise might not exist. Whites and Asians who strive for academic excellence, earning high grade point averages in high school and high test scores on college entrance examinations, often see colleges turn down their applications in favor of blacks or Hispanics with lower rankings. Similarly, white employees who earn high scores on a job promotion test are often denied a job promotion, in the name of affirmative action. A black or Hispanic achieving lower scores is promoted instead. These and other policies destroy racial harmony and good will. Moreover, the offended person might become easy prey for hate groups. On college campuses, we see youngsters who may be the children of black and white parents, who walked arm in arm throughout the South during the civil rights struggle, at each other's throats.

Much of what we see in today's racial arena is simply well-intended, though misguided policy. But a large part of it is motivated by financial interests it serves. A multi-billion-dollar-a-year race industry has been created, involving armies of lawyers, consultants, bureaucratic enforcers, and compliance workers in the private sector. A major part of the time of federal and state judges is taken up with discrimination litigation, creating court decrees and issuing fines.

Lester O'Shea has done yeoman's work in charting the sad history of government intervention in the name of fighting race and sex discrimination. He argues that the supposed basis for government control of private affairs, in the name of fighting discrimination, is in fact a fiction perpetrated by do-gooders, ideologues and opportunists and accepted on blind faith by decent Americans. In telling this story, he has refused to allow himself to be intimidated by "politically correct" talk about racism, sexism, ableism, insensitivity, and the like. He clearly demonstrates how supplanting individual liberty and free markets by official meddling has done more harm than good. It has divided the country and harmed the ostensible beneficiaries by spreading defeatism, dependency and resentment.

WALTER E. WILLIAMS
JOHN M. OLIN DISTINGUISHED PROFESSOR OF ECONOMICS AND
DEPARTMENT CHAIRMAN, GEORGE MASON UNIVERSITY

ACKNOWLEDGEMENTS

I wish to express my gratitude to several persons for their helpfulness in connection with this book. William A. Rusher, Norman R. Phillips, Michael Warder, and Eric Licht read the manuscript and gave me the benefit of their comments. Charles Hallberg, acting as editor as well as publisher, gave the manuscript intensive review and provided numerous editorial suggestions. Last but not least, my wife Camille has my gratitude not only for her thoughts on the manuscript but also for her patience and encouragement.

INTRODUCTION

For who would bear the whips and scorns of time,
Th'oppressor's wrong, the proud man's contumely,
The pangs of dispriz'd love, the law's delay,
The insolence of office, and the spurns
That patient merit of th' unworthy takes

— Hamlet, III, i

Life is still unfair, and victims of the afflictions Hamlet cata-logues still have little legal recourse. Consider the workplace. There, patient merit all too often takes spurns of th'unworthy as people are hired and promoted not on the basis of ability and genuine qualifications but because of things like favoritism, office politics, personal likes and dislikes, and faulty judgment.

Many a candidate is hired not because of objectively demonstrated superior qualifications but because somehow the interviewer takes a lik-ing to the candidate. Is it fair for employment opportunities to hinge on something so insubstantial as a feeling of rapport or the cut of one's jib? And what about where the candidate went to school or college, his hobbies, his politics?

Some people are of unattractive or unprepossessing appearance, and this hurts them in their careers. It is true that if they are to be salespeople, this might be an objective disadvantage in dealing with potential customers; but is it fair to penalize them because of others' tendency to judge a book by its cover? And what about jobs requiring no outside contact?

What about the clever self-promoters who get ahead, once hired, not by honest hard and effective work but by currying favor, playing office politics, advertising themselves effectively, and managing to take credit for others' ideas?

Rudeness and outright cruelty are also found on the job. Cutting remarks are made. People are teased about everything from their weight to their taste in clothing. Hostile co-workers or a hostile boss can make someone dread going to work.

These examples only scratch the surface of the unfairness that Americans experience on the job. The comic strip "Dilbert" has achieved widespread popularity ridiculing workplace folly and injustice.

And that's just the workplace. What about all the other ways in which business decisions and conduct lead to disappointment: choices among potential suppliers, distributors, lenders, borrowers, lawyers, accountants, insurance brokers, and so on: is the objectively best alternative always the one chosen?

No one defends unfairness. So shouldn't it be against the law? That way, if you think it suspicious that all the desirable assignments and promotions are going to those who, like your boss, went to Harvard Business School, whereas you went to Stanford or Wharton, you could do more than seethe internally or grouse impotently, or look for another job; you could go to your local office of the federal Employment Fairness Commission so they would investigate the situation and order that you be given what you deserve. And you could sue your employer for employment unfairness.

In addition, you wouldn't have to put up with unpleasantness at work. If you have a very long nose and a co-worker calls you "Pinocchio," and when you protest and tell him you are sensitive about your proboscis he just laughs and continues to use the offensive name, and when you complain to your boss he laughs at you too, you could sue the company for failing to protect you from a hostile environment, a form of employment unfairness.

And, if you think you didn't get the contract, or the loan, that you hoped for, because the person you were dealing with had somehow taken a personal dislike to you, you could similarly lodge a complaint with the appropriate agency or commence a lawsuit.

In fact, while some lawyers might think it a wonderful thing for all business decisions, or at least all personnel decisions, to be subject to judicial review, no one has openly proposed such idiocy. Would the unfairness have to be deliberate, or would it be enough for someone simply to have made the wrong decision? How would the fairness police, coming in after the fact and having no previous knowledge of the details of the matter, ascertain whether the decision was unfair when it was made? No rational person could seriously advocate having bureaucrats and the courts second-guessing everybody's conduct toward everybody else in the business world. The cure would be far worse than the disease. The costs to society and the economy would be appalling.

We have considerable faith in the fairness and intelligence of our fellow-citizens – this is, after all, a democratic country whose citizens are felt to be equipped to select those who are to govern them – and also a general belief in private enterprise. Certainly events in Russia and Eastern Europe, and the by now obvious failures of socialism elsewhere, do not argue for supplanting decision-making by those on the scene, with a stake in the enterprise, with that of bureaucrats and courts distant in time as well as in place.

Starting in the mid-60s, however, we began taking a very different approach to certain specific types of supposed unfairness, in the workplace in particular: first based on the victim's ethnic background, religion, or sex (the Civil Rights Act), then, due to his being over 40 years of age (the Age Discrimination Act), then, connected with his mental and physical defects (the Americans With Disabilities Act). Unfairness in general remains legal, but unfairness for these specific reasons is against the law, with many business decisions now subject to governmental and judicial review to determine whether they were made for the forbidden reasons.

How is this supposed to make sense? Considering laws against employment discrimination, if socialism is the right approach for human resources management, why should it not be applied to resource management, and to business management generally? Should not knowledgeable and disinterested government functionaries be able to do a better job managing economies than business people interested only in their own profits? But, on the other hand, applying logic in the opposite direction, since socialism has been discredited worldwide, how can it, instead of free markets and free choice, make any more sense in personnel management than anywhere else? How can one recognize the validity of Adam Smith's "invisible hand" everywhere *except* with regard to people?

The rationale for governmentalizing, or socializing, what had always been a matter of individual choice, was that members of certain groups were subject, not like people in general to random acts of unkindness, but rather to systematic mistreatment, either because Americans' general fairness and reasonableness did not extend to these victim groups or because of the power of entrenched oppressors. This would not involve the impossible task of trying to sort fairness from unfairness in an infinite variety of situations but the relatively manageable task of determining whether a particular forbidden motivation had come into play.

Thus, anti-discrimination laws were widely seen as providing a workable mechanism for protecting individuals in these groups from deliberate injustice of a sort no fair-minded person could defend; their administration would be straightforward and easily manageable; their only real burdens would be on those who had brought them on themselves by their own contemptible conduct; and as those with such inclinations came to understand that such conduct would not be tolerated, the problem would wither away, solved by wise use of government power. (When the original, precedent-setting, Civil Rights Act was passed, in 1964, there also was an almost child-like faith in government's ability to solve social problems, reflected also in such enterprises as the War on Poverty and in talk of the Great Society.)

It obviously hasn't worked out that way. In practice, administrative and judicial decisions have eliminated the need for discriminatory intent, and the concept of discrimination has mushroomed to the point that trying to avoid running afoul of the law has become a major preoccupation of businesses across the country and created a whole new industry, with costs in the hundreds of billions of dollars. Yet intergroup acrimony appears to be steadily increasing.

It is widely believed that the crusade is justified; the costs are so great because the evil – Americans' ingrained bigotry – is so great. (This of course is also why race and sex preferences are said to be "still needed.") Is that really the case? This book is intended to answer that question and the closely related one of whether the effects of the governmental anti-discrimination effort justify its costs.

CHAPTER 1

SOMETHING JUST DOESN'T MAKE SENSE HERE

Subsequent chapters will examine the ideological orientation of the groups playing a key role in promoting the view that unfair discrimination is widespread and some of the effects they have had on public discussion of the matter, before going on to analyze, one by one, the principal areas where it is said to be occurring. At the outset, it is worthwhile to consider some reasons for skepticism about such claims.

It is only quite recently, over the last few decades, that Americans have become sold on the idea that so many of them are incorrigibly bigoted that they must no longer be allowed to use their discretion in such matters as the hiring and management of people in the workplace. In a stunningly brief time, the dominant view in public discussion has come to be that the prominent group of white males, in particular, have such animosity toward women, darker-skinned people, older people, and people with every type of handicap, physical or mental, that only if government and the courts have ultimate authority over individuals' advancement can such centuries-old oppression finally be overthrown.

This is quite a change from the traditional view. "You can't keep a good man down." "Cream always rises to the top." "Water always seeks its level." "Land of opportunity." "With liberty and justice for all." It was not that long ago that these were still considered truisms about the United States, expressions of the long-prevalent general conviction that basically God was in His Heaven and all was right with the world in America, the Beautiful. Race was no exception; even at the turn of the century, the great Negro educator Booker T. Washington had written that the "individual who can do something that the world wants will, in the end, make his way regardless of his race."[1] So prevalent was this positive view of America that millions of people left their homelands to come to "the land of the free."

We have now become accustomed to looking upon as recent a decade as that of the 50s, prior to the passage of the Civil Rights Act, when there was no legal barrier to people's discriminating on any basis whatsoever that they chose,[2] as a kind of Dark Ages in which people's bigotry ran unchecked. When a group of Harvard employees a couple of years ago planned an event with a 50s theme, university authorities cancelled it on the grounds that the time had been too oppressive to minorities.

I have a little trouble with this view, because I was alive at the time, and I remember plenty of inter-group fairness and good will.

My junior high school in San Francisco was predominantly white, but there were two (and, as far as I know, only two) students of Japanese ancestry, a brother and sister. This was only a few years after V-J Day, but not only do I not remember anyone expressing anti-Japanese sentiments, the boy was the elected student body president.

I remember also that there were a fair number of Negroes, brought in by bus from around the Hunters Point Naval Shipyard, and that some of them were rather rough and menacing. One of them, in fact, told me that he was not going to go to the high school nearest his home because "there are too many of my people there." Too many of them stole and started fights, he explained. (I assured him that many of "my people" did too, but he insisted that the cases were not comparable.) But I had been brought up to believe that Negroes were just like everybody else except for skin color, and it never occurred to me to think that undesirable characteristics were common to all Negroes. I remember being sure that there were many who were well-behaved and well-brought up, and, indeed, at Lowell, the city's college-preparatory high school, one of my friends, with whom I played chess, was one. Another friend, I remember, was of Japanese ancestry; another of Chinese. But at the time I couldn't have cared less what a schoolmate's ethnic background was, nor did I have the impression that anyone else, student or teacher, did either. I cannot recall witnessing a single instance of racial discrimination in high school.

---

[1] Booker T. Washington, *Up from Slavery*, Pocket Books, 1940 (1900), p. 112.
[2] Except that of union membership, thanks to New Deal labor legislation.

Indeed, looking at my 1955 Lowell yearbook, I can see that all ethnic groups were well-represented among those popular and active in student activities and leadership. That this was so never struck me at the time; I completely took it for granted. To me, in that distant time, bigotry was something I heard about and read of and thought of as of another time or another place. To reasonable people, someone simply wasn't defined by his race.

At Stanford, too, students of different races and sexes seemed to get along fine and treat each other as individuals. Prince Lightfoot, a Yurok Indian, proud that Stanford teams were "Indians," performed his war dances in full regalia to the cheers of the stadium at football games.

Even the Deep South, I know from personal experience, wasn't the total horror story modern views and movies suggest. I had a summer job in Baton Rouge, Louisiana, in 1962. One day my date and I were touring antebellum plantation houses. We were on our way back to the city in the evening on an unpaved back road when I heard a noise under the hood of my old De Soto sedan and the engine immediately overheated. A white truck driver stopped and at once diagnosed and corrected the problem: the fan belt had come loose.

But soon it recurred. This time a car filled with young Negro men, perhaps in their teens and early twenties, stopped. What was the matter? We told them. "We'll fix that for you, sir," was the response. My date offered them some cookies as they worked. "Thank you, ma'am." She held the flashlight. "Who has the flashlight?" asked one of the young men. "The lady does," another answered. Another car with young Negroes stopped. Anything wrong? "We're just fixing the gentleman's car."

What struck me at the time was not that I had no feeling of uneasiness – it would not have occurred to me to have the slightest – but that these young Negroes had, in such a friendly way, gone out of their way to be helpful to a white couple without any obligation or need to do so. They could more easily have simply driven by.

There was of course plenty of unfairness and ill-will in the 50s and 60s. But personal recollections of fairness and good will in that long-ago time make it particularly difficult for me to believe that *now*, after subsequent decades of crusades for fairness including the promulgation of anti-discrimination laws covering everything from race and sex to disabilities, it is really true that America is racist, sexist, ageist, ableist, etc., etc.

Supposedly this currently-popular view reflects a new insight into justice, fairness, intergroup relations, and oppression. But perhaps it is no such thing; perhaps, far from having at long last had the scales of centuries, if not millennia, lifted from our eyes with breathtaking speed, we have instead been sold a bill of goods, a massive conspiracy theory that is fundamentally implausible.

There are some pretty implausible aspects to the supposed new insight.

1. How does maximizing profits – the reason for many a ruthless "downsizing" and for the transfer of production to low-wage countries abroad – fit with the deliberate hiring and promotion of the less-qualified on the basis of race, sex, and other irrelevant characteristics that employers would supposedly engage in if not prohibited by law?

No one has suggested that without a law making such a thing illegal American business enterprises would refuse to avail themselves of cost-effective raw materials, component parts, or finished products because they come from another state, or from abroad, or because of the skin color of the proprietors or workers involved in their manufacture. Indeed, even consumers care little about the ethnic background of the products they buy, as Detroit found to its chagrin years ago when Japanese cars became popular. And Japan had bombed Pearl Harbor and committed terrible atrocities.

Why should the "invisible hand" become inoperative where people are concerned? How could women, Negroes, Hispanics, etc., remain systematically underpaid relative to white males when an entrepreneur could reap windfall profits by availing himself of these neglected human resources? Is it really plausible that entrepreneurs shaped in the so-called "decade of greed," the 80s, who readily close American plants, throwing many white males out of work, and transfer the work abroad to be done by dark-skinned men, women, and children, would persist in hiring less-qualified white men rather than better-qualified women and minorities at home?

It would also be remarkable, in a competitive global economy with little tariff protection, for American enterprises to succeed against those willing to fully avail themselves of human talents and resources if they operated that way.

Only a socialist, or someone without a clue as to how markets and self-interest work – someone to whom the worldwide discrediting of socialism and Communism and acceptance of free-market principles means nothing – could find such a state of affairs plausible.

This doesn't, of course, mean that there is perfect fairness in matters of race, sex, or age, any more than as to any other human dimension that this or that person finds meaningful. Many a person would admit preferring to hire and work with someone "like me." (If "like me" means from the same neighborhood, or the same part of the country, or having gone to the same school or college, or sharing leisure-time interests, such favoritism is legal; if "like me" means coming from the same "old country," or being of the same sex, it is not.) In fact, having employees "like me" can be a plus for an enterprise: for all the currently-popular talk about diversity, cohesiveness also has advantages. Many also like to extend a helping hand to those with whom they feel a bond, of whatever nature. But discrimination here can be only of a marginal, very mild sort, among candidates of nearly equal qualifications, before it runs afoul of the needs of the business or, in the case of a manager not strongly attuned to them, of those higher up who are.

2. For another implausibility, it is a little hard to believe that so many Americans harbor such irrational, bigoted attitudes, particularly after so many decades of education and exposure to – or perhaps one should say immersion in – speeches, films, books, articles, and television programs refuting and denouncing bigotry of all sorts. Films such as *Gentlemen's Agreement* (1947), *Home of the Brave* (1949), and *To Kill a Mockingbird* (1963) – to name just three of many attacks on racism – won critical acclaim and large audiences. "Hire the Handicapped – It's Good Business" was a common slogan decades ago. Has all this been so ineffectual?

3. For that matter, where are all these bigots hiding? Are you, the reader, one who would deliberately hire a less-qualified white or male over a better-qualified Negro or female? Do you hate older people and cripples, and long to deprive them of opportunities to do work for which they are fully qualified? Is your spouse such a person? Your close friends? Do you personally know a number of such people? Study after study shows that something in the area of 95% of Americans surveyed agree that objective merit, rather than race, sex, or other characteristics extraneous to ability to do the job should be the basis for hiring or promotion decisions as well as what the respondents personally say they would rely on, and laws mandating such fairness have been passed with little opposition. As long ago as 1972, according to researchers Stephan and Abigail Thernstrom, 97% of whites surveyed said that blacks should have equal opportunities to get any job.[3]

---

[3]*America in Black and White*, Simon & Schuster, 1997, p. 500.

The country, then, is full of bigots, but they are so surreptitious and secretive about their contemptible attitudes that they do not realize that in fact they are everywhere; and, not daring to show their true colors, they acquiesce in, in fact actively promote the passage of, laws that provide more and more severe penalties for what they yearn to do?

At least in the secrecy of the voting booth bigots ought to show their true colors. The fact that minority-race candidates for statewide office tend to do about as well as whites of the same party – consider the elections of Sens. Mosely-Braun in Illinois and Brooke in Massachusetts and Gov. Wilder in Virginia, and the narrow margin by which Los Angeles mayor Tom Bradley lost his race for Governor of California – also suggests there are not very many around. A January, 1997 Harris poll showed that Gen. Colin Powell was by far the first choice of Republicans and independents for President in 2000, with 37% of those questioned selecting him vs. 13% for the next contender, Jack Kemp.[4] California, which in 1996 passed Proposition 209 banning race and sex preferences by a comfortable margin, is represented in the U.S. Senate by two Jewish women.

In films, indeed, bigots are prominent, but these *are* films. In real life, news stories make clear, there are also a few bigots, but typically they are not prominent businessmen who set their companies' policies but misfits and losers such as "poor white trash" who base such self-respect as they have, *faute de mieux*, on their being white. These people certainly do not shape the country's employment policies and climate.

Among those who do, in leadership positions in major corporations, government agencies and academic institutions, it is, rather, belief in the "politically correct" "affirmative action" or "diversity" that is widespread. Most major corporations have "affirmative action" programs.

The campaigns *against* the Houston and Washington State initiatives barring racial and sexual preferences by government were largely funded by major employers such as Microsoft and Boeing. Is it to be believed that they would like to discriminate *against* women and minorities in their own companies, when they so actively support public preferences *for* them?

The executives profess to believe that preferences are "needed" and right no doubt because of all the bigotry that other, unenlightened, people have been engaging in. Again, the phantom bigots that are so hard to

---

[4] "Powell leads in GOP presidential prospects," *Contra Costa Times*, Jan. 27, 1997.

find,[5] even though so much policy is based on the assumption that they are everywhere.

4. Another element of implausibility in the oppression *Weltanschauung* is the absence of any convincing explanation of how the supposed oppressors have been able to carry it off so successfully for so long. Theirs would be truly a remarkable accomplishment. White males, the usual villains, are a minority in this country, and if you take away those who are also members of supposed victim groups, including the old and those with disabilities, they are fewer yet.

There is nothing mysterious or unnatural about a genuinely superior civilization's becoming dominant, or about exceptionally well-managed companies' doing the same. The strengths of Western civilization and of companies such as IBM are fairly obvious. It would also be natural for the best-qualified individuals to rise to the top, whether in business or in sports. But it obviously would make no sense to call the thriving of the fittest, which is so natural and (without the intervention of outside forces) inevitable, oppression.

It *is* a bit of a tough task, explaining dominance on a basis that recognizes no superiority and thus confers on the dominance no legitimacy. How is it that something other than cream could rise to the top and remain there? This would be a peculiar state of affairs indeed.

Ignorance of economics and history, and receptivity toward victimization theories, can help. One approach is to impute villainy to the successful. Thus, the Nazis, unwilling to attribute the success of Jews in Germany in so many areas, from banking to retailing to the arts, to ability or effort (certainly helped, in the case of banking, by centuries of church opposition to the lending of money at interest), attributed it instead to Jewish trickery and clannishness.

Similarly convincing is the current effort of "Afrocentric" "historians" to explain how it is that Greeks were able to steal all the wonderful inventions made by the Egyptians, who according to them were really black Africans: white people are diabolical.

Another approach, less obviously disreputable, is to blame the dead hand of the past. That women are not as prominent as men in business

---

[5]Unless, that is, bigotry is defined in such a way that only those uncritically enthusiastic about everything about women and minorities, or at least never heard to manifest any impatience or dissatisfaction with them, no matter how justified, can avoid being tarred with this brush. This approach, which will be discussed in a subsequent chapter, worked wonders in the Texaco case.

and the professions and in general outside the home, a state of affairs which has prevailed in all civilizations and cultures throughout recorded history, is now attributed not to people's natural gravitating to what they do best but to the success of an entrenched "old boy network" in holding women down.

The first problem with this approach, however, is suggested by the obvious question, Why is there not an "*old girl* network" keeping *men* down? "Patriarchal religion" is sometimes said to explain men's dominance. On this theory, the sacred writings of the major religions, believed by their adherents to be divinely inspired, in fact were, in significant part, concocted by the then-dominant men to keep women in a subordinate position. But this theory also suggests an obvious question: Why did not dominant *women* create "matriarchal religion" to help them perpetuate *their* dominance?

Another problem with this explanation is that it attributes to established position a power it simply does not have, as is demonstrated by the rise and fall of so many empires, companies, and individuals in past millennia, centuries, and in our own time. What has become of the Habsburgs, the Romanoffs, the mighty U.S. Steel?

This is particularly true in a free-enterprise, free-competition society. Even if it had somehow happened that male losers had come to be in control of existing companies, that would not be the end of the story. This is an era of dynamic change, with large numbers of new enterprises continually being formed. Much of the market value of American common stocks is represented by companies that did not even exist 20 years ago. And being willing fully to utilize all, regardless of race, sex, etc., ought to be a significant advantage in competition with those restricted by bigotry.

When genteel anti-Semitic law firms would not hire Jewish lawyers, they started their own firms, and many largely Jewish law firms are now among the nation's most esteemed and successful. A.P. Giannini, looked down on by the entrenched banking aristocracy, started what has become the gigantic Bank of America. Penniless Asian immigrants have begun extremely successful enterprises. Uncompetitive Old Boys determined to place sex, race, etc. ahead of qualification would have to represent a minor and self-correcting problem in this environment.

5. Yet another reason for skepticism as to the supposed new insight is the very fact that it so thoroughly rejects what had been so long accepted: not only by our parents and grandparents and great-grandparents and so on, but even by ourselves until recently. "Land of opportunity." "You can't keep a good man down." Were we so wrong for so long? Have we really gotten so much smarter so quickly?

It is not supposed to be wise or modest to insist that only we, now, here, are in possession of the truth, and that all that went before or exists elsewhere now is but error and superstition. "Informed opinion" has embraced one brilliant new solution for human problems after another with enthusiasm, from the League of Nations to eugenics to Prohibition to socialism or "central planning" to the United Nations to foreign aid to the Great Society to school busing, only to end up disappointed and disillusioned. This ought to suggest particular skepticism in the case of a radical departure from what had stood the test of time.

The current vogue for "multi-culturalism" in practice amounts largely to denigration of Western civilization, uncritical enthusiasm for anything from primitive cultures, and an insistence that Western Europeans are the villains of the world. It does, however, contain at least one grain of truth that is relevant here: today's "conventional wisdom" could be wrong. This principle deserves to be applied here.[6]

On the basis of all this reasoning, it scarcely seems believable that there should be such intractable and effective rejection of certain groups as to justify placing private business decisions as to their members under the supervision of government and the courts, let alone establishing systems of formal preference for them. And yet this conclusion flies in the face of the impression one gets from newspapers, television news, and public discussion of the matter generally, nearly all of which appears to take for granted that invidious discrimination of various types is a pervasive problem. The explanation lies not so much in flaws in reasoning as in the orientation of those who dominate the public discussion.

---

[6]Indeed, a consistent and honest multi-culturalist would take note, say, of the position of women throughout the non-Western world, in Africa, in the Moslem world, in India, and suggest, "We must be open to the wisdom of the rest of the world and should think twice about the desirability of women's possessing the status and freedoms they enjoy in the West." But devotion to multi-culturalism has definite limits. It is easy to say that *other people's* beliefs should be subjected to multi-cultural scrutiny, but putting the multi-cultural principle ahead of one's own convictions is another matter.

CHAPTER II

THE NEW RELIGION OF THE "POLITICALLY CORRECT"

Professional thinkers, writers, and talkers – roughly speaking, the intellectual and media worlds – play a predominant role in shaping public discussion and the public's view of issues. It is important to understand and keep in mind the orientation of this group: its politics, its biases, its beliefs – in order to give its view of the world the respect, or alternatively the skepticism, that it deserves. When on a particular subject these opinion-shapers demonstrate open-mindedness, reasonableness, and objectivity, their views deserve great weight; where, on the other hand, a kind of religious zeal and dogmatism have supplanted objective inquiry, they need to be taken with many grains of salt.

The latter situation, unfortunately, prevails with respect to the question of whether inequalities among groups occur naturally rather than being the product of sinister forces.

As will become clear in the course of the following chapters, when one area of supposed oppression after another is analyzed objectively in a logical and common-sense manner, what develops naturally in a free society such as that of the United States is a fundamentally fair ordering of position and reward on the basis of merit or market value, not an oppressive state of affairs constantly requiring correction by government intervention on behalf of a variety of groups.

So contrary is the oppression world-view to what straightforward analysis indicates, in fact, that it becomes obvious that it is not held, and preached, primarily because of a few mistakes in reasoning. Bad logic is not enough;

stupidity is not enough. Rather, it is embraced with religious fervor, regardless of the facts, by those to whom inequality is, as a matter of religious belief, a reflection of, a result of, the evil in Americans' hearts.

This conviction, and acting upon it, are at the heart of these people's sense of intellectual and moral superiority, of their image of themselves as an enlightened and virtuous minority set apart from the benighted and sinful masses. Their superiority in intellect and insight are demonstrated by their perception of racism, sexism, ableism, etc., where the insensitive herd see no such thing (whether in society or, worse yet, in their own attitudes and actions). Their superiority in virtue derives from their struggle to stamp out the evil in themselves and to raise up bigotry's victims at the expense of its perpetrators. This is their real, live religion, whether or not they have nominal adherence to one of the traditional formal religions.

It is because the alienated group for whom this radical egalitarianism has become a substitute religion dominates the American intellectual world and public discussion of political issues that this fundamentally implausible outlook has come so widely to shape our policy.

The Alienated Intellectual Class

It is probably a safe generalization that those who go into writing and talking are on the whole less satisfied with their societies than the generality of their fellow-citizens. This is because dissatisfaction with the surrounding society is one of the motivations for going into those fields of endeavor. Those basically satisfied with the way things are do not have that motivation for taking up the pen. As Howard Kurtz, the *Washington Post's* media reporter, acknowledged in the case of journalism, it "seems to attract more change-the-world, left-of-center types than, say, investment banking."

Thus, while some are moved by a desire to sing the praises of, or to defend, a society in which they feel at home and whose values they believe in, such as Kipling, it is relatively common for the intellectual community as a whole to be, as we might put it today, to the left of its society. This is not a new phenomenon. Voltaire detested the *ancien regime* alliance of throne and altar, saying that he looked forward to the day when the last king would be strangled with the entrails of the last priest, and he and the other *philosophes* of what has been called the Enlightenment by subsequent intellectuals were instrumental in bringing about the French Revolution and the resulting Terror. The Bolshevik Revolution in Russia had its roots in the writings of Marx and Engels. A significant proportion of American intellectuals in the 1930s were Communists, an example being Lincoln Steffens, who visited the Soviet Union and wrote, "I have seen the future, and it works." Paul Johnson's *Intellectuals* is a fine study of many prominent intellectuals over the centuries.

The disaffection of the American intellectual community is a relatively new phenomenon. Many college faculties were quite conservative in the early 20s; the socialist Harold Laski had been made to feel so unwelcome at Harvard that he had left for England. But the Great Depression was attributed by many intellectuals not to the business cycle, protectionism as exemplified by the Smoot-Hawley tariff act, actions of the Federal Reserve, Herbert Hoover's misguided efforts to prevent wage cuts, or whatever, but to the fundamental undesirability of the capitalist system.

Even so, after World War II, in the late 40s and 50s, the American intellectual world, while predominantly liberal, was nothing like the radical force it is today. Liberal professors at Stanford in the late 50s were unsuccessful in arousing significant enthusiasm for their causes among my fellow students, which they transformed, with their way with words, into an indictment of us as "apathetic." Even then, however, one had the impression that a conservative would be at a distinct disadvantage in an academic career. Nor would one have accused the traditional liberal professor of uncritical loyalty to American ways of doing things. There was a general snideness toward the hicks out in the rest of the country and their attitudes, such as their simple-minded anti-Communism. Indeed, as late as 1986, John Kenneth Galbraith wrote, after a visit to Russia, "The Soviet system works because, unlike ours, it makes full use of its human resources."

Both the numbers and the orientation of intellectuals began to change dramatically in the 1960s. The number of people able to make a living writing, talking, or teaching had been comparatively very limited. But Lyndon Johnson's Great Society vastly expanded government's role, and government's spending, in the domestic sphere, creating huge numbers of government jobs, funding the "arts," broadly defined, from public funds, financing a massive expansion of higher education, both directly and via federally-guaranteed student loans, and generally facilitating a dramatic expansion of the intellectual class . The number of college and university students rose from 3.6 million in 1960 to 11 million in 1975, with faculty sizes increasing correspondingly. And foundations, whose formation was encouraged by the tax structure, added further impetus to the expansion of professional intellectuals' ranks.

At the same time, the campuses became dominated by angry radicalism. Judge Robert Bork's book *Slouching Toward Gomorrah* discusses this critical era at some length. In his view, the campus radicals basically hated their parents and society, and Viet Nam was something of a coincidence. It may also be that young people averse to leaving the comforts of the campus for battlefield dangers in an undeclared war eagerly rationalized, indeed endeavored to ennoble, their shirking by convincing themselves that their country was an evil force.

Either way, the alienated members of the 60s generation are today extremely influential in the intellectual world, including the institutions of higher learning, whither so many of them gravitated. Even today, after the collapse of the Soviet Union and of international Communism and the emergence of the truth about what an awful system it was, one has to look hard to find any of those who made supporting Communism against their country virtually their religion in the 60s and 70s evincing regret or acknowledging error. Many follow the path on which they began, absorbed with denunciations of their country's supposed depravity – sexism, ageism, homophobia, racism, ableism – as though at least subconsciously validating their course of what, in a real if not a legalistic sense, was treason.

Thanks in large part to public funding, the malcontent who would in previous times have been forced to spend his time in conventional employment, having no time for mischief, because the alternative would have been destitution, can now get a teaching position or a foundation or a government grant. Much of the lunatic ranting against our "racist" and "oppressive" society comes from 60s radicals, such as longtime Communist Angela Davis, who holds the prestigious Presidential Chair, no less, at the University of California at Santa Cruz, supported by the taxpayers through public university paychecks.

Television greatly boosts the ability of the intellectual world to promote its world view. Its compelling combination of visual images with sound induces the average American, from one end of the country to other, to watch it, absorbing its messages, an amazing seven hours a day.

The viewer gets the news, and the emphases, that the editors select. Newspaper editors can emphasize the stories they think important and bury the others in obscure locations in the paper, but they cannot force the reader to read what he does not want to read; but the television news viewer watches what he is given or does not watch the news at all.

He learns what informed, enlightened people are supposed to think. He absorbs what he will in all likelihood remember as fact, presentations "based on" actual events or purporting to present the actual historical events that may be very much at variance with the facts. He watches a wide spectrum of fictional "sitcoms" and other continuing programs from which he will consistently get the impression that businessmen are greedy and irresponsible, that the police are brutal, corrupt, and racist, that unwed mothers, welfare recipients, homosexuals, and minority-group members are the salt of the earth, that bigotry among whites and sexism among males are rampant, that human greed threatens human health and the health of the Earth, that religion is basically irrelevant (except that seriously believing Christians are unbalanced, hate-filled zealots), and similar truths of the new insight as understood by Hollywood.

Hollywood and the media are one part of what may be loosely called the intellectual/media world. Its other parts include the major foundations, the academic and arts worlds, liberal advocacy groups such as the American Civil Liberties Union, and, to a large extent, the organized bar and the "mainline" churches. This group as a whole not only has views very different from those of the American mainstream but also is deeply distrustful of, and hostile to, that mainstream.

A study of the leaderships of over 70 "public interest" groups was conducted by S. Robert Lichter and Stanley Rothman. They concluded, ". . . their alienation was one of our most striking findings . . . Three out of four . . . believe the very structure of our society causes alienation, and over 90% say our legal system favors the wealthy . . . Only about half believe the system can be salvaged." Predominantly, they believed that our private enterprise system was generally unfair to working people. An amazing 96% of these leaders, according to the study as cited by Judge Robert Bork, had voted for George McGovern, in the 1972 election in which Richard Nixon had defeated him in a landslide; and, according to Bork, the figures for the academic and media "elite" were similar.[1]

---

[1]Robert H. Bork, "Why Do The Liberals Rage?" *National Review*, Dec. 8, 1989, p. 26.

Another study, this one of Hollywood decision-makers and creative people by University of Maryland researchers, cited by movie reviewer and media scholar Michael Medved, showed that only 3% of them attend church or synagogue regularly, vs. about 50% for Americans as a whole.[2] Politically, Len Hill, a TV producer and Clinton supporter acknowledged after the 1994 elections, "the all-too-orthodox Hollywood political hierarchy . . . often seemed to insist on political affinity as a condition for power and promotion," referring to "the monolith of Hollywood liberalism." "For years," said another producer, "Hollywood has basically spoken with one voice, the liberal Democratic voice."[3]

The situation is similar in the news media. According to a 1996 survey, 89% of Washington media people voted for Bill Clinton in 1992; 50% described themselves as Democrats and only 4% as Republicans. Of 139 Washington-based bureau chiefs and congressional correspondents, 61% described themselves as moderate or liberal and only 9% as moderate or conservative; only 2% called themselves conservatives.[4] Peter Jennings' response to 1994 Republican Congressional victories, it may be recalled, was that American voters had had a "temper tantrum."

The media outside Washington march to the same drummer. Early in 1997, the American Society of Newspaper Editors released a survey based on responses from over 1,000 newspaper journalists nationwide, showing that 61% identified themselves as liberals or Democrats and only 15% as conservatives or Republicans. In the case of papers with circulations of over 50,000, the percentages were 65% and 12%.[5]

To these news people, stories appearing to bear out their conviction as to the fundamental bigotry of the American people are important, and the reader, or the viewer, is fed a steady diet of such fare. All charges of racism receive prominent and respectful coverage; when, for example, a group of Negro farmers visited the Department of Agriculture in Washington in late 1996 to charge that the number of Negro farmers had been steadily declining because Agriculture Department employees were dis-

---

[2]Michael Medved, "The Hollywood Establishment's War Against Religion," *Human Events*, Mar. 24, 1990, p. 10.

[3]Robert W. Welkos, "GOP ascendance has Hollywood liberals reeling," *San Francisco Examiner*, Jan. 8, 1995, p. A-5.

[4]"Still More Evidence of Liberal Media Bias," *Human Events*, May 3, 1996, p. 11.

[5]Vincent Carroll, "Same Old Slant," *The Weekly Standard*, June 30, 1997, p. 15.

criminating against them, it was the number one news story on CBS news on the network's San Francisco station.[6]

Skepticism is hardly the order of the day. In 1996 came a deluge of front-page headlines: black churches were being systematically burned at an accelerating pace, apparently by a conspiracy of diabolical racists. Eventually it turned out that there had not been an upsurge of such fires at all and that their incidence was in line with that at predominantly white churches and other structures.[7] One black church, the Longridge CME Church in Marshall, Texas, turned out to have been set on fire by one of its members who was a volunteer fireman.[8]

Nowhere is "diversity" more gushed about than in American colleges and universities. Alas, in practice this merely means getting more students and faculty from the supposedly oppressed (because they were "historically under-represented") ethnic groups; it emphatically does not mean seeking meaningful diversity in significant matters such as political orientation. In 1975, Everett Carl Ladd, Jr. and Seymour Martin Lipset, two respected political scientists, conducted a survey of 4,081 professors at 111 colleges and universities and found that only 12% thought of themselves as Republicans. Later surveys give no indication that this imbalance has diminished. For example, a 1995 study showed 186 Democrats vs. 21 Republicans among the faculty in the Stanford departments surveyed.

It is worth looking at statistics such as these as a reminder of how different from America as a whole, in terms of political orientation, its intellectual community is. They are also an aid to understanding why the wildest nonsense – of the left, that is – receives a respectful hearing. Wild nonsense is hardly an aberration among American intellectuals; what is, is skepticism of the oppression world view, or of the sweeping and simplistic egalitarian ideology that underlies it: which says much about the acceptance it has achieved. Statistics alone, however, do not begin to convey how addled those Lichter and Rothman called "alienated" can get.

---

[6]Apparently very selective discrimination is practiced in the Department. A USA Today story on "The Plight of the Minority Farmers," June 7, 1990, stated, "In 1920, 14 percent of farmers were black. Today, less than 1 percent are. The decline for blacks comes as other minority farmers – Hispanics, Asians, American Indians – hold steady or increase . . ."

[7]David G. Savage, "Conspiracy Ruled Out in Church Fires," *San Francisco Chronicle*, June 9, 1997, p. 1.

[8]"Volunteer Firefighters Named in Church Blazes," *San Francisco Chronicle*, July 11, 1996.

The Academic World and Its Adjuncts

Those comfortable with and favorably disposed toward the society in which they live at least give it the benefit of the doubt as to its judgments and values. They are ready to believe that a group that is relatively unsuccessful or widely looked askance at has real deficiencies unless and until they are shown otherwise. With the alienated it is the other way around: every such group is assumed to consist of victims deserving of being identified with and lifted up.

This peculiar *Weltanschauung* is particularly dominant on the campuses, as Dinesh D'Souza's *Illiberal Education*, Alan Bloom's *The Closing of the American Mind*, and *The Shadow University*, by Alan Charles Kors and Harvey A. Silvergate, have well discussed at length. It has been widely derided as "political correctness."

What it *is* that is "politically correct" as in accord with the dominant ideology in Academe is a kind of maniacal egalitarianism. It tries to demonize the rational distinctions made by normal people by coining "ism"s, such as heterosexism, classism, ageism, and lookism. All this reflects the academic world's predominant distrust of the country around it.

"As an American intellectual, I insist on telling the awful truth that American imperialism is a knife at the world's throat," wrote Smith College professor of government Philip Green in *Nation* magazine.[9] His is not a solitary voice.

The 32,000-member Modern Language Association, according to John Leo, has become a hard-edged, politicized academic group that looks on Western literature solely as the ideological expression of white male dominance. At a recent convention, a lecturer from San Francisco State University attacked "white supremacist patriarchal capitalism," saying, "Capitalism must be destroyed in our time." Your tax dollars at work. Sara Suleri, of Yale, ridiculed the idea of setting up a chair of Western civilization at Yale, asking, "Why not a chair for colonialism, slavery, empire and poverty?" The presidential address consisted of a vitriolic attack on white dominance as represented by fraternities at the University of Pennsylvania.

Speaking of that university, it may be remembered that it achieved nationwide notoriety a couple of years ago when a white male student,

---

[9]"Patriotism As Defined By Liberals," *San Francisco Chronicle*, July 4, 1991.

irate at the noisy carrying-on of a group of Negro sorority members under his window around midnight when he was trying to study, called them "water buffaloes," resulting not in disciplinary action against the noise-makers but the hauling of the young man before a tribunal on charges of racism. (In the academic world, any criticism of people who happen to be Negroes is apparently tantamount to racism.) Only after Pennsylvania had become a national laughing-stock because the incident had been publicized in the press, with a lead editorial in the *Wall Street Journal*,[10] were the charges against the man dropped.

At the University of Massachusetts at Amherst, the school symbol, the Minuteman, was the target of protests. "If you're a woman or a person of color, he really can't represent you," declared a protest leader. The Minuteman had only been the symbol for 21 years, since the Indian had been dropped as "racist."[11]

At the University of Alabama at Birmingham, the athletic teams' symbol, a Norseman, met a similar fate. According to university spokes-men, the symbol was "too Aryan," "a white male figure who didn't repre-sent women on campus . . . or the ethnic mix . . ."[12]

At Middlebury College, in Vermont, all fraternities have been banned, and participation in any fraternity activities at all, even off-campus, is grounds for immediate suspension. "To some students and college admin-istrators, traditional fraternities are outmoded institutions that promote sexism and inequality," said the news story.[13]

Universities see initiating their students into the new world view as an important mission. As Heather MacDonald wrote in the *Wall Street Journal*:

> It is never too soon to learn to identify yourself as a victim. Such . . . is the philosophy of today's college freshman orien-tation, which has become a crash course in the strange new world of university politics. Within days of arrival on campus, "new students" (the euphemism of choice for "freshmen") learn

---

[10]"Hackney Watch," May 24, 1993, p. A10.

[11]Janet Cawley, "No more 'Mr. white guy' as college mascot?" *San Francisco Examiner*, Oct. 31, 1993.

[12]"Mascot Who Offended Everyone – 'Blaze' Went Down in Flames," *San Francisco Chronicle*, Sept. 29, 1993,

[13] "At Vermont College, Fraternity is Banned But Unbowed," *San Francisco Chronicle*, Aug. 29, 1994, p. A8.

the paramount role of gender, race, ethnicity, class and sexual orientation in determining their own and others' identity. Most important, they are provided with the most critical tool of their college career: the ability to recognize their own victimization . . . If one can't fit oneself into the victim role, however, today's freshman orientation offers an alternative: One can acknowledge oneself as the oppressor.[14]

At Harvard, the dean who had called for a ban of 50s nostalgia parties organized something called AWARE week, AWARE standing for Actively Working Against Racism and Ethnocentrism. It began with a speech entitled "Racism Among the Well-Intentioned," in which the speaker revealed that 85% of white Americans were guilty of some form of subtle racism, with 15% being overt racists. Minority students were advised later in the week, by an assistant dean, "Overreacting and being paranoid is the only way that we can deal with this system . . . Never think that you imagined [racial insensitivity], because chances are that you didn't."[15]

Free discussion of matters relating to victimhood is not encouraged in this atmosphere. A study at the University of California at Berkeley found that "even liberal educators concede that there is a lack of completely open discussion on many college campuses." One student, who called himself a "moderate Republican," said, "A lot of times I don't want to speak up in class. Otherwise, I'd have 40 percent of the class on me saying I'm a counterrevolutionary racist fascist."[16]

The prevailing view in the academic world is that to question the supposed national dominance of racism, sexism, etc. and its victims' concomitant sacrosanct status and entitlement to special treatment is blasphemy that places those guilty of it outside the community, in outlaw status. "Error has no rights" was a key principle of the Spanish Inquisition. It has become common for copies of student publications taking issue with the prevailing orthodoxy to be systematically stolen and destroyed. This happened to nearly all copies of the issue of the University of California's *Daily Californian* which editorialized in favor of California's

---

[14] "Welcome, Freshman! Oppressor or Oppressed?" Sept. 29, 1992, p. A14.
[15] Robert R. Detlefsen, "White Like Me: The Sensitivity Battles at Harvard," *The Dartmouth Review*, 1989; reprinted from *The New Republic*.
[16] Louis Freedberg, "A Campus Fear of Speaking Freely," *San Francisco Chronicle*, Oct. 30, 1991.

1996 Proposition 209 ending race and sex preferences in state institutions. Over 100 similar instances of theft and destruction of publications expressing "incorrect" views have occurred recently on campuses; and, far from taking action against those responsible, the typical response of campus administrators has been to condemn the heretics. "If it offends people, if people say they are offended by it, it is something we should not tolerate," said Cornell's dean of students when bundles of the conservative *Cornell Review* were stolen and burned.[17]

Curricula have been changed radically in conformity with the new obsession with oppression. At Georgetown University, the English Department has changed the course structure to convey, in its words, "the power exerted on our lives by such cultural and performative categories as race, class, gender, sexuality and nationality." Henry James, Herman Melville and Nathaniel Hawthorne are now lumped together in "White Male Writers," with new courses including "Women, Revolution, and the Media" and "Unspeakable Lives: Gay and Lesbian Narratives."[18]

At Stanford, gone is the required Western Civilization course with reading of Dante, Aquinas, Virgil and Cicero. Works that now must be read include Rigoberta Menchu's book about becoming a Guatemalan revolutionary and "the effects on her of feminist and socialist ideology"; a critique by Zora Hurston of the male domination of American society, and Frantz Fanon's *The Wretched of the Earth*, a celebration of violent revolution. The new choices, according to a professor of French, "reflect a blatantly left-wing political agenda."[19] (The Menchu book, incidentally, was exposed in 1998 as largely fiction.[20])

A 1996 survey of 67 colleges and universities conducted by the National Alumni Forum found that only 23 required *English majors* to take a course in Shakespeare. According to Robert Brustein, artistic director of the American Repertory Theater in Cambridge, Massachusetts, "Most English departments now are held so completely hostage to fashionable political and theoretical agendas that it is unlikely Shakespeare can qualify as an appropriate author."[21]

---

[17]Thor L. Halvorssen, "Burning Issues on Campus," *Wall Street Journal*, July 3, 1997.

[18]Maureen Dowd, "A Winter's Tale For Washington," *San Francisco Chronicle*, Dec. 29, 1995.

[19]Editorial, "The Stanford Mind," *Wall Street Journal*, Dec. 22, 1988, p. A12.

[20]Larry Rohter,"Nobel Winner Accused of Stretching Truth," *New York Times*, Dec. 15, 1998, p. 1.

[21]"Colleges make unkindest cut of all: Bard now optional for English majors," *San Francisco Examiner*, Dec. 29, 1996.

Maniacal egalitarianism even applies to languages. I swear I'm not making this up: "Stanford University has decided to let undergraduate students meet their one-year college language requirement by studying American Sign Language, Quechua and other languages that fall outside the standard curriculum. In doing so, the university joins a broader academic effort nationally to value the languages of smaller nations – or of peoples without nations . . . often, history has determined which language courses are offered . . . The dominant classes and the winners of wars that carved out nations and states triumphed, and the vanquished often were doomed to obscurity. 'They are all viable languages. It is important that we recognize them all and not just be bound by some set of traditions,' said Elizabeth Bernhardt-Kamil, director of Stanford's Language Center and a German language professor."[22] All languages are equal, regardless of their literature or how many people speak them.

What with the continual movement of academics among universities and colleges, foundations, and various education-oriented institutions such as the Smithsonian, it is not surprising that the attitudes dominant on campuses are dominant in these other places as well (as well as prominently represented in Washington particularly in liberal administrations).

The Capital Research Center in Washington reports that only one dollar in five of the large foundations' public policy grants went to conservative causes.[23] Disproportionately, the recipients are at the other end of the spectrum, and see themselves as striving against an unjust and oppressive society. In this struggle, the foundations, such as the Ford, the Rockefeller, and the Carnegie, whose founders of course had no such view of American society, have played a huge role, providing the funding, in effect, to create entire political movements in the women's and minority areas.

It may be recalled that the Smithsonian Institution, a while ago, presented an exhibit on the winning of the West that portrayed this epic period of American history as a shameful exercise in racist, capitalist greed (former Librarian of Congress Daniel Boorstin described it as a "perverse, historically inaccurate, destructive exhibit"[24]), and that the

---

[22]Michelle Levander, "Stanford modifies language standards," *Contra Costa Times*, Jan. 15, 1998.

[23]Austin Fulk, "Corporate Giving Is Funding the Liberal Clinton Agenda," *Human Events*, Feb. 21, 1997, p. 12.

[24]"2 Senators Denounce Smithsonian Projects," *San Francisco Chronicle*, May 16, 1991.

Institution carried its zeal to educate the country about its evil history a bit too far for the public, and for Congress, when it proposed to use the occasion of the 50th anniversary of the dropping of the atomic bomb to present an exhibit that would enlighten Americans to the effect that "for most Japanese, it was a war to defend their unique culture against Western imperialism." In the resulting outcry, changes were made in the Institution's personnel as well as in the exhibit.

As those dominant in Academe see it, their insight, their consciousness of the oppressive character of the country around them, marks them as members of an enlightened elite and sets them apart from the common herd. In fact, these influential people's irrational obsession with oppression – in this land of opportunity, of all places! – says a great deal about their common sense and the state of their mental health, about how nonsense can achieve wide circulation, and about how little respect the cliches about racism and the like deserve when one considers the source.

THE NEW INSIGHT IN ART

The controversies over the National Endowment for the Arts and its support of such expressions of dementia in the form of alleged art as a crucifix in the "artist"'s urine and a woman's "performance art" consisting of dancing nude, smeared with chocolate, while screaming about oppression, called the national attention to the peculiar condition of the current American art world. Indeed, as Irving Kristol put it, "the 'arts community' is engaged in a politics of radical nihilism; it has little interest in, and will openly express contempt for, 'art' in any traditional sense of the term."[25]

John Leo reviewed the 1993 Whitney Museum of American Art biennial show, summing it up by saying, "By current Whitney standards, almost any angry sentiment seems to qualify as art." Among its gems were giant letters running across one room saying, "In the rich man's house the only place to spit is in his face," and a piece of plastic vomit on the floor of a section devoted to "women's rage." As Leo put it, "In two numbing hours at this organized shambles, I learned that the world is neatly divided into good and bad. Good: women, nonwhites, homosexu-

---

[25]Irving Kristol, "It's Obscene but Is It Art?" *Wall Street Journal*, Jan. 11, 1990.

als, transvestites, gang members, glory holes, people with AIDS, gays in the military. Bad: America, straight white males, family, religion, hierarchies, lipstick, liposuction, and penises not attached to gay men. This is one more grim, whining, monocultural show, with all the voices singing the same old song: 'Hey, Hey, Ho, Ho, Western Culture's Gotta Go.' "[26]

Those suitably impressed by such "art" are likely to feel that it is despicable even to question the appropriateness of government intervention on behalf of our society's victims.

The rule appears to be that the new obsession is also to be applied to traditional art as well. If my recent experience with special exhibits at Bay Area art galleries is any indication, whether the exhibit is devoted to the depiction of children in 18th-century English paintings, the wearing of masks in the Venice of Tiepolo, or art and artifacts in California, much of the commentary will deal with income inequality and social injustice.

RADICALISM DISGUISED AS RELIGION

> Still the rich oppress the poor
> And the earth is bruised and broken
> By those who still want more
> — Recessional hymn sung at suburban Bay Area Catholic
> church, Second Sunday of Advent 1996[27]

I used to assume that people went into the clergy out of strong religious feeling and that, when their main thrust became political, it reflected their understanding, however flawed, of their denomination's teaching and scriptures. More typically, what actually happens is that some people with strong political convictions go into the clergy because it provides them with a certain amount of respectability and credibility and, often, a pulpit, to promote what they really believe in. Martin Luther King Jr. does not seem to have been drawn to the ministry by zeal for traditional Christian teachings such as the Sixth Commandment. (During the Viet Nam war, of course, the seminaries were a sanctuary from the draft.)

---

[26]John Leo, "Bashing the Mainstream," *San Francisco Chronicle*, March 28, 1993. "Hey, Hey," etc., of course, had been the chant of students at Stanford, led by Jesse Jackson, demanding the end of the university's required course in Western civilization.

[27]"God of Day and God of Darkness," *Today's Missal, Music Issue 1998*, Oregon Catholic Press (recyclable, recycled, printed with soy ink, union label).

It is difficult to see how someone can find in the Bible a call for radical egalitarianism and the overthrow of private property and the natural order of society. After all, St. Paul said, "If any will not work, neither shall he eat," "Wives, be submissive to your husbands: it is your duty in the Lord," and "Slaves, obey your masters." Envy and sloth are among the traditional Deadly Sins. Jesus condemns the servant who buries his master's coin in the ground instead of investing it profitably. "Is it not lawful for me to do what I will with mine own?" asks the employer who chooses to pay those who have worked but an hour as much as those who have labored all day.

It is, I suppose, possible for someone, especially if he is ignorant of economics, to become sincerely radicalized by focusing on some passages of the Bible while ignoring others, or by seeing poverty first-hand, but the typical explanation for the radicalism prominent among the clergy is that they were radicals to begin with.

Back when Communism was an aggressive force, many of the clergy worked actively to advance it. One remembers the Berrigan brothers, neither still a priest, prominent in their clerical collars at demonstrations urging, in effect, that Viet Nam be left to the Communists. I recall, in the 80s, when I was Republican county chairman in San Francisco, being asked to be on a "panel" on El Salvador at the University of San Francisco, a local Jesuit institution, and being struck by other panelists' fervor for the Communist cause. That the Maryknoll missionary was wearing a red sweater did not seem to me coincidental.

In 1990, a rally in San Francisco demanded, according to a flyer, "END ALL AID TO EL SALVADOR! . . . Boycott Salvadorean coffee . . . End the occupation of Panama. U.S. bases and troops out of Central America. End military aid to Guatemala. NO U.S. INTERVENTION IN NICARAGUA! Respect the gains of the Sandinista revolution. Demobilize the Contras, NOW."

They were certainly covering all the bases to promote a Communist Central America. Not surprisingly, the list of endorsers included the Northern California Communist Party, the Socialist Workers Party, and such old-line front organizations as the Women's International League for Peace and Freedom. Women Against Imperialism and Socialist Action were also on the list.

So were the Sisters of Mercy, Dominican Sisters, Redemptorist Fathers and Brothers, Religious of the Sacred Heart, and the Central American Refugee Organizing Project of Catholic Charities.[28]

With the collapse of Communism, the religious Left is concentrating on the standard domestic victim groups. Purging the liturgies of language now seen as reflective of age-old oppression is a popular project. Presbyterians have eliminated "Stand Up, Stand Up for Jesus" (as "offensive to the handicapped") and "Faith of our Fathers" (as "non-inclusive") from their new hymnal.[29] Rome has thwarted efforts of the American Catholic bishops against the offensive male pronoun, but individual churches sometimes go their own way. The church whose hymn reference to the oppressive rich was quoted at the beginning of this section has changed the Creed so that Christ is no longer "made man" but rather "made flesh," and the Mass reference to "Abraham, our father in faith" became "our ancestor in faith."[30]

The National Council of Churches has enthusiastically accepted the oppression world view, even going so far as to condemn Columbus' discovery of America and its aftermath as "an invasion and colonization with legalized occupation, genocide, economic exploitation and a deep level of institutional racism and moral decadence."[31] More recently, the Council conducted a national campaign to raise money to rebuild black churches destroyed by the nonexistent great wave of racist church burnings mentioned above; the millions of dollars it brought in over and above the cost of rebuilding churches were designated instead for various "anti-racist" programs.

In San Francisco, at Christmas 1995, then-Archbishop Quinn brought modern concepts of victimhood to the Nativity, referring to the shepherds at Bethlehem, in his sermon, as "marginalized by society." From all the references to shepherds in the New Testament, one would seem hard-pressed to consider them even *marginal* in the society of the time; but of course "marginalized" brings in the current vogue for oppression. People may just

---

[28]Needed comic relief was provided by the Mustard Seed Affinity Group, Bay Area Peace Navy, and Bay Area Radical Therapy.

[29]*National Review*, June 11, 1990, "Notes & Asides," quoting the Dec. 31, 1989 *The Living Church*.

[30]In fairness, I should say that when I asked the pastor whether this was because new research had raised doubts about Abraham's sex, he did agree that this was going too far.

[31]*Fresno Bee*, Nov. 24, 1990 (from Scripps Howard News Service).

happen to be marginal; but they are marginalized by someone's oppression.

Leading Catholic churchmen, including the Archbishop of Los Angeles, opposed Proposition 209, the California initiative against state racial discrimination and preferences, apparently convinced that government favoritism is needed as a balance to the public's racism. The frequency with which I have heard sermons against racism in churches suggests that many priests are convinced that their worshipers are bigots.

The traditional concept of the "deserving poor" has been largely forgotten, with all the poor, across the board, and particularly if they are members of relatively unprosperous ethnic groups, considered deserving of special sympathy. The Catholic Bishops' Campaign for Human Development, funded by an annual collection in all Catholic churches, channels large amounts of money to organizations which encourage people to believe that they are victims of injustice.

Some people are poor because of bad luck, including having been dealt bad cards by their Maker at the outset. It is certainly very much in the spirit of Christianity for the more fortunate to share with the less-fortunate. But the notion that people have a special obligation to all the poor, even if they are poor because of laziness, or sloth, which the constant talk about "the poor" from pulpits suggests, requires a belief in the general unfairness of our economic system.

To be sure, many, perhaps most, of the clergy of all denominations are focused on traditional teachings rather than on wealth redistribution. But there are enough with the new view to ensure that God will be solemnly invoked on behalf of all efforts designed to raise up the supposedly oppressed or to pull down their supposed oppressors.

THE LEGAL PROFESSION

It would be hard to overstate the importance of ideologically committed lawyers in effecting the revolution in American society that has taken place in the last three decades. The late William Kunstler, who would not stand for the Pledge of Allegiance and believed ours was a racist, evil society, was an extreme example of these alienated battlers.

They helped draft the battery of anti-discrimination laws pursuant to which a constant stream of lawsuits is filed against private entities, and they are active in filing those lawsuits (although the profit potential in this new industry has attracted non-ideological legal talent as well).

They unceasingly sue public entities seeking to prohibit sensible policies, such as keeping bums from occupying the sidewalks and parks, or hiring employees and awarding contracts on the basis of merit rather than sex or skin color, and to require them, instead, to advance the levellers' agenda of favoring "victims."

And, of course, they concoct tortured legal arguments, either, as lawyers, for the benefit of judges or, as judges, to try to provide some plausibility to what they are doing, explaining how this or that piece of the radical egalitarian agenda is mandated by the federal or state constitution. This wresting of control of public policy away from the people and their elected representatives has been a critical element in the transformation of the United States that has occurred. Even in the case of the civil rights laws, what the courts wrought by "interpretation" went far beyond what Congress thought it was enacting.

And when there is public outcry against some particularly egregious judicial assault on common sense or the Constitution, the legal radicals will solemnly warn against "bringing politics into the judiciary," or "tampering with the Constitution," even though it is they who have done precisely that in the first place.

Most lawyers are either traditional lawyers or entrepreneurs in one of the new litigation areas created by activist judges, rather than crusaders against the existing socio-economic system.[32] But the cause does not lack committed legal warriors. As I came to realize when getting a law degree recently, a significant number of those going into law are, at least in large part, motivated to do so by a desire to overturn what they see as an unjust society. And law professors, a high percentage of whom are similarly motivated, exhort their students to devote themselves to "public interest law," by which they mean litigation on behalf of oppressed groups and the oppressed planet. There was exactly one Republican on the faculty at my law school. The American Bar Association, the most influential lawyers' trade association, is a reliable ally of the supposedly downtrodden, advocating racial preferences and abortion on demand and opposing the death penalty and laws against sodomy.[33] Even partners at

---

[32]That is not to say that the legal profession as a whole does not have a warm spot in its heart for anything, including new anti-discrimination laws, likely to lead to an increase in litigation.

[33]Mark Pulliam, "Extremism in Defense of Federalism," *The Recorder*, Jan. 20, 1999.

leading law firms are predominantly liberal in orientation, with 59% of those sampled having voted for Clinton in 1992.[34]

WORKING TOGETHER FOR JUSTICE: A CASE HISTORY

The 1996 battle over the California Civil Rights Initiative ("CCRI"), Proposition 209 on the November California ballot, is illustrative of what the great majority of the academic, media and arts worlds, working in concert with those with vested interests and a sizeable percentage of religious leaders and the bar, can accomplish, even in as unpromising a cause as defending racial and sex discrimination.

For, indeed, all the measure did was prohibit the state and its subdivisions from discriminating for or against people on the basis of their ethnic background or sex. Early polls showed the measure winning by 2-1 or even 3-1. How, after all, could one defend outright race or sex discrimination by government? But its opponents went to work. Groups benefitting from preferences were mobilized. Proponents of 209 were denounced as racists, and their chairman, who as it happened was a Negro who believed in traditional American principles of fair play, was attacked as a "traitor to his race." Academic leaders, including the head of Stanford University, were quoted as positive that "affirmative action" was needed for the vitally-needed "diversity."

On the law front, a well-known law professor produced a piece of legal nonsense purporting to show that CCRI would make discrimination against women legal, and other lawyers solemnly warned that its passage would result in endless litigation.

As the election neared, news stories were prominently featured in the media to the effect that some ethnic groups were not doing well, proportionally, in such areas as getting government contracts, being admitted to graduate schools, or whatever. The reader or viewer was of course supposed to assume that this was due to discrimination, showing that state favoritism was "still needed" as an offset.

While 209 mentioned discrimination and preferences and nowhere used the term "affirmative action," media coverage almost never referred to "pref-

---

[34]Amy Black and Stanley Rothman, "Shall We Kill All The Lawyers First? Insider And Outsider Views of the Legal Profession," *Harvard Journal of Law & Public Policy*, Vol. 21, No. 3 (Summer 1998), 842-843.

erences," which polls showed voters overwhelmingly opposed, but instead to "affirmative action," which the polls indicated many voters said they favored (perhaps because the term had a fine, positive ring to it or conveyed merely an encouraging attitude rather than actual preferences).

Religious leaders denounced CCRI. The *San Francisco Chronicle's* editorial cartoonist produced a singularly despicable cartoon depicting a burning church marked "affirmative action" from which figures with a gas can, marked "CCRI," were gleefully running,[35] actually suggesting that the no-discrimination initiative was responsible for the at-the-time-not-yet-exposed-as-fiction "wave of black church burnings."

In the event, 209 passed with 54% of the vote, meaning that 46% of the voters had been persuaded that racial and sex discrimination by the State of California was a good thing. Of course, those who had warned of litigation were correct. They knew what they and other opponents of the proposition would do if it passed. The American Civil Liberties Union was in court the day after the election, seeking to prevent its taking effect, and Judge Thelton Henderson Jr., a longtime Negro-rights crusader named to the federal bench by Jimmy Carter, managed to take control of the litigation away from the judge to whom it had initially been randomly assigned and issued an injunction against the initiative's implementation on the absurd ground that prohibiting a state from engaging in discrimination on the basis of race or sex probably *violated the Equal Protection Clause* of the U.S. Constitution. News coverage of the judge's actions was respectful, and editorials reminded the people that they should respect the process of judicial review and the rule of law. And when a crowd of close to 1,000 staged a demonstration against his action, no local newspaper, and only one of four television stations, even covered it.[36]

Judge Henderson's tortured reasoning was soon rejected by a unanimous panel of the Ninth Circuit Court of Appeal, but the struggle by the alliance of media, academe and the bar for the holy cause of race and sex discrimination went on. Academic leaders nationwide signed manifes-

---

[35]June 16, 1996.

[36]Letters to editor: Mike Spellman, "Media Bias," *San Francisco Chronicle*, Jan. 22, 1997, and George J. Mate, "Bay Area media wrong in ignoring Prop. 209 rally," *Contra Costa Times*, Jan. 24, 1997.

toes and took out full-page advertisements in favor of preferences. In California, the party line, focusing on the University of California, became that Prop. 209, and the University of California regents' prior action eliminating preferences at that institution, sent a devastating message to minorities that they were "not wanted" at this prestigious institution. Therefore they would not go, and therefore the "diversity" so vitally needed for a good education would be missing, having a ruinous effect on the flagship institution of higher learning of which Californians were so proud.

Graduate school admissions to the University of California at Berkeley for Fall 1997 showed no significant change in the representation of ethnic groups, prompting a graduate school official to state that there was no sign of a problem with a "negative message"; this news rated a small story far back in the pages of the local papers. Freshman admissions showed moderate declines in Negro, Hispanic, and American Indian admissions and increases in Asian and white, but no spectacular shift; there was little excitement about this development.

Ah, but at the university's Berkeley Boalt Hall School of Law, one of the most difficult in the country to which to gain admittance, only 14 Negroes and 39 Latinos were admitted, vs. 75 and 78 respectively the previous year, and all the Negroes chose to go to other law schools! This "total wipeout," as a Boalt dean characterized it, immediately became the focus not only of front-page news but of President Clinton's San Diego speech defending racial preferences.

Former state supreme court chief justice Rose Bird wrote a strident op-ed piece[37] entitled "A brutal education legacy" likening the results of color-blind admissions to South African apartheid, again displaying the kind of reasoning that had led to her removal from the bench, together with two of her like-minded colleagues, by the exasperated California electorate.

A front-page story in the *San Francisco Examiner*[38] contained a round-up of comments from San Francisco lawyers to the effect that the situation at Boalt Hall would be "unacceptable," "tragic," "disgraceful," and "fundamentally wrong."

---

[37]*San Francisco Examiner*, June 29, 1997.
[38]Annie Nakao, "Big minority dip at Boalt rattles S.F. law firms," July 6, 1997, p. A-1.

The article highlighted a statement by lawyer Eva Jefferson Paterson, scheduled to receive a distinguished-alumni award from Boalt, "Being that I wouldn't be able to get into the school under this year's standards, I found that very ironic." Apparently only her status as a Negro woman had saved her from rejection on the basis of her grades and test scores. Certainly one would not expect her grades in English to have been very high.

Ironic? Ms. Patterson's claim to fame was that she had played a prominent leadership role in the losing effort to defeat Prop. 209 and save racial preferences, not that she had distinguished herself as a lawyer. The implausible theory she had endorsed, that forbidding race and sex discrimination constituted unconstitutional discrimination, had been rejected by the appellate court. Her getting an award for "politically-correct" activism from a "politically-correct" law school said nothing at all about whether she had the legal aptitude, including the ability to reason correctly, that law school admissions are supposed to be about.

Note, too, that she, a Negro woman, was being lauded for working to retain preferences for Negroes and women, hardly a disinterested or selfless effort. It is a very safe bet that a white man would not have gotten a distinguished-alumni award for leading a defense of preferences for whites and men.

For good measure, the line is also that minority-group members are so obsessed with their racial background that they cannot function well without enough others of the same background around. "Boalt Hall grads: new black student won't feel at ease"[39] featured the views of a recent graduate who had been student body president. From her photograph, she appears to be perhaps an eighth or a quarter African and the rest Asian, but she has been sailing under "black" colors. She says that in classes she would "find herself catching the eye of a fellow black student" and that, even with 31 members of her designated race in her class of 270, she still "felt conspicuous."

When the full 9th Circuit ratified its panel's decision and the U.S. Supreme Court also refused to interfere with Prop. 209's finally taking effect, Jesse Jackson led a march across the Golden Gate Bridge, political leaders in San Francisco and San Jose defiantly declared that they would not change their systems of racial and sex preferences, and editorials

---

[39]Michelle Locke, *Contra Costa Times*, July 6, 1997, p. A29.

urging respect for judicial review and the rule of law were noticeably absent in the local press.

RELIGIOUS FERVOR

One thing you will never hear advocates of racial or other group preferences express is an interest in looking at the facts and calmly analyzing whether inequalities among groups are really due to discrimination. Nor are they troubled by the obvious randomness with which preferences operate, their automatic rewards and penalties based solely on group membership. That is because radical egalitarianism is the religion of those in its grip, and its fundamental tenet is that inequality is the product of pervasive injustice. This is the essential element of their faith, and it is not subject to being rationally disproven. It is as Paul Johnson wrote of the liberal approach to crime: "It has been tested to destruction. It has failed everywhere, overwhelmingly and manifestly – except in one region: the minds of its advocates. For them liberalism is a religion, an article of faith, born of conviction and not susceptible to proof or disproof."

No U.S. President has suggested that it is time for a "national dialogue on religion," aimed at moving toward conclusions as to which religion or religions are most deserving of Americans' adherence. Rather few people try to argue others out of their religions. President Clinton's call for a "national dialogue on race" runs up against a similar problem. As columnist Dan Walter observed concerning California's constitutional amendment banning race and sex preferences, on the one side "those who pushed for . . . the enactment of Proposition 209 . . . have maintained a high tone. Even the most overtly political of the advocates, Gov. Pete Wilson, has cast the conflict as one between two versions of moral fairness." The advocates of preferences, however, "have used shameful words and acts," including denouncing their opponents as engaged in "ethnic cleansing."[40]

The intolerance and self-righteous zeal of ardent levellers is reminiscent of religious fanatics of old. The epithets they hurl are not "blasphemer," "heretic," or "enemy of God," but rather "racist," "sexist," and "bigot." "Hate," which seems equivalent to holding traditional religious views as to what constitutes moral and immoral conduct, is also very popular. When objections were raised to federal funding of obscene "art," the National Advisory

---

[40]Dan Walters, "Prop. 209 debate tone getting ugly," *Contra Costa Times*, Aug. 27, 1997, p. A13.

Endowment for the Arts' advisory theatre panel, in 1990, passed a resolution denouncing critics as "zealots, bigots and homophobics."[41]

The new religion is, when you think about it, rather analogous, in an upside-down way, to traditional Catholicism. It is still common for Catholics to supplement their worship of God, and nearly universal veneration of Mary, with special devotion to one or more of the other saints. St. Ann novenas are common. St. Jude, patron saint of hopeless causes, has many popular shrines. Particular countries are devoted to their patron saints, for example St. Patrick in the case of Ireland and St. Elizabeth in Hungary. Occupations have their patron saints, such as St. Thomas More for lawyers.[42] Each saint's worthiness of veneration stems from his devotion and relationship to God.

The new religion also has many shrines, at which the new faithful can express their devotion to particular victims of the common oppressor, the Great Satan, mainstream America. The cult of the Negro is the most popular, but the Woman, the Disabled, the Homosexual, the Hispanic, the Homeless, and the Indian have their special devotees too.

So do the Criminal Suspect, the Convict, and the Murderer Sentenced to Death. The Worker, popular in the 30s, has fallen out of fashion, having become too prosperous and, often, "politically incorrect," but the Farmworker has a substantial following.

Celebrity victim cults, such as those of the Rosenbergs, the "Chicago Seven," the Black Panthers, and Mumia Abu-Jamal, have their vogues. So do Exploited/Bullied Foreign Countries, such as Cuba, Viet Nam, and El Salvador. Even Animals (subgroups Endangered, Laboratory, Fur-Bearing, and Cute) and inanimate things such as the Forest, the Rainforest, and the Earth.

And just as the old-fashioned Catholic expresses devotion to God by devotion to His faithful saints, so here the new believer opposes the common evil by devotion to its victims. The truly religious, such as are found in particular abundance on college campuses, adhere to all the victim cults.

To be sure, as Freud said, sometimes a cigar is just a cigar. It is certainly possible to be moved to take up a particular cause because of its

---

[41]Allan Parachini, "NEA Advisers Slam Art Agency Critics," *San Francisco Chronicle*, June 16, 1990.

[42]It is *not* true, however, that St. Martin of Tours is the patron saint of travel agents, St. Gregory the Illuminator of electrical contractors, and St. James the Lesser of landlords.

perceived merits rather than as part of a general conviction as to the nastiness of American society. But in the case of multiple cultists, such as the man who lost his legs lying in front of a train protesting arms shipments to El Salvador and soon after recovering was featured at a rally against the cutting of redwood trees (and the tenth anniversary of whose amputation was marked with extensive and reverent coverage in the local press), or the San Francisco motorist whose bumper stickers included U.S. OUT OF EL SALVADOR, REPRODUCTIVE RIGHTS FOR ALL WOMEN, HOMOPHOBIA IS A SOCIAL DISEASE, and ROBIN HOOD WAS RIGHT, it is a safe bet that general alienation is the problem.

The latter part of William Butler Yeats' line, "The best lack all conviction, while the worst are full of passionate intensity," comes to mind in connection with the radical egalitarian crusaders. Certainly extreme ideas and irrational hostility toward normal American customs, as expressed in some of the examples earlier in this chapter, can produce a negative reaction, as with the widespread current ridiculing of "political correctness." Yet strong beliefs, and quasi-religious zeal, can also be a great help to a cause. The French Revolution, the Bolshevik Revolution, and the Nazi takeover of Germany were not accomplished by reasonable, moderate people.

Those who believe that this is a fundamentally unjust society whose numerous unfairly-treated groups must be rescued from mistreatment at the hand of the oppressors do not all hate ordinary Americans. Their feelings toward them are found on a broad spectrum running from mere distrust through dislike to real hatred.

For the most seriously disturbed, "Amerika" is always wrong, and those at odds with it are always in the right, whether they are foreign enemies or domestic criminals. Demonstrators in San Francisco responded to the U.S. invasion of Panama by chanting not only "U.S. out of Panama!" but also "We love Noriega!" The enemy of my enemy, whether Viet Nam, or Cuba, or the Soviet Union, or Iraq, or Libya, is my friend. Nothing the United States does abroad, whether in Central America or Granada, is ever right. Ramsay Clark, who actually was attorney general in the Kennedy administration, participated in a "Crimes of America" conference in Teheran, denouncing the attempt to rescue the long-imprisoned American hostages as "lawless and contrary to constitutional government." Subsequently he accused his country of "war crimes" in the Persian Gulf war. At home, he called murderers on Death Row "helpless people that we have in our power," saying that executing them would say something terrible about us as a people.

The more moderate merely dislike or distrust ordinary Americans. This degree of negative feeling, at least, is, when you think about it, essential to the insistent belief that American society is unreasonably hostile to so many groups. If you have a positive feeling about people, you give them the benefit of the doubt and do not convict them of mistreating others without proof. And if they tend to look askance at a particular group, you take that as suggesting that there is probably something wrong with that group, not with the American people as a whole.

Years ago, in his book *Capitalism, Socialism, and Democracy*, Joseph Schumpeter predicted that the prosperity which capitalism would create would, ironically, bring into being an influential and disaffected intellectual class that would bring about the system's destruction. At this point, it would seem that he underestimated the resiliency of our system. But he was certainly right as to the intellectuals' alienation, which has been so critical in selling the country on the need for laws against all sorts of discrimination as well as the appropriateness of open preferences.

CHAPTER III

THE NEW RELIGION'S EFFECT
ON DISCUSSION AND ANALYSIS

An uninformed person from abroad would be unlikely to get the idea from reading newspapers and magazines and watching television that the population of the United States actually consists predominantly of heterosexual white people in at least reasonably sound financial, physical and mental condition. If one were to judge from media coverage of these matters, racial minorities, homosexuals, mistreated women, the physically or mentally disabled, and the impoverished make up the bulk of the population.

Or, at least, to the extent that there are any significant number of Americans not themselves in one or more of these constantly-discussed and apparently long-neglected and long-victimized groups, they must think of little else. In their fascination with them, they apparently cannot get enough of films, books, or articles dealing with these arresting matters. Book review after book review deals with books on these subjects. The whole nation apparently waited with bated breath for weeks to know whether a particular television actress was lesbian or not, and her announcing that she was, was treated as one of the major events of the year. Race, sex, disability, sexual orientation – this is what everyone constantly thinks about.

Not quite. Even Americans' appetite for being reminded of the evils of slavery is not unlimited. Asked Sharon Waxman of the *Washington Post*, "Will American audiences have nothing to do with movies about slavery? That may be one conclusion drawn from the dismal showing of

Oprah Winfrey's "Beloved," . . . praised by critics and rejected by audiences . . . Not even those expected to show up – African American audiences and Winfrey's core female audience – turned out to support the film." Nor did "Amistad," also intensively promoted, do well.[1]

But the media and intellectual community are obsessed with these matters and think the population must be inundated with them. Some news organizations have formal policies requiring that a certain percentage of stories deal with minority groups. But formal policy or no formal policy, it is clear that the media believe that educating the public about the unfairness that they think has "marginalized" what are now properly to be considered holy groups and making up for past neglect by giving their readers and viewers a saturation diet of them is a moral imperative.

They are not without help in their virtuous work. An endless stream of reports and studies issues from academics and advocacy groups, highlighting some disparity or other, some over-representation or under-representation of some sort, affecting one "disadvantaged" group or another, ready to be publicized as, presumably, yet more evidence of American society's pervasive injustice. Lawsuits alleging mistreatment based on race, sex, disability, or whatever are constantly being filed. Accusations of bias are made at press conferences and in press releases every day. From this steady diet, the reader or viewer can be expected to get the impression that unfair discrimination is practically ubiquitous.

This is particularly true because of the now-common practice of presenting every instance of inequality among groups as news of "bias" or deliberate mistreatment based on animosity. Such simple-mindedness would be relatively understandable in a high-school newspaper, where it might be attributed to impressionable and naive youngsters influenced by alienated left-wing teachers. But that is the way things are at a respected adult publication such as the New York Times.

All too typical is a current example. In the "Business Digest" highlights of key business news appears a summary headed "Bias Against Minority Stations": "Radio stations aimed primarily at black and Hispanic audiences receive significantly less ad revenue per listener and have also been forced to offer deeper discounts than their mainstream counterparts, an F.C.C. study has determined."[2]

---

[1] "Beloved's' Message Isn't Being Heard," *San Francisco Chronicle*, Nov. 12, 1998.
[2] Jan. 14, 1999.

Deep within the article itself one does find that the report "cautioned that racial discrimination might not be the only reason for [the stations'] lagging revenues," but the whole thrust of the piece, and of its headlines ("The Government's first study on discrimination in radio advertising finds a lot of fodder" was that of the article itself), is to present as unquestioned fact the preposterous idea that the lower ad rates commanded by radio stations aimed at relatively low-income minority groups reflect not market forces but advertisers' antagonism toward the minorities.

FORBIDDEN DISCUSSION

The claim that a group's relative lack of success or respect is the product of unfairness and oppression rather than simply the group's own deficiencies is unlikely to be refuted if any such suggestion is, like skepticism about the Emperor's new clothes, ruled out of bounds at the outset. And, in public discussion today, any reference to such deficiencies has become taboo. Unless it is presented in the context of assigning blame to someone else, it is likely to be greeted with accusations of racism, sexism, heterosexism, or some other -ism.

For good measure, "blaming the victim" is a likely charge. It suggests truly reprehensible conduct: as the disheveled, bloody rape victim sobs, a heartless monster growls, "She was wearing make-up, wasn't she?" No one wants to be guilty of being so lacking in basic decency.

And no trial is held, with all the evidence carefully considered, before a group receives certification as a victim group and society stands condemned as its oppressor. To the egalitarian community that dominates discussion, inequality of success or respect is sufficient proof of victimhood.

If there are real past injustices to the group, however long ago or far away, the public is likely to be reminded of them constantly by books and motion pictures. Hollywood's current wave of films about the sufferings of Negroes, perhaps designed to counteract growing impatience with racial preferences, is a case in point. Not only are they enslaved: they are used as human guinea pigs, their syphilis left untreated in the 30s, in *Miss Evers' Boys*; they are murdered by crazed racists in Florida in the early 20s in *Rosewood*; in other recently-prominent films, Negro airmen experience bigotry in World War II and civil rights workers are murdered in Mississippi in the 50s. Hang your head in shame, white man, and never forget your guilt!

The victim group has a kind of holy status. It is exempt from normal criticism, blame, or reproach, and any negative comment or reference is a sign of mean-spiritedness or bigotry, or, at the least, "insensitive." Group members are to be portrayed positively in the media (unless it is made clear that they are unrepresentative of the group); all demands and claims made by the group or those who purport to speak for it are to be treated with seriousness and respect. The most exacting standard of "sensitivity" is *de rigueur*, and the group's members must *never* be accused of hypersensitivity, over-reacting, or unreasonableness.

There is no room for levity here, or for dismissing a complaint as something no grown-up could mean seriously: not where victim status can be asserted. And people are on the alert, ready to take offense and exact apologies. "Activists" keep a sharp eye on real estate advertisements: "'Walking distance' could suggest that disabled persons aren't welcome."[3] California Governor Wilson accused Democrats of "trying to welsh on that deal" and apologized after being accused, by the Welsh-American Legal Defense, Education & Development Fund, of a degrading slur against the Welsh.[4]

Don't Say It!

In April 1990, the assistant manager of a large San Francisco Bay Area public transit system was talking candidly to a group of visiting transit experts, and he told them that "in an effort to reach affirmative action goals relative to minorities and women, AC Transit did not always exercise stringent screening and hiring practices, which resulted in some unqualified employees."

All hell promptly broke loose. A wildcat strike was threatened. "AC Transit Aide Suspended for Biased Remarks" was the headline. The unfortunate executive was immediately suspended without pay from his $90,000-a-year job; he would "voluntarily" attend "sensitivity and awareness training to improve his performance" (such would also be mandatory for all managers); and he would also "volunteer" to "help the NAACP in 'workshop' programs for minority youngsters who are interested in careers in the transportation field."[5]

---

[3]"Housing ads: Do 'code words' discourage some buyers?" *San Francisco Examiner*, March 12, 1995.
[4] Letter, "Wilson's Slur," *San Francisco Chronicle*, Aug. 7, 1995.
[5]Michael Taylor, *San Francisco Chronicle*, May 12, 1990, p. A7.

In the same year, the U.S. Attorney for Northern California, preparing to return to his old law firm, commented that San Francisco was a logical place for drug dealers because of its "strong Hispanic community that could provide protection and insulation from law enforcement," noting that there were a "disproportionate amount of drug dealers of Hispanic ancestry." Local Hispanic organizations went on the warpath, the county board of supervisors joined their demand for his resignation, picketing began, with threats to seek to bar the law firm from recruiting at law schools and promote a general boycott of the firm for harboring such a person,[6] and soon the attorney engaged in the prescribed groveling ritual, agreeing that parts of his statement could have been viewed as "insensitive and damaging" and insisting that he was sorry if he had implied that the "Hispanic community in the Bay Area, or indeed anywhere, is not law-abiding."[7]

There was no discussion in the press of whether the transit man or the attorney had said anything that was contrary to the facts.

Across the continent, in 1999, the superintendent of the New Jersey State Police, Carl Williams, who had been criticized because, of those stopped and searched for drugs on the state's highways, a high percentage were black or Hispanic, was interviewed by a Newark newspaper. The veteran of 35 years on the force emphasized that he would not tolerate stops based on race as such but pointed out that according to New Jersey's Uniform Crime Report for 1997, 50% of drug arrests in the state in 1997 were of blacks and 13% of Hispanics. While "predominantly white" motorcycle gangs were prominent in the methamphetamine market, he said, in the case of cocaine or marijuana, it was "most likely a minority group that's involved with that."[8]

A coalition of "black state legislators, ministers and civil rights advocates" immediately denounced Williams. "His views are dastardly, his thoughts are ill and sickened, and he's unfit to hold such a critical, important office. He's a racist of the worst kind, because he doesn't even know it,"

---

[6]Maitland Zane, "Hispanic Leaders Urge Boycott of Firm That Hired Russoniello," *San Francisco Chronicle*, Feb. 24, 1990, p. A6.

[7] "U.S. attorney 'sorry' for remark," *Contra Costa Times*, Feb. 25, 1990.

[8]Joe Donohue, "Boss warns troopers: Don't target minorities," *The Star-Ledger* (Newark), Feb. 28, 1999.

was the interesting analysis of assemblyman Leroy Jones, and Governor Christine Todd Whitman immediately fired the superintendent.[9]

In contrast to the typically uncritical dissemination by the media of charges of racism, the *Star-Ledger's* story took pains to try to rebut the superintendent's position that the police were acting properly. Of the Uniform Crime Report statistics he cited, it said, "National statistics do not seem to support Williams' claims." Having thus reduced the official New Jersey statistics to "Williams' claims," the story went on to say that "just 38.4 percent" of all drug arrests nationwide in 1996 were of blacks. How could *national* statistics either "support" or "not seem to support" the New Jersey ones? Negroes' percentage of the population nationally (about 12%) is not the same as that in New Jersey. In any case, 38.4%, even with "just" in front of it, is not dramatically different from 50%, and both are huge in relation to either population percentage.

The *Star-Ledger's* story also cited a study by a Temple University professor as suggesting that "minorities are no more involved with drugs than whites." On a highway in Maryland, 75% of motorists stopped and searched were black even though blacks make up only 17.5% of Maryland traffic violators, the study found; and, also, that nearly the same percentage of blacks as of whites statewide (about 28%) were found with drugs. But what this actually shows is that blacks *are* far more likely than whites to be involved with drugs: for if the disproportionate number of blacks stopped were being stopped capriciously, and only the whites for good reason, the percentage of blacks found with drugs would be far lower than that of whites.

RESPECT IS MANDATORY: DOUBLE STANDARDS

If Polish-Americans began insisting that the ancient Greeks were really Polish, one doubts that anyone would bother to contain his laughter. But some American Negroes are seriously arguing that the ancient Egyptians (despite all the evidence) were really black. According to Irving Kristol, writing in the *Wall Street Journal*, five leading Egyptologists were asked whether there was any substance to the claim that the Egyptians were black and all replied that the claim was total nonsense; but none was willing to have that view attributed to him by name.

---

[9]Robert D. McFadden, "Whitman Fires Police Chief Over Comments on Race," *New York Times*, March 1, 1999.

The African-American Baseline Essays, published by the Portland, Oregon public schools as a guide to "Afrocentric" education, inform the reader that "Africa was the birthplace of mathematics and science," and that ". . . The discovery of time, the control and use of fire . . . tool technology, language and agriculture . . . were first accomplished by Africans . . ."[10]

Negroes have sometimes been unfairly treated because of their race, but it does not follow that they are always blameless. In 1944, for example, 258 Negro sailors were court-martialed for refusing to load ammunition in Port Chicago, California, after a disastrous explosion that had killed over 200 men; they were convicted, imprisoned, and dishonorably discharged.

Forty-five years later, 24 Congressmen demanded that the Navy re-open the case. There was "new evidence," they said, indicating that the ammunition loading was not being done safely (not a startling conclusion considering the result), and they contended that the sailors had refused orders "because of well-grounded fears for their personal safety, not because they were challenging military authority."[11]

"That's right, Lieutenant! I'm not following you over the top! But I want to make clear that this is because of well-grounded fears for my personal safety, not because I am challenging military authority."

Munitions loading stateside undoubtedly had its dangers, but considering the amount loaded and the fact that this disaster was unique, hardly on a par with serving at the front. (To its credit, the Navy upheld the convictions after reviewing the case.)

In 1990, Betty Dopson, identified as "chairwoman of the Committee to Eliminate Media Offensive to African People," was reported as saying, "The New York Post is the most virulent, despicable publication in New York City, and we are determined to rid our community of it." Her complaint was that its "coverage of blacks was limited to crime, social dependency and dysfunction, entertainment and sports," and "added that the organization considers all of the city's mainstream papers to be racist in their coverage."

No one apparently laughed, or decried a threat to press freedom, and the Post's editor actually asked the committee to meet and discuss grievances.

---

[10]Gary Putka, "These Teaching Guides Credit Blacks For Math, Science and the Pyramids," *Wall Street Journal*, July 1, 1991.

[11]"Port Chicago courts-martial review urged," *Contra Costa Times*, May 31, 1990.

Nor did Betty Dopson's ludicrous offensive make a laughingstock of her. On the contrary, in 1998 she achieved a towering success in her chosen work of browbeating spineless white people. The New York borough of Queens was named after Catherine of Braganza, who became Charles II's queen, and it was decided to erect a five-story-high statue of Queen Catherine at Hunters Point in the borough. After the expenditure of $2 million, largely a gift from the people of Portugal, and six years' work by the sculptress, the Queens Borough President, Claire Shulman, withdrew the site. Betty Dopson was the most vocal leader of a group formed to oppose the sculpture, saying its "hands are bloody with the murder of millions of Africans." How so? In the 17th Century, Portugal and England were both involved in the slave trade.[12]

The predominantly Negro Oakland, Calif. school board unanimously passed a resolution in late 1996 calling the fractured English of uneducated Negroes "Ebonics," or "African Language Systems," declaring it to be "genetically based and not a dialect of English," stating that the board "officially recognizes" it as "the predominantly primary language of African-American students," and referring to "instructing African-American children both in their primary language and in English" and "imparting instruction to African-American students in their primary language for the [purpose] of maintaining the legitimacy and richness of such language . . ."

The board members were not ridiculed for applying the silly and pretentious term "ebonics" to Negro slum talk. Editorial writers and others strained to explain that those who thought the resolution meant what it said, obviously indicating that its authors were guilty of sappy nonsense, misunderstood. A news story referred to "sections that caused some to believe that students would be instructed in black English," as though it was not perfectly obvious that it had unequivocally provided for precisely that. And "Ebonics" and its "rules," such as the absence of tenses, received a lot of serious discussion in the press.

Wrote a Nigerian journalist on a Hubert Humphrey fellowship in an op-ed piece, "To me, 'Ebonics' is totally unrecognizable and those who argue that it has a West African origin are merely contriving a thesis to justify nonsense."[13]

---

[12]Barry Bearak, "The Queen of Ethnic Nightmares," *New York Times*, Jan. 9, 1998, p. C18.
[13]Reuben Abati, "Stranger in a strange world of Ebonics," *Contra Costa Times*, Jan. 26, 1997.

More than innocent silliness may well have been behind the Oakland effort. Jesse Jackson's initial sensible reaction, that it was "borderlining on" the absurd, changed when he sensed the possibilities. On a visit to Oakland, he led a chant, "Limited-English proficient FUNDS! Limited English-proficient FUNDS!"[14] The nonsense might facilitate a raid on the Treasury. If that had been the idea behind "ebonics," the school board members were even more deserving of contempt. But they did not get it from the respectful press.

The "politically correct" never scoff at charges of racism or reject them out of hand, even when they themselves are accused. The Sierra Club can be counted on in every liberal vs. conservative battle, even one far removed from the mountains and the environment: it opposed Judge Robert Bork's confirmation to the Supreme Court. But when Benjamin Chavis Jr., at the time director of the United Church of Christ's Commission for Racial Justice (subsequently NAACP head until ousted for using NAACP funds to pay a woman who had accused him of sexual harassment, after which he converted to Louis Farrakhan's Nation of Islam with the name Benjamin Chavis Muhammad), and the Rev. Fred Shuttlesworth of the Southern Organizing Committee for Social and Economic Justice accused the Sierra Club (along with the Natural Resources Defense Council, the Audubon Society, and Friends of the Earth) of racism in its hiring practices and demanded that it take steps within 60 days to ensure that 30-40% of its staff would be members of minority groups, it did not get indignant but rather humbly vowed to mend its ways.[15]

All normal standards give way when an accredited victim group is involved. Reporting on an effort by something called the Sentencing Project, a recent article in the Knight-Ridder Newspapers began, "Since the nation's founding, almost every state has stripped criminals of the right to vote. Today, as more and more black men are imprisoned, those laws mean that black America is losing a big part of its voice in the democratic process." Putting an interesting twist on the matter, an "expert on black politics" with the Joint Center for Political and Economic Studies warned, "In a country that has a history and legacy of slavery, it's pretty significant that here we are almost into the 21st century and 15

---

[14]Nanette Asimov, "Jackson Calls for Ebonics Funds," *San Francisco Chronicle*, Dec. 31, 1996, p. 1.

[15]Philip Shabecoff, "Environmental Groups Faulted For Racism," *San Francisco Chronicle*, Feb. 1, 1990.

percent of black men are still disenfranchised."[16] We should, in other words, give the vote to felons in order to increase Negro voting power.

Women also occupy a special position. Anita Hill's accusations against Judge Clarence Thomas were entitled to unquestioning belief because "women don't make these things up." But ideology trumps sex. Paula Jones' charges of far more serious misconduct against Bill Clinton got no sympathy from Prof. Hill's enthusiasts. Some contended that her association with conservatives discredited her. They had not found Anita Hill's association with liberals a problem, however.

In the liberal college town of Davis, California, in 1991, a woman told the police that she had been gang-raped by a group of skateboarders. She would, however, tell the police neither exactly where the outrage had occurred nor which doctor she had consulted. This reticence engendered some skepticism, outraging the local university's Rape Prevention Education Program coordinator: "It just makes me want to throw up." But, according to a local newsman, people began talking "in hushed voices at street corners." "It seems that men are afraid to say it at all because they know how politically incorrect it would be to even hint it may not have happened," he said; but "women feel like they have more license to say it. They're the ones who, under their breath, are saying, 'I know I'm not supposed to say this, but I'm just not sure.'"

Finally the woman confessed having made the whole story up after an accident on her bicycle.[17]

It Can't be What it Looks Like

In 1994, in honor of Martin Luther King Jr.'s birthday, a teacher at Oakland, California's Castlemont High School took his students to see *Schindler's List*, the dramatic true story about the Holocaust. According to the lead story in the *Oakland Tribune* a couple of days later, "To the horror of many in the audience . . . some of the African-American and Latino teenagers seemed to[18] laugh and applaud at scenes depicting Nazi atrocities." The theatre's management responded by evicting 60 students, "whose departure was applauded by the remaining patrons."

---

[16]Lori Montgomery, "Convicts' vote loss raises race issue," *Contra Costa Times*, Jan. 30, 1997.

[17]Marjie Lundstrom, "Gang rape that tore Davis apart was all a lie, police say," *Sacramento Bee*, Aug. 18, 1991, p. 1.

[18]Diana M. Williams, "Field trip to 'Schindler's List' backfires," Jan. 19, 1994, p. 1. Note that "seemed to": some sort of auditory mirage, or mass hallucination on the part of the audience?

Could anyone defend or excuse such conduct? Of course. These were not white students laughing and applauding a lynching in a film, which would probably have occasioned at least a week of nationwide agonizing. Tanya Dennis, "head of discipline at Castlemont," who was present, did acknowledge that "her students' behavior was inappropriate, because of cultural differences." But their reactions, she insisted, were "misunderstood." "Actually, it made me feel good that they reacted to that scene, because that's when I knew it affected them."

The *Contra Costa Times'* story, a day later, made no mention of the students' racial background,[19] while the *San Francisco Chronicle's* offered the suggestion that their laughter was understandable because in the film "the body contorted in a way they thought was a strange fashion." These kids have a keen eye for detail. A student was quoted: "The theater manager is prejudiced . . ."[20]

It was soon decided that the popular modern culprit, lack of education, was to blame. A special presentation, to be developed by the school district together with the Holocaust Center of Northern California and the Anti-Defamation League of B'nai B'rith, would give the high school students that heightened understanding of modern history without which it is of course natural to laugh at atrocities on the screen. Thus, snatching glory from the jaws of shame, Castlemont became one of five recipients of a "Courage to Care" award presented by the Governor.[21]

SOMEONE ELSE IS REALLY TO BLAME

Those who are familiar with "informed opinion" as communicated by the media know that when there is an urban riot, with its standard burning, looting, and violence against innocent individuals, it is never ultimately the fault of the Negro and sometimes Hispanic slum-dwellers who typically are involved.

Back in 1965, right after the passage of the Civil Rights Act, when Watts, in Los Angeles, erupted in a riot after a drunk driver was arrested, *Time* magazine declared, "Most responsible Negro leaders also fear that such insensate outbursts of anarchy can only discredit the Negro's legitimate struggle

---

[19]Michelle Locke, "Students ejected from movie about Holocaust," Jan. 20, 1994.

[20]Sandy Kleffman, " 'Schindler's List' Opens Oakland Teenagers' Eyes," Jan. 20, 1994, p. A17.

[21]Donna Hemmila, "State to honor school embroiled in 'Schindler's List' controversy," *Contra Costa Times*, Jan. 29, 1994, p. 1A.

for civil rights."[22] But the dominant thinking has changed. When Chicago burned, the federal Kerner Commission put the blame on white racism. Since then, whenever there has been a major outbreak of rioting and looting, the focus has almost immediately shifted to the supposed real culprits, viz. racism, police disrespect, and white people – or, more recently, as in the Los Angeles riots a couple of years ago, white and Asian people.

Less serious misbehavior is also somebody else's fault. A 1992 story in a San Francisco newspaper, headlined "Study Blames Oakland Schools For Truancy, Dropout Rates," began, "Oakland's public schools contribute to low self-esteem and high dropout rates, particularly among blacks, and educators must find other means of discipline to keep children in school, according to a report . . ."[23] The report stated that during the 1990-1991 school year "80.2 percent of the suspended students were black." Negro boys, 28.6 % of the students, accounted for 53.3% of the suspensions. And heavens, most of the suspensions were not because of drugs or weapons but just "defiance of authority, fighting and profanity." The fault was the schools' for suspending so many disruptive students, not the students' for unacceptable conduct or the parents' for failing to raise their children properly.

The same shift in blame occurs in higher education. Negroes, Hispanics and American Indians are not doing well in college? "U.S. Universities Failing to Educate Minority Students," says the *Wall Street Journal* headline.[24]

Poor eating habits? The *Journal* was equal to the challenge. In a three-part, front-page series,[25] it focused on the real culprits. "Fast-Food Chains Play Central Role in Diet of the Inner-City Poor," the second part was headed. "They Offer Pleasant Refuge . . ." according to the subhead. A customer was quoted: "The atmosphere makes me feel comfortable and relaxed and you don't have to rush . . . Ain't no hip-hop [music], ain't no profanity. The picture, the plants, the way people keep things neat here, it makes you feel like you're in civilization." There is even a picture of George Washington Carver on the wall.

That's just what's so insidious, the article makes clear. These clean, inviting places seduce people into eating things like Big Macs. The president

---

[22]*Time*, Aug. 20, 1965, p. 19.
[23]Yumi L. Wilson, *San Francisco Chronicle*, Sept. 11, 1992.
[24]Hilary Stout, *Wall Street Journal*, Dec. 7, 1990.
[25]Dec. 18-20, 1990.

of a South Bronx health center charges, "the industry is public enemy no. 1 to the health of poor, working-class people." J. Jerome Cooper, pastor of the Berean Presbyterian Church, declares, "The underclass is held in a fast-food dietary prison, which produces nothing but bad health."

These people have apparently been lured away from their traditional diets of salads and yoghurt. But no; apparently they do not eat such foods at home either; and the blame for that, another article in the series suggests, lies with the supermarkets for failing to emphasize healthful foods.

And of course the blame for excessive drinking and cigarette smoking in minority communities lies with the liquor and tobacco industries. "Minorities Decry Target Ads," says the *San Francisco Examiner* front-page story.[26] A man resembling Ho Chi Minh with dark glasses, identified as the chairman of La Raza Studies at San Francisco State University, is shown with the damning evidence: a Spanish-language display showing a can of Mexican beer, half a lime, and a saltshaker on a bed of ice cubes.

"They are targeting with ethnic-specific kinds of images, making it culturally acceptable," is his complaint; "The images are that to be Mexican or Latino is to drink and smoke." That seems a bit much to read into advertising in Spanish. If the advertisements were all in English, one suspects, the chairman would be complaining about the marginalization of Spanish-speaking people.

Similar indignation has been voiced about malt liquor advertisements aimed at Negroes. The fearsome alcohol content of these beverages has been much stressed.[27] But it is only around 6%; higher than beer's but similar to ale's, and tame indeed compared to chablis' 12% or bourbon's 50%.

When all is said and done, advertising is placed where it is expected to produce results. To the extent that it is feasible to target an audience, brands of alcoholic beverages are advertised to those disposed to drink, not to teetotalers. Rather than causing the drinking, advertising is a response to it. Were the brewers and distillers of Ireland better marketers than their counterparts elsewhere in Western Europe? Is Russian vodka advertising uniquely effective? It is simply nonsense to blame the liquor industry for an ethnic group's drinking problem.

---

[26]Annie Nakao, Aug. 13, 1991.

[27]See, e.g., Alix M. Freedman, "Malt Advertising That Touts Firepower Comes Under Attack by U.S. Officials," *Wall Street Journal*, July 1, 1991, p. B1.

New Vocabulary

If you have to take a lickin'
Carry on and quit your kickin'
— From school song, James Lick Junior High School,
San Francisco, c. 1952

The reason I remember these old lines, I suspect, is that they were sung to a very catchy tune, originally "Don't Give Up the Ship." But the sentiment did not seem particularly noteworthy at the time. Whining and complaining, even by those with legitimate grievances, was generally looked on with disfavor in American society.

The transformation of common terminology that has occurred since the days when it was thought proper for people's career progress to depend on individual choices rather than governmental intervention provides an immediate indication of the success of the alienated in shaping the discussion.

In the days when we thought things were basically fair in this country, those whose complaints reflected general dissatisfaction with matters rather than the individual grievances of "whiners" were "malcontents" and "chronic complainers." Those convinced the whole system was unjust and oppressive were called "crackpots," "loonies," "anarchists," "Bolsheviks," or "Commies."

And when they actively tried to impart their insights to those they regarded as oppressed, they earned names such as "troublemakers," "agitators," and "rabble-rousers."

When did you last see these terms in print? Today's troublemakers and agitators are "activists" or "advocates," and whiners and malcontents are "activists," "militants," "victims," or "people with grievances." Complaining is a badge of honor, entitling someone to sympathetic coverage on the evening news, not an indication of contemptibility.

These things can happen very fast. Consider the case of bums, or derelicts, seen from time immemorial on the sidewalks of urban skid roads. A sorry lot, typically with alcohol problems, they had long been considered their own worst enemies. Suddenly, in the early years of the Reagan Administration, they disappeared, having overnight been transformed into "homeless people," a reproach to Republican policies and capitalist society.

Transforming the language so as to make sensible analysis an uphill battle is certainly one of the most significant contributions the intellectual community has made to the spread of the injustice-and-oppression world view.

"DISCRIMINATION"

These requirements discriminate. They are going to treat these residents differently than if they were not mentally ill.
"Advocate" on proposed provisions affecting a proposed Berkeley group home for insane people

Couple With Cursing Disorder Sues Airline for Discrimination
Newspaper headline

The use of "discrimination" in wildly inappropriate fashion has had a far-reaching effect on the general perception of the fairness or unfairness of American society, turning the most reasonable and innocent recognition of human differences into something apparently sinister and crying out for governmental intervention.

Webster defines "discriminate" as "to make a distinction; to distinguish accurately." In this sense one might speak of a "discriminating palate," which could tell a fine Bordeaux from jug red wine. Webster also provides a second definition: "to make a difference in treatment or favor (of one as compared with others)."[28] Here is the meaning that is the problem; for while a difference in treatment or favor *can* be made for improper reasons, such as skin color, no such impropriety is inherent in the concept. Different treatment or favor can reflect eminently reasonable and proper considerations, as when a fast runner rather than a slow is picked for the track team or a hard worker rather than a slacker for a job promotion.

But the context in which "discrimination" rose to prominence in our times was discrimination against Negroes. In *that* context, discrimination constituted *unfair* discrimination, denial of opportunities or equal treatment purely on the basis of color and not by virtue of any real deficiency. Fundamental to the unfairness was the fact that the basis was *altogether*

---

[28]*Webster's New Collegiate Dictionary*, G. & C. Merriam, 1956.

irrelevant to actual qualification. If a Negro had been rejected for work where color really mattered – undercover police work in the Mafia, or testing tanning creams, for example – no one would have been silly enough to employ the opprobrious word "discrimination."

But "discrimination" has been running amok. With all its invidious connotations from the racial-discrimination area, it is now freely applied where objective lack of qualifications is precisely the problem, not where an irrelevant factor is overriding the qualifications. A deaf woman was turned down for admission by a nursing school; she sued, charging that she had been illegally discriminated against because of her handicap. The law said that no "otherwise qualified person" was to be rejected because of a handicap. The Supreme Court finally ruled that the law was not intended as an affront to common sense: "otherwise qualified person" meant someone qualified despite the handicap, not someone who would have been qualified had the handicap not been present. It prohibited, in other words, unreasonable, not reasonable, discrimination.

This distinction is often lost. No one in his right mind would hire a blind man to drive a bus, someone confined to a wheelchair to herd sheep, or a terminal cancer patient with a year to live to begin the six-month training program at a brokerage firm. As the term has come to be used, this means "discrimination against the blind, the crippled, and the sick." When conduct dictated by elementary common sense is characterized as reprehensible by current word usage, something is radically wrong with that usage.

But it has rolled merrily on. The law has taken on the evils of "discrimination against people with AIDS" and "age discrimination." That language suggests kicking someone when he is down and shabby treatment of older people. But in fact the potential for long-term employment *is* seriously diminished in both cases. This is true in the case of the old, in the inevitable nature of things, even without a mandatory retirement age. To be sure, if one is hiring a hit man or an arsonist, a short life expectancy can be a plus, and in some cases, as sales on commission from the employee's home, life expectancy may not matter, but, particularly where it takes time and training to get a worker up to speed, a diminished period of potential work availability is a minus.

Formal marriage has real practical consequences. Those in it have an entitlement in each other's earnings and liability for each other's debts.

It also typically is a more stable and long-lasting relationship than mere cohabitation. One party's moving out is not sufficient to terminate it. One would thus expect a rational bank to be more comfortable lending to a married couple than to a couple merely living together and for its loan terms to reflect this. But this is "another example of discrimination," according to a member of the San Francisco Board of Supervisors, who has proposed legislation to outlaw it. "These sweeping changes will allow San Francisco to have the strongest anti-discrimination laws in the nation," she said proudly.[29]

All sorts of reasonable distinctions now provoke charges of "discrimination." Apartment complexes for the elderly, offering them the peace and quiet many of them understandably seek, are accused of "discrimination against families with children." Men's clubs are said to "discriminate against women." After the 1989 earthquake, the Federal Emergency Management Administration decided to withhold earthquake-damage funds from a San Francisco boys' and girls' club on the ground that it was guilty of "age discrimination": it "discriminated against" those not between 6 and 18 years of age. This decision was soon reversed, but it is indicative of the extreme lengths to which misuse of words can lead apparently sane people to go.

With this usage, clearly, the Society of Mayflower Descendants "discriminates against the foreign-born" and the Veterans of Foreign Wars "discriminates against non-combatants."

There is little if any suggestion, however, in coverage of "discrimination" charges in the media, that the term is being ludicrously misused. Rather, it appears taken for granted that language that suggests reprehensible conduct accurately conveys the truth about yet another manifestation of the national beastliness.

A story tells of a policeman who is suing his department "because, he says, it discriminated against his color-blindness." A sympathetic story tells of a woman who has developed a program whereby volunteers and tandem bicycles make it possible for blind people to go bicycling. A fine thing, you say, but surely there is nothing here suggestive of anything reprehensible? Oh, but there is, if you use the right language: the story quotes the bicycle-program originator: "Visually impaired people have

---

[29]Yumi Wilson, "S.F. Plan to Protect Unmarried Couples," *San Francisco Chronicle*, April 4, 1997.

been denied access to basic recreational outlets." Shame on those who did such a dastardly thing. Who are they? How did they do it?

A woman "who lost her hearing in a punk rock band" sues a theatre chain, and the headline is, "Bias suit claims . . . theaters withhold listening aids." "Withhold": "Naah! Look at it and weep! We're not going to let you use it!"

In case after case, the simple facts of everyday life are turned into a reproach of society through the misuse of language. STOP KILLING BLIND PEOPLE, said placards carried by demonstrators in San Francisco. It may indeed be a good idea to install rubber strips along the edges of subway platforms, as the demonstrators wanted, but imputing the purposeful slaughter of the sightless to the transit authority goes a little far.

In their attitude, of course, these angry demonstrators were following in the footsteps, or perhaps one should say following in the tracks, of the squads of wheelchair-bound protesters who some years back demanded (successfully) federal legislation requiring virtually every nook and cranny in the country to be made wheelchair-accessible. They would barricade buildings and chain themselves to gates with a grim fury that would have been altogether appropriate if wheelchair ramps occurred naturally and, once ubiquitous, had been systematically destroyed by vicious Americans for no reason other than sadistically to impose further misery upon the crippled.

In fact, what they were demanding was very far-reaching and very expensive; considering how few people in wheelchairs there are, for example, it would seem quite reasonable to require one car on each commuter train rather than every car to be equipped for wheelchairs. But that proposal was rejected in Congress as "back-of-the-bus" philosophy. Similarly borrowing civil-rights terminology in service of their cause, advocates of extensive and expensive new provisions for crippled patrons at San Francisco's sports stadium, even though existing facilities were going unused, was justified on the grounds the existing facilities constituted "segregated" seating. All this is very, very costly. As a California architect put it, "this idea of 'equality' at any price – regardless of actual need – is bad for business and the public, who ultimately foot the bill. Cost is no object. Up to 25 percent of typical construction budgets go to meet handicapped standards" for "an arguable one to two percent of the public" that is genuinely disabled.[30]

---

[30]Letter by Richard Deight, *Design/Build*, April 1997.

It is understandable, although far from admirable, that those seeking advantages would seek to clothe themselves in the aura of strugglers against oppression in order to enhance their prospects for getting what they want. The important point is that this sort of thing consistently works because, with its predominant mind-set about pervasive injustice in America, the media and intellectual community are predisposed to believe claims of victimhood. In this climate, people are reluctant to question such claims for fear of being made to appear monsters.

An additional dimension of lunacy is achieved through the widespread acceptance, in public discussion, of the notion that if an employer seeks to avoid characteristics undesirable in particular jobs and they are disproportionately present in particular groups, this constitutes objectionable discrimination *against the group*.

For example, it would seem reasonable for airlines to exclude alcoholics from employment as airplane pilots. But does this constitute illegal discrimination against American Indians, who disproportionately have a drinking problem?

Not yet, fortunately for air travelers. But in an exactly analogous situation, the National Labor Relations Board held that for airlines to require flight attendants to be at least 5'2" tall (so that they could easily reach the overhead bins) was impermissible discrimination against Orientals, since a higher percentage of Orientals than of whites or blacks are shorter than that height.

And in New York State, because a higher percentage of Negroes than of whites have criminal records, inquiry as to whether a job applicant has a criminal record is against the law as being racially discriminatory.

Consider the 1999 Clinton Administration proposal to ban "discrimination against parents."[31] Are employers taking anger over the growth in population out on employees with children? Of course not. But employers tend to reward employees willing to work overtime or finish a project on a weekend, when necessary, relative to those who refuse because they have a better use for their time. For those for whom that better use is tennis or some other sport or exercise rather than time with the children, we can ban "discrimination against the health-conscious." Laws like this are really about banning discrimination on the basis of suitability for the job.

---

[31]"Bill Would Protect Parents From Bias In the Workplace," *San Francisco Chronicle*, April 17, 1999, p. A3.

What is being objected to is not discrimination against members of the group but rather their being held to the same standards as everybody else.

In analyzing the issues involved here, which are central to the basic question of the appropriateness of laws against discrimination, it is critically important to recognize that differences in treatment of individuals reflecting their actual, relevant differences are appropriate and not to be deplored, and that applying the term "discrimination," with the connotation of unfairness it has acquired, in such cases is inappropriate and a serious impediment to rational discussion. It makes drawing reasonable distinctions sound like something evil.

It is also important to understand that real discrimination, treating people less favorably solely because of their group membership rather than because of their individual characteristics, has a variety of forms, ranging from the inexcusable to the inevitable; and that is inappropriate to lump them all together as the same reprehensible thing. (In almost any other area, such distinctions would be drawn as a matter of course, but here religious zeal, feelings of guilt, and fear militate against straightforward analysis.)

The first type of discriminatory treatment regardless of individual merit is rejection of all members of a group because of animosity. "I don't like Jews, and I'm never going to hire one, no matter how good he is." Many groups have been the targets of this kind of nastiness. "The only good Indian is a dead Indian." "All whites are devils." Sometimes the animosity is religious in origin, as manifested in places such as Bosnia, Northern Ireland, and the Near East. Sometimes the animosity has roots in envy, as toward Jews in Germany or East Indians in Africa or Koreans in South Central Los Angeles. Sometimes it reflects a real or perceived competitive threat, as manifested by hatred of Chinese by white laborers in 19th-century California or of Negroes by poor whites. The terms "hate" and "bigotry" are properly used in connection with this type of discrimination, which is usually based on race or religion.

A second type of discrimination occurs when different treatment is accorded to an identifiable member of a given group because of the deficiencies that the discriminator believes, rightly or wrongly, are particularly common in that group. These may be deficiencies of character, intellect, qualification, or attitude. This is properly called prejudice, from the Latin *prae*, before, and *judicium*, judgment.

In the extreme case, the individual is rejected out of hand. "I will not consider any woman for this job; no woman can do it." The rejection is as automatic and total as in the case of bigotry, but there is no hate involved, just a closed-minded equation of group membership with disqualification. The discriminator may be a fool, but he is not a hater.

Usually group membership represents not conclusive demonstration of lack of qualification but a preliminary indication of more or less importance. No one whose mind is not a blank slate can fail to have his expectations as to an individual affected by what he knows or thinks he knows, favorable or unfavorable, about groups to which the individual belongs (or appears to belong). But cavalier overgeneralizing – "stereotyping" – can lead to discrimination. The interviewer's first reaction, when the job applicant comes in and hands him his resume with the name O'Leary on it, is, "Great: another drunk." Or he sees a Negro and thinks, "Just what we need: another incompetent paranoid looking for a chance to file a discrimination lawsuit." Or he assumes that a woman applicant is just looking for a job until she finds a husband.

These initial reactions may not prove decisive, if the interviewer is open-minded enough, recognizing that every individual is different, and takes the time to judge the applicants on their merits. If not, and he thinks he has better things to do than waste his time with people he thinks have very slim odds of measuring up, his initial reaction will carry the day, and in some cases qualified people will be discriminatorily rejected. This is true even if he is right that a particular group has a disproportionate percentage of members with defects.

Sometimes, of course, there is no time to go beyond first impressions. Is the store security guard to keep his eye on the elderly Asian woman or the young Negro man?

This is a very different kind of discrimination than the first. It is discreditable to hate people because of their race, but it is not discreditable – indeed it is inevitable – to have expectations or to figure the odds based on one's understanding of reality. Where people can and do take the time to give someone a fair shake despite initial negative expectation, they are hardly to be criticized.

A third kind of discrimination that should be distinguished occurs where a person is recognized as qualified but nevertheless rejected because of his or her group membership, not because of animosity or prejudice, but because of practical considerations.

One form of this discrimination has to do with attitudes of co-workers and/or customers or clients. An employer of laborers on the East Coast around the turn of the century with a work crew of men from one part of Italy knew better than to hire some additional workers from another part. There would be trouble.[32] If he had two crews he might have one of men from Genoa and another of Neapolitans, but if he only had one and its members were Genovese, the sons of Naples were out of luck, and not because the employer disliked Neapolitans or though ill of their average qualifications. (Similarly, when the Transcontinental Railroad was built, the Central Pacific used Chinese crews and the Union Pacific predominantly Irish.)

This type of discrimination sometimes comes about because there are bigoted people in the picture: the other employees, or, for example when companies avoid hiring Jews for work in Saudi Arabia, the demands of customers or clients. In other cases, it is simply a matter of choosing employees thought most likely to relate easily to those with whom they will be in contact. Is a Sikh with a turban or a woman from Brooklyn likely to be best able to get rural Southern dealers to stock your line of tools? Is it a smart move to send a man to sell needlepoint supplies? Today, taking customers' sex into account in selecting sales representatives constitutes illegal discrimination.

Employees also need to relate to each other within the workplace, and sometimes discrimination reflects neither animosity nor negative views of ability but merely the desire to have a smoothly-functioning workplace. Amidst all the talk about "diversity" as a rationale for preferential hiring, it should not be forgotten that cohesiveness and compatibility can also be of benefit in a workplace. In particular, in the area of sex, diversity can be disruptive. As everyone knows, men and women are attracted to each other. Exposure to each other in the workplace can result in sexual activity, physical and romantic attachments, and various consequences, including jealousy, favoritism, pregnancy, and marriage, not without some adverse effects on the efficiency of the organization. The likelihood of such results is enhanced when employees must work in

---

[32]Thomas Sowell, *The Economics and Politics of Race*, William Morrow, 1983, p. 177.

close or extended physical proximity. A modicum of privacy and separa-tion of the sexes for things such as dressing and undressing and personal needs is also considered a matter of common decency in our civilization. And the atmosphere of a nearly all-male workplace, particularly a pre-dominantly lower socio-economic class one, has long been regarded as "no place for a lady."

Individual employers have traditionally taken these facts into consid-eration using their own judgment based on the particular case. In the office setting, physical strength was not a significant requirement and large numbers of women were qualified for the work; middle-class mores predominated; physical intimacy was limited; and privacy was no prob-lem. Women were readily hired (although for many years the railroads hired only men as executive secretaries, since they would need to go on extended trips with their bosses on the roads' business cars).

On the other hand, where the potential for trouble was exacerbated by the need for close and extended contact, particularly where strength requirements ruled out all but a few women, women were often auto-matically rejected. Women did not man freighters or firehouses; and the extreme case was represented by the military. There is no privacy in the trenches. And while romantic attachments in the office can be disrup-tive, they are not likely to have life-or-death consequences. You do not want to have an officer deploying his troops even on the basis of friend-ship (one reason for forbidding fraternization between officers and en-listed men), let alone passionate attachment. You do not want Lt. David to send Sgt. Uriah into danger to eliminate his rival for Pvt. Bathsheba (or Pvt. Bruce: homosexuals have not been welcome in the military either). Nor do you want military personnel on duty distracted from their duties by sexual attraction or activities or using their rank to obtain sexual favors, as – surprise! – has now become commonplace at posts such as the now-famous Aberdeen Proving Ground.

Apart from the matter of distractions on the job, an employer might feel that it made sense from the standpoint of efficiency and simplifying operations, in a particular case where suitable employees were predomi-nantly of one sex and there was no shortage of them, to employ only men or only women. A man would have not found it easy to get a job as a telephone operator 50 years ago. When Fred Harvey opened his chain of restaurants along the Santa Fe Railroad in the late 19th Century, he found that waiters' drinking, and their getting into fights with customers, presented a problem. So he replaced them entirely with waitresses – the famous "Harvey Girls," a fixture of the old West that could never have passed muster with the EEOC.

In summary, not only is the reproachful term "discrimination" often used where the characteristics for which someone is being penalized *are* manifestly relevant, but even where that is not the case the discrimination may not be unreasonable or reflective of animosity.

"Racism," "Stereotyping," and Other Ethnic Word Games
"Racism" is another veteran of the civil-rights struggle that has, thanks to the orientation of those who shape public discussion, taken on new life. This word did not need to take on odious baggage from that struggle. Its original meaning was bad enough. The 1940 edition of Webster's Collegiate Dictionary did not contain "racism," but it had "racialism," defined as "race hatred." The New Collegiate edition of 1956 defined "racism" as "assumption of inherent racial superiority or the purity and superiority of certain races, and consequent discrimination against other races . . . Also, less specific, race hatred and discrimination." For the true racist, race is critically important, and he rejects the idea that individual qualifications can override a person's race.

Both race hatred and the idea that all members of certain races are inherently inferior or undesirable are nearly universally regarded as reprehensible and indefensible, and rightly so. Racism is something of which, understandably, no one wants to be accused. (Indeed, the extent to which people cringe at the prospect says a lot about how non-racist American society is.) Conversely, it ought to be something of which no one accuses someone else without convincing proof and careful consideration.

The substance of major supposed manifestations of racism will be analyzed in Chap. VI. Here, the point needs to be made that an intellectual atmosphere and climate of discussion have developed in which not only are charges of racism, even unfounded to the point of frivolity, routinely made with impunity, but the opprobrious term itself is bandied about with no apparent understanding of its meaning: for example, as if it were racist to be aware that there are races.

An opponent of anything demanded by minority-group leaders is likely be called a racist, as San Francisco Mayor Willie Brown called those supporting California's Proposition 209 against state racial discrimination and preferences.[33]

The charge has also become standard whenever a Negro is accused of wrongdoing. The noncommissioned officers accused of sexual offenses at Aberdeen Proving Ground and elsewhere in the 1997 scandals claimed they were the victims of racism. The San Francisco school board president, who had made a campaign issue of parental responsibility, was revealed to be behind on child support payments himself; he accused the newspaper that printed the story of being racially motivated.[34] Years earlier, when that ultra-liberal city's tax collector, a Negro, whose parking meter collectors had been pocketing much of their collections, was suspended from his job, a prominent local minister of the same race (now a member of the county Board of Supervisors) blamed "the sinister forces of institutionalized racism." Washington, D.C.'s mayor Marion Barry charged that he had been singled out for prosecution on drug charges because of his race.

No one seems to get indignant at such charges of racism. Even totally false accusations produce little condemnation. A Negro girl at Emory University received nationwide publicity for her charge that she had received hate mail and death threats and that racial slurs had been scrawled on the walls of her dormitory room. It turned out that the girl had written the letters and done the scrawling herself while under suspicion of cheating in chemistry class. Otis Smith, president of the Atlanta NAACP chapter, who had attacked the university for its alleged racism, was not critical of the girl. "It doesn't matter to me whether she did it or not, because of all the pressure these black students are under at those predominantly white schools. If this will highlight it, if it will bring it to the attention of the public, I have no problem with that."[35]

In other words, whether a charge of racism is true or not is not really of any consequence since we all know that racism is everywhere in this racist society.

The press helps this sort of thing along by its coverage. Reflecting the media's orientation, headlines can be very misleading. "Black and His-

---

[33]John H. Bunzel, "Brown told students: 'Terrorize' the professor," *San Francisco Examiner*, Oct. 29, 1995.

[34]Nanette Asimov, "School Board Chief Lags in Child Support," *San Francisco Chronicle*, May 12, 1997, p. 1.

[35]Peter Applebome, "Harassment Case Is Called a Hoax," *San Francisco Chronicle*, June 1, 1990.

panic Women Face Bias More Than Whites, Labor Study Shows"[36] is an instructive example: it began, "Twice as many black and Hispanic working women *say* [emphasis added] they face discrimination, says a Labor Department study that paints a bleak picture of opportunities in America." "S.F. Accused of Bias in Contracting Program / City excludes American Indians from bid process" was about Indians' desire to get in on the bidding *preferences* San Francisco accords Negroes, Hispanics, and Asians; they were angry at being treated the same as ordinary whites.[37]

Charges of "racism" now do not even require alleged negative feelings about a group. Any reference to race at all is subject to being pressed into service as evidence of racism, as though the mere awareness that there is such a thing as race and ethnic background was a sign of an evil mind. Attacking athletic teams' names such as "Indians" as being racist is a case in point: never mind that this is obviously a compliment to Indians; the mere use of the word apparently is the sin. The cigar store Indian, which reflected the fact that smoking tobacco, a New World plant, originated with the indigenous inhabitants, has been denounced as racist. Some complained that the typical specimen was a "stereotype": that is, he apparently did not cut a fine enough figure. But when a California tobacco-store chain placed noble-looking new Indians in front of their stores, it was immediately denounced as racist nevertheless.[38]

A bill was introduced in the California legislature to allow bat-boys under 16 to work past 7 p.m. on school nights at professional baseball games. One bat-boy, at the committee hearing, volunteered to the committee that he played baseball for a Mexican American league; whereupon the committee chairman, there being two Hispanic women on the committee, joked, "Well, that will get you two votes." "Lawmaker Quits Panel To Protest Racist Remarks," was the news story headline.[39] Dear me. Was the chairman supposed to be unaware that Martinez and Escutia are Hispanic names? The suggestion, even in jest, that his colleagues might be favorably disposed toward a youngster of their ethnic background was unspeakable? It is fine for the boy to announce that he plays in a Mexican-

---

[36] Asra Q. Nomani, *Wall Street Journal*, Oct. 17, 1994.

[37] *San Francisco Chronicle*, March 26, 1997.

[38] Glen Martin, "Cloud of Controversy Thickens Over Statue," *San Francisco Chronicle*, Oct. 4, 1996, p. A21.

[39] *San Francisco Chronicle*, June 28, 1997, p. A15.

American league, fine for there to be such a league, fine for legislators from ethnic minorities to talk constantly about ethnicity, affirmative action, and the like, but it is racism for a white male to be aware of their ethnic background?

"Stereotyping" is another contribution to muddled reasoning by the ever-seeing-injustice writing and talking community. One day, the *San Francisco Examiner* had a front-page headline:

S.F. a lure for Gypsy con artists[40]
Inside the paper was another story, entitled:

Gypsies can't shake criminal image
Stereotype has followed the Rom for 1,000 years[41]

The fact is that stereotypes reflect something *real*: something disproportionately present in particular groups. A committee of white males didn't get together and say, "Let's see: who shall we say tends to drink too much? Hasidic Jews? Sicilians? Hey, how about Irish? Let's pick Irish for that." In fact, Irish people, and Irish-Americans, on average do drink more than members of most ethnic groups. Practically everyone understands that so-called stereotypes reflect broad generalizations rather than rules universally applicable to every member of a group, so attacking "stereotypes" is merely one more barrier to recognition of the now resented and rejected reality that group differences are real rather than mere creations of white male oppressors.

Since advocates of racial preferences are beginning to try to scare people with the spectre of what they call "segregation," it is worth remembering that that now long-outlawed practice involved *assigning people on the basis of race*, so that, for example, children might *not* go to their neighborhood schools. When they did, and the school was all of one race because the neighborhood was, whether Negro in Harlem or white in rural Minnesota, no one called this naturally-occurring result "segregation."

When liberals attributed magical properties to "racial balance," thinking that a proportional mixture of the races in each school would raise up

---

[40]Steven A. Chin, July 3, 1994.
[41]Eric Brazil, July 3, 1994, p. A-11. If the second piece was intended to avert criticism for running the first, it failed: letters to the editor (July 10, 1994) expressed "shock" and "outrage" at the front-page story.

the Negroes rather than pull down the whites, they concocted the term "*de facto* segregation" to give a bad name to the natural results of housing patterns. It is an oxymoron; the only kind of segregation is *de jure* – by law. It would be similar nonsense to call an extended vacation abroad "*de facto* exile." Segregation and exile must be imposed by law. Neither the absence of Negroes from a law school nor of whites from a basketball team pursuant to the application of objective standards constitutes the ancient ogre of segregation.

"Multiculturalism" sounds wholesome. Should not the many cultures represented in this "nation of immigrants" get appropriate respect? But in practice "multiculturalism" basically amounts to denigrating Western civilization. "Affirmative action" has a fine, positive ring to it, sounding much more appealing than racial and sex preferences, but now that it is widely understood to mean the same thing "diversity" has sprouted all over. Surely it is to be preferred to monotonous uniformity? Alas, in practice it does not mean meaningful diversity at all, but simply giving preferences based on race and sex. (One term that the press consistently avoids using for preferences is "preferences." Thus the *New York Times'* account of the University of Washington's response to passage by the state's voters of the 1998 initiative banning preferences was headed, "Citing Vote, U. of Washington Is Ending Race-Conscious Admissions."[42])

A very peculiar thing has suddenly happened to the prevailing view of the significance of race. Once upon a time, one may remember, it was the old segregationists who insisted that people were defined by their race. No Negro, no matter how well-mannered, intelligent or educated, was qualified to eat in this restaurant or attend that school or college. "They're happier with their own kind," the Mississippian might have said. All right-thinking people rejected such foolishness with indignant scorn. "How can you define someone, or someone's 'kind,' by something as utterly extraneous and superficial as skin color? Why not hair color or height?"

Martin Luther King, Jr. eloquently denounced such wrong-headedness in his famous speech.

But now we have "diversity." It is supposed to be a very valuable thing to have a certain percentage of Negroes in a workplace (or a college, or wherever). And why? Because all Negroes, by virtue of having at least a drop of

---

[42]Nov. 7, 1998.

African blood, have unique characteristics for want of which the workplace and employer would be worse off. They *are*, in fact, defined by membership in a race (and a very artificially and arbitrarily defined race at that).

This is of course nonsense. It is true that diversity can be desirable; but this assumes *real, meaningful,* diversity: of things such as education, background, outlook, and interests. No one cares about the percentage of people with red hair or 5'8" in height. (Nor is all diversity desirable, either. A biology laboratory is no place for a Greek and Latin scholar with no scientific background.) "Negroes should not be rejected because of the color of their skin because it has nothing to do with their qualifications, but they should be hired because of the color of their skin because it gives them unique qualifications" is a logical absurdity.

As the Fifth Circuit Court of Appeals put it in its *Hopwood* opinion on racial preferences at the University of Texas School of Law, in response to the law school's talk about "diversity," preferences don't produce meaningful diversity, only a student body "that *looks* different."

There is no "black viewpoint" that someone with some African ancestry will automatically provide. The entire spectrum of views and outlook is found, whether in lawyers and Supreme Court justices (compare Thurgood Marshall and Clarence Thomas), writers (Carl Rowan and Thomas Sowell), or political leaders (Jesse Jackson and Ward Connerly). Nor is there such a thing as "black personality" or "black character." Looking at the sports world, Mike Tyson, Latrell Sprewell, Tiger Woods, and Arthur Ashe are hardly peas in a pod.

There is no universal "black experience." With Negroes as with everyone else, individuals' experiences are infinitely varied. A Negro may be the child of a Mississippi farm laborer, a Chicago millionaire, a Washington bureaucrat, a Los Angeles teacher, a New York musician, or a San Francisco welfare mother.

There is no special expertise in familiarity with discrimination. According to a 1997 CNN-Time poll, only 23% of Negro teenagers, and 53% of Negro adults, believe they personally have experienced discrimination – and that is despite the endless talk about it that encourages them to think it is there.[43] And there are plenty of others with creden-

---

[43]Clarence Page, "Survey shows black teens know freedom's not free," *Contra Costa Times*, Nov. 30, 1997, p. F12.

tials in this area. Japanese-Americans, who were interned during World War II, know a lot about discrimination. So do Chinese-Americans. So do many whites; I recently read a letter to the editor in the *New York Times* whose writer recalled walking to school in a group with fellow Jews so they would not get beaten up. A New York security analyst of Italian ancestry once told me of his unhappy experiences growing up in an Irish neighborhood in Boston.

Whites and Asians are not identical, cookie-cutter, bland, white-bread, interchangeable people. The idea that replacing a white or an Asian with a Negro automatically makes a contribution to worthwhile diversity is in fact racist nonsense.

There are, of course, those who think of themselves as "authentic blacks." Obsessed with their skin color and convinced that they are the targets of a ubiquitous racism, they tend to separate themselves from those of other races, seethe with resentment at what they perceive as constant slights, display lower-class mannerisms, and focus much of their attention on racial matters. They would bring to the workplace a real diversity that would no doubt be enthusiastically received by those who would welcome a bad headache to enliven an otherwise uneventful day. But selecting by color alone is not the most effective way to get disagreeable and paranoid lower-class people.

What percentage of those who enthuse about "diversity" actually think they are promoting something of substance, as opposed to doing the best they can to justify and sell the racial favoritism they like, I will not attempt to guess. But they would not be getting away with it to the extent they have been, with this phony "diversity" widely taken seriously as a reason for racial preferences, if the media and the other principal players in public discussion had a different orientation.

If the old segregationists had had the intellectual community on their side, they might well have been waging battles for "harmony," "cohesiveness," or "compatibility." And states' rights would have been a holy Constitutional imperative comparable in force to the rights of criminal suspects, never before detected in the Constitution, that the Supreme Court made up in the Warren years.

Other Egalitarian/Obscurantist Twaddle

Those whose religion is egalitarianism not only see differences among groups as imposed by oppressors and their recognition as a mark of moral deficiency, they also struggle against them by eliminating straightforward language and, where feasible, by substituting terms whose use promotes their objectives.

Supposed victim groups are assumed to be preoccupied with their status and easily devastated by any reference to or reminder of it. The Presbyterian Church's new hymnal dropped "Stand up, stand up for Jesus" as "offensive to the handicapped." Real estate agents have been advised to avoid the terms "sweeping view" and "walk-in closet" as offensive to the blind and crippled, respectively.

"Crippled," of course, is out. "Physically challenged" is popular. "Universal baths and bathrooms" are being designed by people who want to "eliminate the stigma that older people often feel with the installation of grab bars and other geriatric devices," according to the *Wall Street Journal*. Perhaps we should all walk with canes, whether we need them or not.

The feeble-minded are long gone, and the retarded are on the way out, the meaning of that term having over time become too clear. "People with learning disabilities" has the advantage that one is not completely sure whether they have some peculiar problem such as dyslexia or are simply feeble-minded. "Developmentally disabled" has similar non-specific properties. The headline "'Mentally Challenged' Man Held in Slaying of Family"[44] presents yet another possibility. Particularly in the case of children, "special," which used to be a doting parent's term for an especially darling child, also commonly means "feeble-minded" now.

Much of the new terminology does not simply obscure facts about human differences but conveys a political message. "Homeless persons" sound a lot more sympathetic than bums or derelicts. Slum-dwellers, traditionally regarded as having some responsibility for the squalor of their surroundings, have become "inner-city residents." The inner city apparently just happens to be a bad place to live. It is subject to a "crack epidemic" that seems to have swirled in like a fog. People "suffer from" "disabilities" such as "chemical dependency."

"The children" have become quite prominent recently, with efforts to curb welfare and income redistribution opposed as threatening children. "Do not cut down the flow of funds to promiscuous women on welfare" doesn't have quite the punch of "Let's not hurt the helpless children." In fact, of course, "the children" are not living as independent bands, and

---

[44]*San Francisco Chronicle*, Oct. 3, 1997, p. A8.

hoping that welfare money sent to their mothers gets spent on them rather than on drugs or alcohol is a pretty iffy way of helping children, but arguing in terms of "the children" was an effective tactic, although ultimately unsuccessful, in the attempt to stave off 1996's welfare reform.

Unwed mothers have vanished, too, suddenly replaced by "single mothers." As with "disabilities," this usage muddies the waters; one is not sure whether such a mother is divorced, widowed, or unwed.

Many children, sadly, particularly in minority slums, kill each other, frequently in connection with gangs or drugs. A recent front-page headline, however, "U.S. leads in killing its children,"[45] was suggestive of the Slaughter of the Innocents.

These introductory chapters should make clear that the American intellectual and media world, broadly defined, has a predominantly negative view of the fairness of the country's traditional socio-economic system, and that it has had a tremendous influence in shaping public discussion of political issues along the lines of that negative view. It is still remarkable that Americans have allowed themselves to be sold a bill of goods widely thought to justify not only such intrusions on individual freedoms and private property rights as government control of personnel management and lending practices but even open favoritism, in order to save their fellow citizens from mistreatment at their hands, but it is understandable in the light of the brainwashing that has been carried on.

---

[45]Kelly Ryan, *Contra Costa Times*, Feb. 7, 1997, p. 1A.

CHAPTER IV

WHY WOULD OTHER AMERICANS WANT TO TREAT NEGROES UNFAIRLY?

The obvious place to begin in analyzing whether government intervention is appropriate in order to prevent people from being unfairly treated because of their membership in a group is with the group whose cause started the country on that road, Negroes.

I am of course well aware that the currently most "correct" term is "African Americans" or perhaps "African-Americans," with "blacks" fairly acceptable. Before that "blacks" was the preferred term, with a period of competition from "Afro-Americans." Before that, "colored people" strove to supplant "Negroes," which was the standard term when I was a child, with the word "black" used only in a pejorative sense. Through all this time whites have remained "whites." I have a strong disinclination to change, *a fortiori* to change repeatedly, perfectly good words, and I have no feelings of guilt leading me to think I should jump through verbal hoops by way of atonement.

Furthermore, implicit in both "black" and "African American" is something that in the case of an estimated 75% of those so called is not true: that they have no European ancestry. In fact, many have a great deal. If "white" means, as it always has in this country, being 100% European and 0% African, then by analogy "black" suggests precisely the reverse; and to call someone who may be half or more European "African American" is even more obviously misleading. "Intercontinental American" is not very informative – what continents? – and "European and African American" is cumbersome to the point of absurdity.

Defining anyone with any African ancestry at all in this way, regardless of the term used, is a unique approach – no one would automatically call an American who was seven-eighths German and one-eighth Chinese "Chinese" or "Chinese-American" (even in the South African scheme of things, "black" refers to those with no European ancestry, with those of mixed background in a separate category, "colored"). The practice goes back to the old racist idea that African ancestry constituted a taint, hardly a respectable basis for classifying people today. The famous golfer Tiger Woods, refusing to categorize himself in that way, likes to call himself "Cablinasian," reflecting his Caucasian, African, Thai, and American Indian ancestry.[1]

It would have been equally logical to define anyone with any *European* ancestry at all as a "Blanco" and reserve the term "black" for those purely African, in which case we would have a very different but equally artificial racial division. The term "Negro," at least, is a reminder of how the group we are talking about is defined and does not muddy the waters further.

Not only did the language of the movement for equal treatment for Negroes, called the civil-rights movement, provide a model or form readily adaptable for other groups by, in effect, filling in the blanks differently, it provided an effective vocabulary of words charged with emotional impact from connotations acquired in what was widely viewed as a just and virtuous struggle.

In addition, its eventual outcome served as the precedent for similar intervention on behalf of other groups, bringing government into areas of private property and individual choice in ways that would previously have been well-nigh unthinkable.

There were significant differences. Women, for example, were half the population, not a tenth; men did not lynch women but married them, and had voluntarily given them the vote; and no one claimed that differences between men and women, including different average size and strength, were merely figments of bigots' imagination. Hispanics had never been slaves in the United States nor subjected to segregation by law. Old people really do lose effectiveness and die, on average, a good deal sooner than young people. And people with disabilities by definition have real handicaps rather than merely being a different color.

---

[1]Thomas Sowell, "Tiger Woods gets beyond race issue," *Contra Costa Times*, May 19, 1997, p. A11.

No matter. What was sauce for the goose was sauce for the steak, the oyster, and the artichoke.

The case of the Negro is thus particularly important, not only because such a high proportion of claims of bias involve race, but also because in view of past history it is here if anywhere that one might expect to find fairness and economic self-interest inadequate to overcome prejudice and ill-will and produce a basically equitable result.

Even if there is significant discrimination against Negroes, of course, it doesn't automatically follow that free choice in this area should be replaced by government control.

Even if the governing principle is maximum fairness regardless of cost, or at least up to the point where it becomes manifestly absurd, there is no guarantee that socialized human resources management will produce better results. It still relies on fallible and flawed human beings, and these farther from the scene. Intervening to punish A for hiring B instead of C may in fact be unfair to both A and B. Proving that many companies make bad capital investments doesn't prove that industry should be nationalized.

A question that deserves to be asked at the outset is why people would *want* to hold someone's African ancestry against him. We are of course not talking here about perceived undesirable characteristics which naturally inspire aversion but about real racial discrimination, based on race *in and of itself*. What could cause such an attitude?

It is true that Negroes are in general readily recognizable. No matter how strong someone's dislike of a particular ethnic group may be, he will have trouble discriminating against its members if he can't tell them from other people. (If in fact we have reached the point where fiendishly clever people are able to design "culturally biased" examinations whose apparently innocent and reasonable questions members of particular groups are uniquely unable to answer correctly,[2] sufficiently sophisticated bigots no longer face this problem even with people who look "just like anyone else.")

But why should people *want* to hold Negroes' ancestry against them? This elementary question is rarely asked. Wariness toward people of different background, in more pronounced form xenophobia, is indeed a common human trait, as people tend naturally to be more comfortable with people with whom they have much in common and feel "at home,"

---

[2]"Culturally biased tests" will be discussed in the next chapter.

and this has been true even of white Americans, as Yankee "WASPs" distrusted Irish, both distrusted Italians, all three distrusted Jews, all four distrusted Eastern European Jews, all five distrusted Chinese and Japanese, etc. But somehow as time has gone on and all these groups have gotten to know each other better and become more like each other, we have reached the point where no one suggests that government must today step in to stop the free market from giving any of these groups, all but the Yankee once the target of discrimination, the short end of the stick.

The reason can hardly be that it is impossible to detect ancestry in these cases. The ethnicity of many names is obvious, physical appearance provides some clues, and Orientals, at least, can instantly be distinguished from whites. So the fact that Negroes are on the whole readily recognizable does not answer the question why people should have it in for them and not for Chinese or Japanese.

One possibility is that people have an irrational hatred of the Negro appearance: that is, apparently, of dark skin. Given the popularity of sun tans, it is hard to believe a dark complexion by itself is adequate to inspire implacable aversion. And after all Negroes run the gamut from nearly black to a very light tan, a great deal lighter than many people of East Indian ancestry.

A more plausible explanation, at least initially, is that the "legacy of slavery," often blamed for some persisting Negro handicap, includes an unreasonable negative attitude toward Negroes on the part of other Americans. Because they were once slaves with the lowest status, the theory would be, their color still automatically triggers in the minds of a significant number of non-blacks a sense of them as inferior beings.

At least a brief review of the relevant history is in order. Slavery is as old as the hills and had been around thousands of years before the birth of Christ. There were slaves in ancient Egypt, in Greece, and in the Roman Empire. There were slaves in Asia and in Africa. Slaves were of all nationalities and races. Often enslavement resulted from the fortunes of war, as in the case of the Israelites' lengthy slavery in Egypt.

By the time of the discovery of the New World, slavery had become a rarity in Western Europe, although it was relatively common in the Moslem world. Colonization of the Americas' vast lands, however, created a demand for large amounts of cheap labor.

And a convenient source of extra-cheap labor – slaves – was discovered: sub-Sahara Africa. West Africa was relatively close to the Americas; more importantly, its people were in a primitive state of development. This condition was remarked on by early Asian and European explorers; whether the Africans' primitive state was due to climate, genetics, or something else, it unquestionably was not caused by those who discovered them. It made it relatively easy for traders to capture African slaves or, more often, buy them from Arab slave traders or from African tribes who had captured them in tribal warfare.

Buyers were interested in live slaves fit for work, so it was obviously in the traders' interest to get the slaves to their destination in that condition, but even so conditions on slave ships were notoriously bad and an estimated 20% of slaves did not survive the long sea voyage (The mortality rate on the "coffin ships" carrying Irish emigrants to North America in the Potato Famine year of 1847 was about the same[3]).

Life expectancy of American slaves appears to have been about the same as for free American working people, and by the time of the Civil War their numbers had reached 4,000,000. A slave was a valuable asset – the going rate in 1860 was $1,400-$2,000 – and in the pre-Civil War South Irish laborers were often used in work considered too dangerous for slaves.[4] Nonetheless, slaves of course lacked basic human rights; families might be broken up by sales. Some slaves were allowed to buy their freedom or were freed by their owners, but their numbers were relatively small.

Education was limited; in some Southern states, it was illegal to teach a slave to read and write. Thus it is certainly true that slavery left American Negroes in a predominantly uneducated condition, even though it did not put them – that is, their ancestors – in that condition to begin with. The original cultural state of the imported Africans, the consequent prevalent belief that they were of an inferior race, the desire on the part of slaveowners to justify slavery by holding to that belief, and the failure to provide education for Negro slaves, taken all together, could be expected to leave both a widespread view of Negroes as intellectually inferior and a prevailing condition that could easily be taken as confirming rather than refuting that view.

---

[3]Thomas Sowell, *Ethnic America*, Basic Books, 1981, p. 22.
[4]*Ibid.*, p. 27.

Many, of course, particularly in the North, were strongly opposed to the institution of slavery or in any case did not regard the culture and achievements of Negroes under it as indicative of their true potential. Certainly many individual cases of successful Negroes (one had even been a prosperous slave trader in early New England) gave the lie to the notion that all members of the race were intellectually inferior. Nevertheless, when slavery was abolished in 1865, American Negroes were predominantly poor and lacking in education and marketable skills.

It is true that they were in a more advanced condition than would have been the case had their ancestors not been taken from Africa and brought to America. As Booker T. Washington, himself born a slave, wrote, in his 1901 autobiography, Up from Slavery:

> Then, when we rid ourselves of prejudice, or racial feeling, and look facts in the face, we must acknowledge that, notwithstanding the cruelty and moral wrong of slavery, the ten million Negroes inhabiting this country, who themselves or whose ancestors went through the school of American slavery, are in a stronger and more hopeful condition, materially, intellectually, morally, and religiously, than is true of an equal number of black people in any other portion of the globe . . . This I say, not to justify slavery – on the other hand, I condemn it as an institution, as we all know that in America it was established for selfish and financial reasons, and not from a missionary motive – but to call attention to a fact . . . [5]

Still, they had been slaves, they were in a relatively backward state, and the general view was that they were members of an inferior race. This view lasted a long time.

Once Reconstruction ended and the Southern states regained self-government, their whites soon succeeded, by means of the ballot box and also by intimidation, in retaking political power, and they enacted the so-called Jim Crow laws, establishing racial segregation in everything from schools to railroad cars. The United States Supreme Court, in its 1896 Plessy v. Ferguson case, held that segregation that was "separate but equal" did not violate the equal protection clause of the Fourteenth

---

[5]Pocket Books, 1940 (1901), pp. 11-12.

Amendment. Yet, unquestionably, segregation having been not the Negroes' idea but rather imposed by whites, it constituted an official badge of inferiority applied to all those with any black African ancestry.

Segregation, of course, was not an example of the free enterprise system at work but of the political system's being used to override individual choice. Segregated coaches had not been the railroad companies' idea. Businessmen tended to be more interested in profits than race; during the era of slavery, when white workers at a Virginia factory objected to working with slaves, the owners fired the white workers and replaced them with more slaves.[6] After the Civil War, however, it became accepted that some jobs were "white jobs" and others "Negro jobs."

Outside the South, official segregation was relatively rare but not absent; the armed forces became resegregated during Woodrow Wilson's administration. In the private sector, many jobs and neighborhoods were closed to Negroes.

For decades after the end of slavery, few Negroes were qualified for the better jobs. W.E.B. Du Bois, the founder of the National Association for the Advancement of Colored People, recognized, around the turn of the century, that "representative Negroes" were "probably best fitted for the work they are doing," and if prejudice disappeared overnight it "would not make very much difference in the positions occupied by Negroes" as a whole.[7]

Booker T. Washington believed it a "great human law, which is universal and eternal, that merit, no matter under what skin found, is in the long run, recognized and rewarded."[8] The response to those who acquired skills at his Tuskegee Institute, in Alabama, suggests that his view had validity even in the Deep South at that time. Companies were eager to hire Tuskegee students because of their reputations; one, for example, having learned advanced agricultural techniques, was hired to take over the operation of a large white-owned farm.[9]

As the artificial hindrance represented by slavery slipped further and further into the past and Negro skills grew relative to white, the gap between

---

[6]Thomas Sowell, *The Economics and Politics of Race*, William Morrow, 1983, p. 179.
[7]Sowell, *Ethnic America*, p. 293.
[8]Booker T. Washington, *Up from Slavery*, Pocket Books, 1940 (1901), p. 29.
[9]Elizabeth Wright, "The Movable School," *Issues & Views*, summer 1995.

black and white earnings steadily diminished. At the same time, many gifted and able Negroes overcame prejudice by refuting it through showing what they could do and achieving success as businessmen and professionals. An example was C.H. James, who began a wholesale fruit and vegetable business in West Virginia in 1881 which expanded steadily; former President Theodore Roosevelt wrote him, "I think I have spoken of you at least a hundred times, pointing to you as the man who actually is by his actions and not merely by words solving the race problem in this country."[10]

Thus, even though racial discrimination remained completely legal and many white workers and their unions strove to reduce competition for jobs by demanding that employers not hire Negroes, more and more jobs became open to them as the costs of refusing to consider Negroes for employment grew. Jackie Robinson played for the Brooklyn Dodgers and San Francisco's Municipal Railway hired Negro streetcar motormen and conductors. According to Thomas Sowell, for example, in the period between 1954 and 1964, the decade *before* the passage of the Civil Rights Act outlawing discrimination in employment, the number of Negroes in professional, technical, and similar high-level positions more than doubled. In fact, the percentage of employed Negroes who were professional and technical workers rose less in the five years following the Act than in the five preceding it. In other kinds of occupations Negroes' advance was even greater "during the 1940s – when there was little or no civil rights policy – than during the 1950s when the civil rights revolution was in its heyday."[11] As University of Chicago economist Gary S. Becker (subsequently Nobel Laureate in Economics) showed in his 1957 book, *The Economics of Discrimination*,[12] racial discrimination was costly to those who practiced it.

White attitudes changed as Negroes progressed. In 1940, 87% of Negro families were in poverty; the figure was down to 47% in 1960.[13] In 1940, only about a third of white Americans said that it would not "make any difference" to them if "a Negro with the same income and education" as theirs moved onto their block; by 1956, the percentage had risen to over 50%; by 1966, to 71%; and in 1972, it was 85%.[14]

---

[10]*Wall Street Journal*, Feb. 2, 1995.
[11]Thomas Sowell, *Civil Rights: Rhetoric or Reality?* William Morrow, 1984, p. 49.
[12]University of Chicago Press; rev. ed. 1971.
[13]Stephan and Abigail Thernstrom, *America in Black and White*, Simon & Schuster, 1997, p. 18.
[14]*Ibid.*, p. 221.

President Truman eliminated segregation in the Armed Forces after World War II, and the Supreme Court's *Brown v. Board of Education* decision in 1954 declared that racial segregation by government violated the Equal Protection clause of the Constitution. (Before long, however, the courts were *requiring* race-based pupil assignments in the form of busing.)

For the next ten years, as segregation in tax-supported institutions was dismantled, the long-standing rule as to individual rights in the private sector remained the same. Private individuals and businesses could hire or do business with whomever they wished.

That included the operators of lunch counters and restaurants, which became a target of those demanding that discrimination in the private sector be outlawed. This was, at the time, controversial and strongly opposed as unconstitutional. Never before, except in the case of a New Deal law forbidding firing people for union membership, had the government forbidden private individuals or businesses to hire or not hire people, or to do business or not do business with them, as they chose, for whatever reason, sensible and fair or otherwise.

But, how could anyone defend racial discrimination? All the Act would do, its proponents insisted and its plain language said, was outlaw provable discrimination. Hubert Humphrey, a leading advocate, assured the Senate that claims that it would lead to quotas or preferences or deny employers the right to apply reasonable standards across the board lacked any factual basis. In an attempt to kill the legislation, opponents added sex to race as a forbidden basis for discrimination. But the whole apparatus of "enlightened opinion" was in high gear; the issue, including the huge "March on Washington" to whose vast throng Rev. Martin Luther King Jr. gave his now-famous "I have a dream" speech, was front-page news day after day. The Civil Rights Act passed.

Under the Act, someone who sued for damages claiming to be the victim of job discrimination was entitled, if he proved his case, only to pay actually lost; punitive damages, as to which the sky is the limit, were ruled out. Also, these cases were to be tried before a judge, not a jury. And it was generally thought that someone had to actually prove that he had been purposefully discriminated against, for example by a Negro's demonstrating that he had been rejected for hiring or promotion in favor of a less-qualified white or having other evidence, perhaps remarks that had been made, of discriminatory intent. A federal Equal Employment

Opportunity Commission was also set up, with the assumption that it would look into specific complaints of discrimination much as commissions set up in some states in the 40s had done.[15]

This stage did not last long. The proponents of the Civil Rights Act clearly had had more things in mind than outlawing provable discrimination. Disdaining a case-by-case approach to specific charges of discrimination, the EEOC set to work attacking the use of standards that screened out a higher percentage of Negroes than whites, and in 1971 the Supreme Court, in the *Griggs v. Duke Power Co.* case, accepted this radical divergence from the clear intent of the 1964 Act. Unless an employer could show a "business necessity" for a standard, it was forbidden if it had a "disparate impact" on applicants of different races, regardless of absence of discriminatory intent.[16] If an employer didn't want to spend a lot of time in court, he was well-advised to make sure he hired enough Negroes. According to a 1989 survey in *Fortune*, only 14% of Fortune 500 companies claimed to hire on merit alone; 18% admitted to racial quotas and 54% said they had "goals."[17] Except during the Reagan years, when Clarence Thomas refocused the EEOC on individual cases of deliberate discrimination, the federal government's agencies have typically been aggressive in attacking employers for alleged discrimination based on different percentages of whites and minorities in their work forces. A 1993 *Wall Street Journal* study found a widespread pattern in companies reducing their work forces of laying off more experienced white men in order to retain junior women and minority-group members and found that this was occurring not because the white men were less cost-effective but in order to avoid becoming vulnerable to enforcement actions and lawsuits.

The companies, of course, are not home free once they have the right percentage of Negroes on board. In the nature of things, under-qualified employees get relatively few promotions. The problem then becomes one of disgruntled employees who got jobs because of the color of their skin com-

---

[15]An example was that of Massachusetts. A study by sociologist Leon Mayhew of complaints to its commission from 1946 to 1962 found that typically the complainers' own deficiencies, not discrimination, were found to be the source of their problems.

[16]See Paul Craig Roberts and Lawrence M. Stratton Jr., "Color Code," *National Review*, March 20, 1995, for an excellent summary of the transformation of the Civil Rights Act.

[17]Roberts and Stratton, "Proliferation of Privilege," *National Review*, November 6, 1995.

plaining that they are being held back because of the color of their skin: the employer is still accused of discrimination, but now of a different type.

In 1989 the Supreme Court undid some of what had been wrought by rejecting the basing of a prima facie case of discrimination on statistical disparities alone, but the 1991 Civil Rights Act changed that. For good measure it also made jury trials available in discrimination lawsuits and made punitive and compensatory damages available as well, thereby attracting the serious attention of the lawsuit industry. Large companies are a particularly attractive target, not only because of the potentially large number of employees who can join in a class-action lawsuit, but because the Act's limit is $300,000 per employee in companies with over 500 employees vs. only $50,000 for those with under 101.[18]

In less than 35 years, thus, the state of American employment law as regards race has gone from complete individual discretion to the statutory prohibition of deliberate discrimination to, additionally, presumption by government enforcers of guilt on the basis of "under-representation" of minorities in a work force and the creation of far-reaching exposure to lawsuits on a similar basis.

For good measure, the federal government and many states and cities have adopted programs giving minorities preference in employment and contracting. These have been restrained by recent Supreme Court decisions holding such preferences to violate the Equal Protection clause of the Constitution unless narrowly tailored to remedy actual past discrimination by the particular governmental entity. Such entities have eagerly hired consultants to try to show that they have been guilty of such conduct in the past, creating a new industry, but these studies have typically been rejected by the courts as showing only that Negroes had seldom been selected, not that they had been rejected for discriminatory reasons.

We have indeed traveled a long, long road since the days of slavery, and traveled it in large part because of white Americans' sense of justice and fair play and determination to be fair to Negroes. This didn't happen overnight, just as acceptance of other "different" groups didn't happen overnight, but for all its imperfections Americans' comparative openness and

---

[18]The Civil Rights Act forbids discrimination against whites too, but not only is demonstrating such discrimination on the basis of statistics rarely an available option (since, even with preferences for Negroes, the higher-level jobs are disproportionately held by whites), the Supreme Court's *Weber* decision held that Title VII was not meant to outlaw discrimination against whites.

fairness to those of different ethnic backgrounds has long helped make the country a Mecca for immigrants and justifies more pride than shame.

Manifestly, the "legacy of slavery" in the form of the view of Negroes as inherently inferior was a waning and, ultimately, a dying one. The typical view now is that the era of slavery was an epic injustice casting no adverse reflection on those who were slaves but rather calling for shame on the part of white Americans. We have still not found an answer to the basic question of why other Americans should want to treat Negroes differently than those of other ethnic backgrounds.

Nor does the case of American Negroes fall into any of the common patterns of racial discrimination found in history and in the rest of the world.

One basis for discrimination involves religious as well as ethnic differences. But America has seen nothing approaching the religious hatreds manifested in the Old World in places such as Northern Ireland, the Balkans, Czarist Russia, the Near East, and India. Animosity toward Irish "Papists" in the 19th Century United States was negligible by comparison. And in any case the predominant religion of American Negroes is Protestant Christianity, which is exactly the religion particularly prevalent among Southern whites (and not by coincidence, since the Negroes typically acquired the religion of their masters in the days of slavery).

Another classic type of racial animosity is that toward particularly hard-working and successful minority groups, born of envy and resentment. The cases of Jews in Germany, Armenians in the Ottoman Empire, Chinese in Malaya, East Indians in Africa, Ibos in Nigeria, and Koreans in Harlem are among those that fall in this category. But this pattern is hardly applicable in the case of American Negroes, whose relative *lack* of success is precisely what causes the suspicion that they are suffering from discrimination.

A third type of racial antagonism arises out of direct competition for livelihood. Violence against Chinese workmen in California in the 19th Century is an example. White South African workers, early in this century, agitated against blacks and demanded laws excluding them from certain occupations in order to reserve the job opportunities for themselves. Similarly, racial antagonism has consistently been strongest among poor whites, by whom competition from Negroes was perceived as a real threat. In areas of the country where labor unions became powerful, they often served as a means of keeping Negroes, together with other non-union workers, away from jobs, by denying them membership. Legislation was sought for that purpose as well; the proponents of the Davis-Bacon Act, requiring "prevailing wages" on publicly-funded construction projects, acknowledged that one purpose was to eliminate competition from non-union firms employing Negro workers.[19]

But antagonism born out of a struggle for jobs would not explain why employers and managerial employees, who certainly are not in a struggle for jobs with those they interview and supervise, should be anti-Negro. True, some may have recently risen from the factory floor themselves, or be from a family whose breadwinner saw himself as in a struggle for work in competition with Negroes, and that may influence their attitude. Those higher up, however, who set company policy, are rather unlikely to be part of this culture, and even less likely to be so much a part of it as to want to place the indulging of racial animosity ahead of getting the best people for the company's jobs.

In any case, the United States today is not Birmingham or Pittsburgh in 1936. The idea that there are enough white and Asian workers to whom a threat from low-wage Negro competition has such an immediacy as to engender pervasive racial antagonism throughout the country has to be considered altogether far-fetched[20].

Summing up, Africans were originally brought to the New World as slaves not because people disliked dark-skinned people but because they were primitive and available. They were, with relatively few exceptions, artificially held back by the system of slavery; but once the nation repudiated and abolished that system as an evil, they progressed, despite segregation and discrimination, both because of their own efforts and because white Americans, more and more and, ultimately, overwhelmingly, became convinced that race was irrelevant to merit. Although until 1964 legally free to discriminate, fewer and fewer chose to do so. Nor is there any obvious reason why they should wish to do so. It would be strange and irrational behavior indeed gratuitously to mistreat inoffensive indi-

---

[19]Scott Alan Hodge, "Davis-Bacon: Racist Then, Racist Now," *Wall Street Journal*, June 25, 1990.

[20]There is, to be sure, a good deal of white resentment at the preferential treatment of minorities that has become widespread. But that is a very different thing from opposition to fair, color-blind treatment of members of other racial groups.

viduals whose ancestors practically everyone agrees got a raw deal.[21] If Americans actually have it in for Negroes because of the color of their skin, this is a mysterious thing indeed.

But they really don't seem to. Take the case of Siskiyou County, in far northern California bordering Oregon. According to a recent newspaper account, "The county is still pretty much the Wild West hinterland it was in the mid-1850s"; "with a black population of about 2 percent, [it] helps define the terms rural and redneck." Unemployment, due to lumber mill closings, is high. It is of course in backwaters such as this that racism is widely believed to be particularly deep-seated.

The county sheriff, who grew up in the county in the town of Weed, has been elected and re-elected for 12 years and is so popular that even suspicions that he had been drinking in his car made no dent in his re-election prospects. "Hell, Charlie – he's a down-home boy like the rest of us, and who cares if he was drinking or not? Most of us have been fishing with him or barbecuing with him. We all know him," said a local businesswoman. The sheriff, Charles Byrd (who also is president of the state Sheriff's Association), is a Negro.[22]

If, of course, Mr. Byrd had slum manners and values, exuded anger and resentment, had been promoted over others with better qualifications because of his skin color, and was in the habit of accusing anyone who criticized or opposed him of racism, it is a safe bet that he would not be the popular sheriff that he is. But it would not have been his race that had held him back.

---

[21]If your reaction is, "That may be so, but 'inoffensive individuals' is not the most apt description for the kind of blacks most likely to be discriminated against," be careful: you are confusing behavior with race. As pointed out in Chap. VI, this confusion underlies many accusations of racism, including self-accusations.

[22]Kevin Fagan, "Wild West Sheriff Is Hard to Beat," *San Francisco Chronicle*, June 2, 1998, p. A15.

Chapter V

Relative Success and Racial Discrimination

D o we normally assume that if an individual is not doing well finan-
cially this is because others have it in for him? Or that if a country is
relatively poor this must be because prosperous countries bear it ill-will?

Some years ago a news story focused on the contrast between the
failure of British companies to make sales in certain markets and the
success of their Japanese competitors. The reasons were straightforwardly
discussed. They were that the British products were not competitive in
price or in quality and/or that the companies had a bad attitude toward
their prospective customers in terms of cooperating with them and ac-
commodating their needs.

It seemed to have occurred to no one to suggest that deep-seated
antagonism toward Great Britain might be the problem, let alone to
proceed as if that was the obvious explanation. Indeed, Japan's newly-
won customers included countries that had had very unhappy experiences with it in World War II.

Nor was the problem due to ancient stereotypes: on the contrary.
When in the 50s a Japanese delegation met in Washington with American leaders to discuss Japan's economic problems and needs, Secretary of
State John Foster Dulles found the suggestion that Japan might be able
to earn needed foreign exchange by selling finished goods in the United
States laughable. He suggested that the Japanese ought to direct their
attention to markets in Asia where the quality of their products might be
acceptable. It was the Japanese who had to convince prospective buyers
that they were now offering quality goods. And, when they did that, they
found ready buyers.

Out of respect for Adam Smith, let us similarly consider the hypothesis that Negroes do poorly relative to other ethnic groups for reasons similar to those that were holding British exports back: not because people have it in for them but because a relatively high percentage of them are poorly qualified and/or have a bad attitude.

It seems almost brutal to suggest such a possibility about a group that has been so consistently portrayed, in the media and in public discussion, as victims. But it is also rather brutal to attribute intransigent bigotry to such a large part of the American people. If the accusation is false, they are being slandered outrageously. And if the result of spreading this view has been to poison the attitudes of Negroes so as to further hamper their competitiveness, they have been done a grave disservice as well.

No one is unclear as to the fact that Negroes, on average, do less well than whites, or Asians, in terms of financial and occupational success. Statistics to that effect are publicized constantly.

The percentage of whites who own homes, for example, rose from 69.1 in 1983 to 70.8 in 1995, while in the same period the percentage for Negroes dropped from 45.6 to 42.2.[1] In terms of income, the Census Bureau reported in 1994 that the median income for Negro families was 54% of that of white in 1992, compared with 61% in 1969. Even though the statistics are affected by the disproportionate increase in illegitimacy and decline in two-parent families that has occurred among Negroes, their basic message as to inequality of average success, decades after racial discrimination was outlawed, is valid.[2]

This overall state of affairs reflects near-invisibility at the top levels in the private sector (for example, of the 102 executives in major San Francisco Bay Area companies with reported earnings of $1 million or more in 1997, not one was a Negro[3]), disproportionately high representation on welfare rolls and in low-paying jobs, and a relatively limited presence in well-paying, skilled occupations. "Blacks and Latinos," according to a 1998 study, "are largely missing out on the Silicon Valley technology boom – [California's] most powerful economic engine since the Gold Rush."[4]

---

[1] Source: U.S. Census Bureau.

[2] The Census Bureau reported that when both husband and wife worked, the average Negro couple earned 85% of the white couple's income.

[3] "The Million-Dollar Club," *San Francisco Chronicle*, June 1, 1998, p. E2.

[4] Julia Angwin and Laura Castaneda, "The Digital Divide," *San Francisco Chronicle*, May 4, 1998, p. 1.

POOR QUALIFICATIONS

To those whose intellect is no match for their egalitarian yearnings or egalitarian religious convictions, such disparities are conclusive proof that Negroes are the victims of discrimination. Indeed, such data are frequently publicized by the advocates of racial preferences on the theory that they prove that they are "still needed."

But they prove no such thing. On the contrary, many of the specific disparities in success that are publicized clearly suggest to an objective observer that differences in ability or in qualifications rather than discrimination are at work. Consider the following news items, whose language in many cases also demonstrates the media world's widespread conviction as to the pervasiveness of discrimination.

> . . . in Pennsylvania . . . some public officials and lawyers are calling for abolition of the bar examination. They have charged that the tests are "culturally biased" against Negroes and that a high percentage of them do not pass . . .
> — New York Times News Service, Feb. 1, 1971

> RACISM IS SAID TO PERVADE NEW YORK COURTS
> . . . The report . . . by the . . . Commission on Minorities . . . notes that while 82% of the prison population is non-white, 81% of court personnel is white . . . Part of the problem seems to be that such a low percentage of minority law students pass the bar exam . . . Between 1985 and 1988, the passing rate for blacks was 31%, for Native Americans 33%, and for Hispanics 40%. During the same period, the passing rate for whites was 73.1%.
> — Wall Street Journal, June 5, 1991

> Eight black college graduates from Chicago filed a lawsuit against the Civil Service Commission yesterday . . . Statistics cited in the legal brief indicate that while 49% of all people who take the test pass, only 3 percent of those who attended black colleges do so. As a result, they say, only 1.2 percent of all federal employees in the high grades of GS 16 to 18 are black.
> — Times-Post Service, February 5, 1971

US Study Finds Bias In Job Exams
The scores of minorities on a test used to screen job applicants must be adjusted in order to assure that blacks and Hispanics are given equal consideration with whites, experts from the National Research Council said . . ." With no score adjustments, very low fractions of minority-group members will be referred for employment," it said.

— Associated Press, May 24, 1989

Minorities Flunk Test, City Orders New One
San Diego – The Civil Service Commission ordered that a new test be developed for fire fighters aspiring to higher rank after none of the minorities who took the test passed.

— Associated Press, 1986

Deputy FBI Director Floyd Clarke told more than 250 field agents this week that the bureau would be unable to hire specially targeted groups, including "females and minorities," if it did not lower minimum passing scores on its written entrance test, according to bureau sources.

— Washington Post, July 25, 1991

In 1993, the San Francisco Police Department tested 255 applicants, including 22 Negroes; but the highest a Negro woman placed was 70th and the highest-scoring Negro man placed 106th, so none of the sergeants promoted to lieutenant was a Negro.[5] "In the entire history of the San Francisco Police Department there have been only two African Americans who have ever managed to reach the permanent rank of lieutenant," complained the president of Officers for Justice. "That in itself is an indication that there is something dangerously wrong with the system."

Hardly. As Daniel Seligman wrote in *Fortune* magazine when tests in Washington, D.C. produced similar results in 1981, "The proposition that nobody seems willing to utter out loud . . . seems at least as obvious . . . The proposition: members of minority groups might actually not make as good cops, on average, as white people. Any speculation along this line tends to be repressed by all concerned because years of brainwashing by the equal-opportunity establishment have left conscientious citizens . . . persuaded that such thoughts are racist and impermissible."[6]

---

[5]Dennis J. Opatrny, "No blacks in new cop promotions," *San Francisco Examiner*, August 29, 1993, p. B-1.
[6]"Naked in Washington," *Fortune*, Oct. 5, 1981, p. 101.

In fact, aptitude tests in connection with employment are carefully and scientifically developed by the same specialists who devise the Scholastic Aptitude Test ("SAT") and the other examinations on the basis of which people are admitted to college, law school, etc. They know that their whole objective, which they are being paid to achieve, is to determine aptitude for the positions involved and not penalize applicants for irrelevant characteristics. They are part of the academic/educational world so overwhelmingly committed to fairness to minorities. The idea that they are unwilling or unable to develop tests that fairly test the relevant qualifications of all applicants is preposterous.

A silly exercise commonly engaged in until it was exposed was called "race norming." A test administrator would, for example, test 20 Negroes and 80 whites for 20 job openings. Then, when none of the Negroes placed in the top 20, he would add enough points to their scores so that 20% of those with the top scores, to be referred for employment, would be Negroes. This required simultaneously rejecting the test as fairly testing whites vs. Negroes while accepting it as fairly testing Negroes against each other, the logic of which would require some agility to defend.

Usually, tests are rejected altogether as "culturally biased." A typical recent case was that of California's Basic Educational Skills Test, designed by the respected Educational Testing Service of Princeton to test teacher competence. Before it was used, state officials, leaving no stone unturned, conducted independent studies of *every* test question, asking bilingual teachers and administrators whether it was relevant to the job and equally fair to all applicants.

But, after the test was administered, a group of minority-group teachers filed a lawsuit charging that it was "culturally biased": for, while 80% of white takers had passed it, only 35% of Negro, 51% of Latino, and 59% of Asian had. The teachers' lawyer was unable to cite any specific examples of the bias that had eluded such careful scrutiny. "You're not going to find bias on an individual question. The bias is very subtle." Fortunately for California's schoolchildren, the court rejected this nonsense and refused to prohibit the use of the test.[7]

Although examinations for employment typically test for knowledge specific to the job, they also to some extent test general intelligence and problem-solving ability. This is what IQ tests are designed to do.

---

[7]Nanette Asimov, "State Test Upheld for Teachers," *San Francisco Chronicle*, Sept. 19, 1996, p. 1.

The publication of *The Bell Curve*[8] in 1994 again thrust IQ tests into prominence. In particular, its view that consistently lower average Negro IQ scores appear partly genetic in origin inspired the usual thoughtful discussion. *Atlanta Constitution* editorial page editor Cynthia Tucker referred, in one column, to the "ugly and racist" book, its "vile theories," "warped theories of racial superiority," "insidiousness," and "the infection of the poisonous book."[9]

Perhaps among those infected was the president of Rutgers University, Francis L. Lawrence, a consistent advocate of preferential admission of racial minorities. In 1995, defending such policies at a faculty meeting, he argued, "The average SAT for African Americans is 750. Do we set standards . . . so that we don't admit anybody with the national test? Or do we deal with a disadvantaged population that doesn't have that genetic hereditary background to have a higher average?" Days of demonstrations and outrage erupted. Lawrence's defense was that his tongue had a mind of its own; the university board of governors agreed "that he was guilty of nothing more than inadvertently uttering some words that represented the opposite of what he meant."[10] He also "met daily with student and faculty groups to deliver his apology personally."[11]

The phenomenon discussed in *The Bell Curve* was hardly new. Negroes have consistently done relatively poorly on IQ tests, and the question of whether this is due to a "cultural bias" in the tests that invalidates their conclusions as to Negroes who take them has received intensive study. More than ten years earlier, the London *Economist*, never considered a racist rag, devoted seven pages in its Science and Technology section to "The great IQ debate." It addressed the question of IQ differences straightforwardly.

> Begin with the unpalatable fact, accepted by most people on both sides of the debate over race and intelligence because based on literally hundreds of studies: typically, American blacks score 15 IQ points (or one standard deviation) below American whites. Then ask three questions. Does the gap matter? Is it real, or merely an artifact of the tests? If important and real, what does it actually mean: is it a measure of the impact of

---

[8]Richard J. Herrnstein and Charles Murray, The Free Press.

[9] "Language of Bigotry," *San Francisco Chronicle*, Feb. 10, 1995.

[10]Jon Nordheimer, "Rutgers Race Controversy," *San Francisco Chronicle*, Feb. 1, 1995.

[11]Doreen Carvajal, "Protest Stops Ballgame," *Ibid.*, Feb. 8, 1995.

past and present discrimination or of something else as well? The answer to the first question is easy. It matters . . . Consider just one example. Cut-off IQ scores of 70, or even as high as 75-80, are used by many educational authorities to define mental retardation . . . Given the typical profile of IQ scores . . . a cut-off of 70 would affect roughly 2% of whites but 16% of blacks.

As to the second question, the *Economist* went on, "A lot of research, much of it by people convinced blacks were getting a raw deal, has been done on this." Specifically, was the fact that IQ tests use "standard" English and are administered by white examiners causing low black scores? No: cited was a 1982 study by the National Academy of Sciences concluding that blacks' scores do not consistently go up when a black examiner administers a test or when test directions are given in "black English."

> Are the results biased simply because blacks are 'verbally deprived,' learning a smaller vocabulary in their homes and classrooms? One study . . . showed that the black children used only half as many different words as the white. That might explain why blacks score lower compared with whites on verbal tests.
>
> Awkwardly, however, blacks tend to score as low on non-verbal tests as they do on verbal ones.

Do predictions based on tests results consistently underestimate the actual performance of blacks? "In fact, quite extensive research mostly shows that IQ predicts equally well for blacks and whites. Indeed . . . the common prediction equations used at American undergraduate colleges tend, if anything, slightly to overestimate the grades actually achieved by black students."

The conclusion: ". . . most researchers, of all political stripes, accept that a substantial black-white gap in IQ scores is no mere artifact." As to the third question, the conclusion was that we do not really know.[12]

These conclusions as to IQ tests strongly suggest that aptitude tests used in employment are validly assessing Negroes' qualifications, and therefore that it is lack of qualification that is holding Negroes back and

---

[12]*The Economist*, Dec. 24, 1983.

that their relative lack of success does not demonstrate a national racial discrimination problem.

Indeed, in a 1996 study published in the *American Sociological Review*, University of Texas sociologist George Farkas analyzed the "wage gap" that University of Cincinnati sociologist David Maume Jr. had attributed to racial discrimination. He found that Dr. Maume had failed to control a key variable – mathematical and verbal abilities as measured in standardized tests – and, based on his own study of over 6,000 employees tested in 1979-80 and reinterviewed in 1990, concluded that when differences in these skills were factored in, there *was no wage gap* between blacks and whites.[13]

Similarly, a 1993 California study, by the state Assembly's Commission on the Status of African American Males, found that among college and professional school graduates, there was little difference in terms of employment levels from one ethnic group to another (so few Negroes fit in that category, however, that "State's Black Males Facing Grim Situation" was not inappropriate as the headline).[14]

Similar results were reported in *The Bell Curve*. The National Longitudinal Survey of Youth, or NLSY, is a nationally representative sample of youths (over 12,000 at the outset) aged 14-22 in 1979, when the survey began, and followed ever since. "Controlling for age, IQ, and gender . . . the average wage for year-round black workers in the NLSY sample was 101 percent of the average white wage" in 1989.[15]

It Doesn't Start at the Employment Office

It is a tribute to the powerful effect of religious dogma that the proponents of the oppression-and-discrimination view of America can not only brush aside all the evidence that Negroes' relative lack of success in the workplace reflects their relative lack of qualification but also somehow disconnect the situation from all the factors that combine to make up people's career preparation and qualification. They do not dispute the basic facts about these factors (in fact, they often proclaim them as additional condemnations of American society), yet they exhibit no understanding as to how they must inevitably result in poor performance in

---

[13]*Wall Street Journal*, August 7, 1996. Interestingly, however, the article was entitled "Race Still Plays Role in Wages, Study Says."

[14]Sonia Nazario, *Los Angeles Times*, Dec. 11, 1993, p. A1.

[15]*The Bell Curve*, p. 326.

competition for jobs and promotions, *without* discrimination in the work-place. Illegitimacy, welfare, truancy, anger, failure in studies, drugs, crime: no one denies that these disproportionately affect Negroes; yet somehow they are supposed to reach the employment office in a condition totally equal to that of whites and Asians.

BLACKS LOSING GROUND IN MED SCHOOLS
— San Francisco Examiner, Feb. 21, 1984

LARGE SHORTAGE OF BLACK PROFESSORS
IN HIGHER EDUCATION GROWS WORSE
— Wall Street Journal, June 12, 1984

In early 1994, the American Council on Education reported, "With the exception of blacks, the number of minorities who received doctorates increased substantially between 1982 and 1992," by 27%, but "blacks saw a 9.2% decline, finishing 1992 with 951 degrees earned, compared with 1,047 in 1982. The drop was due to a sharp fall in degrees awarded to black males, who had a 20% decline. Black females showed minimal gains."[16]

Some years ago, Scholastic Aptitude Test scores were 937 for non-Hispanic whites, 934 for Asian-Americans, 811 for Mexican-Americans, 766 for Puerto Ricans, and 737 for Negroes, who were also the only group failing to show a gain. In 1998, test results being computed differently, combined test scores were 1,060 for Asian-Americans, 1,054 for whites, 927 for Hispanics, and 860 for Negroes, with the Negro-white gap having widened in the past decade.[17] Other results are consistent. In one recent year, tests of California 12th-grade students showed scores of 12.2 and 12.5 on reading and mathematics, respectively, for whites and 9 and 8.5 for blacks.

Mathematics is particularly important in an increasingly high-technology world. Yet a 1998 city-wide test of eleventh-graders in Boston showed "only two percent of blacks," vs. 30% of whites, "proficient" or "advanced" in grade-level math.[18]

---

[16]"Minorities With Ph.D.s Rose 27% Over Decade," *Wall Street Journal*, Jan. 19, 1994.

[17]June Kronholz, "SATs Change Little; Black-White Gap Widens Further," *Wall Street Journal*, Sept. 2, 1998.

[18]Tamar Jacoby, "Color Bind," *The New Republic*, March 29, 1999, p. 23.

Writing Scores Decline Among Montgomery
County Minority Students

*The percentage of Montgomery County ninth graders who passed the
Maryland functional writing test rose by one point this year, but the passing
rate among black students fell by five points . . .*

— Washington Post, September 1989

Blacks' Low Test Scores Sparking Controversy

*. . . In 1982, the College Entrance Examination Board released, for
the first time data showing the median scores of black students, on a
scale of 800 points, were 200 points below those of whites on the
Scholastic Aptitude Test. Since then, one school district after another
in the Washington area have [sic] released test data showing blacks
trailing whites by 20 to 48 percentile points . . . white classmates
scored in the 75th percentile . . . black . . . in the 27th . . .*

— Washington Post, Sept. 9, 1985

San Francisco Blacks Blame System For Low Scores

— San Francisco Chronicle, Aug. 25, 1989

*If it weren't for quotas it would be almost impossible to get minorities into
schools and trained for such professions as medicine and law.*

— Donald L. Reidhaar, general counsel for the University
of California Regents, on the Bakke case, c. 1977

*"I don't think we will ever achieve, without taking race into account . . .
the kind of diversity that we have had in the past, especially among the
African-American and Hispanic population."*

— UC-Berkeley Chancellor Robert Berdahl, quoted in
the Contra Costa Times, Sept. 14, 1997,
after racial preferences at the University
of California had been banned

'Troubling' NCAA Study On Athletes

*A National Collegiate Athletic Association survey released yesterday
found that white student athletes are twice as likely as their black counterparts to graduate from college within five years. Only 26.6 percent
of blacks graduated from the schools they enrolled in while 52.4 percent
of whites earned degrees . . . The study showed that only 9.2 percent*

*of black athletes graduated from college in four years, as compared with
30.8 for whites . . . Furthermore, blacks are much more likely than
whites to flunk out of school in their fourth or fifth years.*
— San Francisco Chronicle, July 4, 1991

Even if one entirely ignores the issue of IQ, there are in turn plenty of
obvious explanations for Negro scholastic difficulties. The illegitimacy
rate among Negroes has always been somewhat higher than among whites,
but in recent decades it has soared to over two-thirds of all Negro births,
and over 80% in some slum areas. Growing up in a single-parent home,
much more likely than the average to be dependent on welfare, very
possibly in an environment pervaded by drugs, alcohol, gangs, and violence, is not likely to encourage good study habits.

Neither is the widespread attitude in the Negro community toward
learning. A recent study by university anthropologists conducted in
Washington, D.C. schools concluded that "many black students may
perform poorly in high school because of a shared sense that academic
success is a sellout to the white world." Among the taboos mentioned in
the study were speaking standard English, studying in the library, and
being on time.[19] A 1994 *Wall Street Journal* front-page feature story described the ostracism experienced by good students in a predominantly
Negro Washington school; the school gives out awards for academic
achievement without advance notice so the winners will not be able to
absent themselves to escape "the sneers of classmates."[20]

Across the continent, a San Francisco student wrote, in a letter to the
editor after the anthropologists' study had been reported, "I remember
hearing words like 'Oreo' and 'wanna-be white girl' all through my school
days and the taunts continue to a lesser degree in college."[21]

Not surprisingly, a relatively high percentage of Negroes drop out of
school and a relatively low percentage go to college. In fact, more young
Negro men are in prison than in college,[22] and a third are either in
prison, out on parole, or otherwise under the supervision of the criminal

---

[19]Seth Mydans, "Academic Success Seen as Selling Out, Study on Blacks Says," *San Francisco
Chronicle*, April, 1990, p. B6.
[20]Ron Suskind, "Against All Odds," *Wall Street Journal*, May 26, 1994.
[21]Kymberlyn Toliver-Reed, letter "Taunted for Success," *San Francisco Chronicle*, April 29, 1990.
[22]Rep. Ron Dellums, quoted in *Sacramento Bee*, Sept. 16, 1991.

justice system.[23] Among those in school, from elementary school to high school, a disproportionate number experience suspension and expulsion due to behavior problems.

Not helpful is the common practice of ignoring family and community conditions and attitudes and instead denouncing the schools. One nonsensical claim is that it is teachers' low expectations of Negro slum children (which apparently come out of the blue) that causes them to fail in school.

Another is that grouping students by ability for instructional purposes is somehow the culprit. A 1990 study by the Rand Corporation showed, according to the lead of a *Wall Street Journal* story, that "racial segregation inside public schools creates inferior opportunities for black and Hispanic students to learn mathematics and science." But what the study actually showed was that "the fewer whites in the 7th to 12th grades, the higher the percentage of low-ability math and science classes"; "At mixed-race schools, blacks and Hispanics were also over-represented in low-level classes . . . and under-represented in high-level classes."

"However," the article conceded, refuting the message of its lead, "critics have found it hard to convince courts that placements are being made on racial grounds, and not on the basis of demonstrated ability." Norman Chachkin, an attorney for the NAACP Legal Defense Fund, nevertheless called tracking "institutional discrimination," complaining that it was "tremendously resilient [sic] to change."[24]

A *San Francisco Chronicle* news story headed "Gaps in Blacks' Education Called a 'Sin' " focused on another culprit. According to "religious leaders," Negro students are "suffering from a narrow curriculum that lacks any sense of cultural diversity or ethnic perspective." Ah, so. "Motivation and self-esteem rise immediately when people find out who they are."[25]

Of course! The painstaking attention given by the public schools of turn-of-the-century New York to Eastern European Jewish, Southern Italian, Hungarian, etc., etc. culture was crucial to the educational progress made by immigrant children. And how, after all, could a child possibly know who he is unless his teacher told him?

---

[23]Louis Freedberg, "New Jump in Rate of Incarceration For Black Males," *San Francisco Chronicle*, Oct. 5, 1995, p. 1. In the case of the District of Columbia, the proportion is one-half, with an estimated 80% locked up at some point by age 35 ("Half of D.C.'s Black Men In Trouble With the Law," *San Francisco Chronicle*, Aug. 26, 1997.)

[24]Gary Putka, "'Tracking' of Minority Pupils Takes Toll."

[25]Leonard Greene, *San Francisco Chronicle*, May 25, 1990.

This sort of twaddle not only wastes time and energy that might be directed constructively, it is likely to reinforce the pernicious notion that application to studies is selling out to the enemy. Considering how devoutly so many educators believe in the injustice and oppressiveness of American society, as discussed in an earlier chapter, and how desperately eager they are to help its supposed victims, blaming "racist teachers" for Negro scholastic failings is unusually ridiculous.

Discontinuing preferential college admissions for Negroes and Hispanics has made their disproportionate failure to meet competitive admissions standards obvious and inspired a chorus of denunciations of the "terrible schools" that are "failing minority students."

This does not mean the private schools and schools in good neighborhoods to which the children of prosperous professionals and businesspeople go, and whose white and Asian graduates do very well in meeting regular college admission standards, while their Negro graduates do not (which of course suggests right away that the schools are not the real problem); rather, it means the schools in poor, predominantly Negro and Hispanic, areas, extremely few of whose graduates qualify.

What distinguishes these "terrible schools" from the others? The buildings meet the same basic state standards (litter, graffiti and broken glass are the work of the students, not the school district). So do the teachers and administrators. Class sizes and money spent per pupil are comparable (in fact, the per-pupil expenditure in "inner-city" schools is often higher than average because of their many "special needs" students). Curricula and textbooks are the standard ones.

What really distinguishes these schools is that they are full of ill-raised slum kids with bad attitudes with regard to behavior, authority, study, learning, and the rights of others. With today's craziness about "mainstreaming" disturbed and feeble-minded children and rules against the expulsion of the disruptive, it would be hard enough for teachers to maintain conditions conducive to learning were all the children white; what with racial resentment and paranoia among students and the readiness of parents to charge racism when they are disciplined, it becomes well-nigh impossible.

Add the fact that, with nature and nurture both against them, these slum children are not going to be of high average intelligence, and it hardly makes sense to concentrate blame on the schools for their graduates' failings.

But no matter. In particularly daffy San Francisco, school superintendent Bill Rojas announced that schools whose students continued to perform exceptionally poorly on tests would have their entire staffs, from janitors to principal, removed. Months of intensive effort failed, however, to produce silk purses, and he carried out the threat, prompting one student to say, at a meeting, "It's not the faculty that has to be reconstituted – it's the students!"[26]

Poor learning doesn't conduce to success in later life. Neither does poor health or problems with drugs or alcohol.

Blacks Blame Bad Health On Low Self-Image
— San Francisco Chronicle, July 17, 1989

New Racial Statistics On Life Expectancy
After narrowing for decades, the gap in life expectancy between blacks and whites has grown for three years in a row and most of the disparity is due to patterns of behavior . . . The causes of death that increased much more for blacks . . . and were the chief factors in the widening gap were, in order: AIDS; drug overdoses and other drug-related factors; diseases and disabilities that kill infants in their first year; accidents . . . and chronic liver disease, including cirrhosis caused by alcoholism.
— New York Times, Oct. 9, 1989

Life Expectancy For Blacks Drops Again
. . . black life expectancy dropped for the third straight year – largely because of heart disease, homicides and AIDS . . .
— San Francisco Chronicle, July 26, 1991

In New York City, a 1991 study showed that the incidence of stroke among Negro men was 61% higher than among white and 85% higher than among Hispanic men. National Cancer Institute statistics indicate a cancer death rate for Negro men 44% higher than for white, with some of the differences due to "life-style factors such as smoking, diet and alcohol use."[27] Syphilis rates among Negroes more than doubled from

---

[26]Nanette Asimov, "S.F. Would Oust Teachers In Shakeup at 3 Schools," Feb. 9, 1994; "Staffs to Be Replaced at Two Worst S.F. Schools," May 10, 1995," *San Francisco Chronicle*.

[27]Sally Squires, "Gap is Widening: Cancer Death Rate Higher for Blacks," *San Francisco Chronicle*, Jan. 17, 1990, p. A5.

1985 to 1989.[28] According to *The Black Women's Health Book*, 35% of Negro women from age 20 to 44 and 50% from 45 to 55 are overweight, and Negro women's alcoholism rate is three times that of white women.[29]

BLACKS FALLING FURTHER BEHIND IN HEALTH
— San Francisco Chronicle, Jan. 26, 1998

It is common to present Negro health problems as somehow yet another indictment of American society. But while it is easy enough to produce a headline such as "Health Care Systems in U.S. Called Separate and Unequal," the facts don't cooperate. The main complaint of the survey, conducted by a predominantly Negro medical school, in fact was that there is not *enough* separateness: "Among the significant findings was that far fewer blacks and Hispanics than whites had a doctor of their own race or ethnicity. Among whites, 90 percent had a white doctor; 40 percent of blacks, a black doctor, and 50 percent of Hispanics, a Hispanic doctor." This is hardly surprising, considering how few members of these minority groups have achieved admission to medical schools. It's probably also true that the percentage of Gentiles with Gentile doctors and lawyers is lower than the percentage of Jews with Jewish doctors and lawyers. Is this a problem? The survey's next finding cited is that "blacks sought medical advice more often than whites, or Hispanics. Eighty-five percent of blacks surveyed had seen a doctor within the past year, compared with 76 percent of whites and 70 percent of Hispanics."

Finally, "another cause for concern was that compared with whites and Hispanics, a higher percentage of blacks – 36 percent – did not take their medicine. Among whites and Hispanics, the rates were 18 percent and 15 percent."[30] All this means the *health care system* is "separate and unequal"?

It would really be nothing short of a miracle, and hardly to be believed, if in the light of all these disadvantages in preparation, education, life style, and even health, Negroes, on average, should achieve, in the workplace, on a par with whites and Asians.

---

[28]"Syphilis Hits Highest Rate In 40 Years," *San Francisco Chronicle*, Sept. 19, 1990.

[29]Patricia Holt, "Health and Black Women," review of Evelyn C. White, ed., Seal, 1990, *San Francisco Chronicle/Examiner*, June 24, 1990.

[30]Holcomb B. Noble, *New York Times*, April 27, 1999, p. D8.

And that is so even if one ignores, or goes into denial about, the 15-point difference in average IQ between Negroes and whites that all studies confirm but few dare mention. This apparent gap has implications far beyond the validity of employment qualification tests discussed above.

It is an interesting commentary on the extent to which egalitarianism has become our national religion that it is perfectly acceptable to say that the Catholic Church is a fundamentally pernicious institution, or that American whites and Asians generally are tainted by hatred and bigotry, but completely taboo even to take note of evidence that Negroes are of lower average intelligence.

Is to do so an unbearable insult to Negroes? One can hardly deny that it can be hurtful to their sensibilities. But every individual is an individual. He is not defined by the color of his skin. His self-esteem cannot rationally be based on his ethnic background rather than on his own character, worth, and accomplishments. My mother was Austrian and my father, born in 19th-century Riga, was Latvian (he changed his name from Oscha when he became an American citizen after the Russian Revolution), but if studies showed that the average Austrian or Latvian IQ was lower than that of other European ethnic groups I would not be crushed, any more than if it turned out that people of my height or hair color had a lower average IQ. I am I, not the average of people with whom I share one particular characteristic among many.

In any case, if a large proportion of Chinese- and Japanese-Americans were seething with resentment at what they perceived as the systematic exclusion of Orientals from professional football and basketball and the rest of the country was agonizing about the situation, while no one dared discuss the possibility, suggested by measurements, that Orientals are shorter and lighter, on average, than whites and Negroes and that it is this rather than bigotry that accounts for their underrepresentation on sports teams, it would not be a healthy situation.

The undeniable fact is that tests consistently show that the average IQ of American Negroes is 85 vs. 100 for American whites. That this is not some kind of illusion or mirage is painstakingly established in *The Bell Curve*. It certainly fits rather neatly with other undeniable facts.

For one thing, it seems consistent with the 85 found in the case of South African "coloured" (who are, like most American Negroes, of mixed European-African ancestry). To a non-scientist, at least, it would also seem reasonable to expect that if mixing whites with an average IQ of 100 with black Africans produces an average IQ of 85, the black Africans must have an IQ lower than 85, and, indeed, the figure that tests indicate is 75 or lower.[31]

In turn, a very low average African IQ[32] would help explain both the original primitive state of Africans when first encountered by Europeans and Asians and the current miserable state of Africa. The manifest retrogression since the end of colonial rule, the apparently endless childish savagery, the poverty, the egregious misgovernment by thugs and thieves, that periodically compel the civilized nations, moved by human decency, to endeavor to help, certainly do not suggest a high level of intelligence.

Accepting the evidence of the IQ tests as valid and meaningful also provides a rather plausible explanation for why Haiti, independent since the 18th century, the Western Hemisphere's only long-independent nation with a population predominantly of African ancestry, is consistently the hemisphere's basket case, with its lowest standard of living. Haiti does not, after all, suffer from uniquely bad climate or a unique lack of natural resources; it shares the island of Hispaniola with the Dominican Republic. (In fact it is infinitely better-endowed with natural resources than outstandingly-prosperous Hong Kong or Singapore, and far less densely populated as well.)

It might also explain Brazil's experience. This huge country was settled by nonchalantly-intermarrying Portuguese free of the racial prejudice of those who settled the United States. It had slavery until 1888, but never any sort of racial segregation or color bar. In one recent census, Brazilians offered 135 different descriptions of their skin colors. Yet, while blacks and those of mixed race comprise 45% of the country's population, they are only 1% of those who qualify, by entrance examination, for admission to Brazil's largest public university, their illiteracy rate is twice that of whites, and their income is less than half that of whites.[33]

It is hard to reconcile all these facts with the equality of black-white intelligence that has become such a dogma today. And, while the consis-

---

[31]Herrnstein and Murray, The Bell Curve, p. 289.

[32]According to the classification proposed by Terman, an IQ of 100 is average, 80-90 denotes mental dullness and 70-80 borderline mental deficiency, 50-70 is the moron range, 20-50 the imbecile and below 20 denotes idiocy. (Nathaniel Weyl and Stefan Possony, The Geography of Intellect, Regnery, 1963, p. 152.)

[33]Wall Street Journal, Aug. 6, 1996.

tent relative failure of American Negroes by so many measures, as discussed above, can be understood even with the assumption of equality of intelligence, it becomes even more understandable when IQ tests are taken as valid. Indeed, to a large extent the "cultural factors" cited by writers such as Thomas Sowell and Dinesh D'Souza as holding Negroes back *themselves* suggest low intelligence. It is just not very *smart* to reject learning as "selling out," or to damage one's health with fatty foods, alcohol, and drugs.

The great mediaeval philosopher William of Occam, known for "Occam's Razor," counseled against unnecessarily rejecting simple explanations in favor of complex ones. When accepted scientific methodology overwhelmingly indicates that something is the case, and accepting it provides a simple and straightforward explanation for many things that otherwise defy ready explanation, normally, at the very least, it becomes the working hypothesis, even if it cannot be proven to a mathematical certitude. People operate on the basis that it is true unless and until such time as it is proven false. So it is that nearly everyone long operated on the assumption that cigarette smoking is hazardous to health, despite tobacco companies' insistence that this had not been conclusively proven.

Not so when religion is involved: neither in Galileo's day nor today.

Practically everyone, I suspect, would prefer that all races be equal in average intelligence. And perhaps they are. Perhaps the problem is in the geography of sub-Saharan Africa. It largely lacks good natural harbors and navigable rivers, important to contact with others and cross-fertilization of ideas, and it is terribly hot and humid. But while these conditions might well hold people back while they were there, conceivably even to the extent of causing them to do poorly on IQ tests, they have no direct bearing on Africans' descendants in the United States.

Perhaps Africa casts a long shadow in ways not really understood. Perhaps the juxtaposition of slavery with previous backwardness has somehow produced a defeatist attitude toward problem-solving so that underlying equality of intelligence is unable to make itself known through IQ tests and other indications. Who knows?

But intelligence for practical, real-world, as opposed to theoretical, purposes, does appear well measured by IQ tests and the like. An intelligence that couldn't express itself by following directions and solving problems would be terribly nebulous. Inability, or refusal, to come to grips with this reality contributes significantly to the endless accusations against educators of failing to educate, and against just about everybody of discriminating against, Negroes.

Recognizing that a gap in average IQ appears to exist is not an argument for racial discrimination. Many Negroes score far higher on IQ tests than the average white, and many whites lower than the average Negro. There are Negro geniuses and white imbeciles. No one hires, or otherwise deals with averages, but rather specific individuals, and, regardless of averages, people of all races are found at all points on the IQ spectrum.

BAD ATTITUDE

The gap in objective qualifications represented by below-average education, preparation, and health is not the only impediment to equal workplace success by Negroes. There is also a gap in attitude.

Reference was made above to the common view among Negro students that working hard in school was "selling out." This reflects what has become a common view among Negroes, that white America is an adversary implacably opposed to them because of the color of their skin.

Among other manifestations of this attitude is the reported belief by something like a third of Negroes of such wild fantasies as that AIDS was developed to kill Negroes and that the prevalence of crack cocaine addiction in Negro slums is due to a government plot.

The lower part of the "black underclass," which the doctrine of ubiquitous racism has done much to create (see Chap. VII), is not really part of the work force, a fact worth bearing in mind whenever a comparison is made between Negro *population* and Negro representation in some occupation. In the case of those seeking work, their own racial hostility often compounds the problems of lower-class mores. As reporter Lesley Stahl commented on a "60 Minutes" story on a Harlem program called "Strive," which has had considerable success in getting slum Negroes employed, "Attitude has kept a lot of these folks from getting jobs, or keeping them. They were surly or didn't show up on time or didn't show up at all." Said a staff member: "My job is to help people who want to be helped, not people who need help. You got some sense of entitlement? You special? You do what you always done, you're gonna get what you always got."[34]

---

[34]Cal Thomas, "How Thousands Find Work Through 'Strive'," *Human Events*, May 30, 1997, p. 11.

But anger and resentment are not confined to the slum. Ellis Cose's *The Rage of a Privileged Class* described their widespread presence among Negro professionals. A 1992 *Wall Street Journal* lead article described at length the "indignant fury" and "quiet despair" of Negro lawyers and bankers living "with a surging river of indignities dammed up inside."[35]

Just the kind of people you would love to hire and work with. Particularly since it became clear from a careful reading and re-reading of the article that, with a solitary exception, what these people were so worked up about amounted to nothing more than understandable, and reasonable, cases of mistaken identity to which a chuckle would be an appropriate response. A lawyer, going to see a client after many telephone conversations, is mistaken for a messenger; a bank chairman, for a bellman. So? Not everyone is Sherlock Holmes.

It is not particularly surprising or blameworthy, however, that Negroes should have such feelings. There is no reason to expect them to have been less exposed than Americans generally to the media's endlessly repeated message of pervasive racism and discrimination. They may also have had the benefit of being told by a college dean that they should never think they might just be imagining a slight. Well-meaning teachers convinced of the importance of self-esteem have succeeded so well that, on average, while Negro students do relatively poorly in terms of mastering subject matter, they have among the highest scores reflecting how well they think they are doing;[36] people with an inflated idea of their abilities and accomplishments are particularly likely to feel they are being denied their due.

In these circumstances, human nature being what it is, the temptation must be very strong for a Negro to attribute career disappointments to racism rather than to his own deficiencies, particularly if he has grown up with a similar explanation for difficulties in school in a milieu where it was taken for granted that all the problems of his race were the white man's doing.

An angry and hypersensitive individual is likely to inspire exasperation in those with whom he works and thereby reduce his effectiveness. Even if he is somehow able to keep his resentments to himself and nev-

---

[35]Alex Kotlowitz and Suzanne Alexander, "The Gulf," May 28, 1992.
[36]Tom Loveless, "The Academic Fad That Gave Us Ebonics," *Wall Street Journal*, Jan. 22, 1997.

ertheless radiate cheer, his internal state is likely to impair his performance, even if his talents and qualifications are of the highest order.

But often he is not successful in covering up his anger and resentment. It will be quite clear to co-workers and bosses that he thinks he is getting a raw deal; that he is being unfairly criticized, denied attractive assignments or promotions, etc., because of the color of his skin. Blaming others rather than one's own faults for failure is not an endearing trait, and when people are falsely accused of anything reprehensible – and racism is certainly reprehensible – it does not cause them to like the accuser more. And, as is well known, people often do get ahead not solely on the basis of mental power and skill but in significant part because they are liked.

All in all, when differences in attitude as well as objective qualifications are considered, it is hardly surprising or suggestive of discrimination that Negroes are doing relatively poorly in the workplace.

But you would never know that from press coverage and public discussion. There, every achievement of less than proportional representation (in desirable positions) by Negroes is treated as a "problem" reflecting American racism. It is indicative of how relentless the drive to find racism is that this approach is followed even where it is altogether implausible and that even proportional representation will not avert it if human ingenuity can find a way.

Consider the fact that, according to Derrick Z. Jackson, a *Boston Globe* columnist, "10 percent of [the head coaches in the National Football League] are African-American."[37] That's right in line with the overall population percentage: any problem here? Oh, absolutely, according to a current complaint; for, as William C. Rhoden writes in a *New York Times* piece entitled, "In the N.F.L., Justice Is Still Denied," "The rosters of N.F.L. teams are about 70 percent African-American; many of the starting offensive and defensive units are 80 to 90 percent African-American."[38] The fact that "only" 10% of the head coaches are Negroes, thus, according to Jackson, "is central to the current debate on racism."

Rather than recognize the obvious – that the fact that 70% of those hired to play professional football are Negroes makes the suggestion that

---

[37]Derrick Z. Jackson, "African-American head coaches lacking in NFL," *Contra Costa Times*, Feb. 1, 1998, p. F11.
[38]*New York Times*, Jan. 31, 1998.

the owners are racists utterly implausible[39] – these complainers incredibly attribute the absence of correspondingly skewed representation at the head coach level to racism. Yet the size, strength and speed so important in playing football are not what are needed in coaching. Indeed, Jackson acknowledges that only 11 of the 30 current or most recent head coaches ever played professional football. But no matter: he knows what is motivating the owners.

OTHER ETHNIC GROUPS

This book addresses the issue of racial discrimination primarily in terms of the Negro case, which is widely thought to best demonstrate the consequences of American bigotry and the need for corrective action by government. It should be clear from this chapter that it doesn't; that, regardless of the injustices of the past, it is primarily Negroes' own present deficiencies rather than discrimination on the part of others that account for their relative lack of success.

The same holds true in the cases of other presently under-performing ethnic groups. In the case of Hispanics, for example, many factors, including dropping out of school, trouble with the law, and alcohol and drug problems, are the same as in the case of Negroes. Indeed, the drop-out rate is even worse, 30% vs. 13% for Negroes.[40] Others are different, but similarly of straightforward impact. Among Hispanics a relatively high percentage are immigrants without proficiency in English, an obvious competitive disadvantage. An appallingly high percentage of American Indians are alcoholics. For whatever it's worth, both groups (except for a tiny minority of Hispanics of purely Spanish ancestry) have origins in the Western Hemisphere, where, as in sub-Saharan Africa, neither

---

[39]*Anti-Negro* racists, that is. The charge of bias against whites, Asians, and Hispanics would be quite plausible. After all, these groups comprise about 90% of the population and have only 30% of these highly-paid and glamourous jobs, while Negroes, a mere 10% of the population, have 70%. That's *seven times* the 10% they "should" have, on a proportional basis. Where are the complaints of discrimination, suggestions that player selection procedures are biased and invalid, hints that whites are made to feel unwelcome in the sport, and denunciations of colleges and high schools for failing their non-black students in athletic preparation?

[40]"Latinos Trail Other Groups in Education, Report Says," *San Francisco Chronicle*, July 22, 1998 (report compiled by National Council of La Raza).

written language nor the wheel had been developed prior to the arrival of Europeans.

The notion that relative failure reflects the bigotry of the larger society rather than the group's own differences is devastatingly refuted by the case of those of Chinese and Japanese ancestry. Particularly on the Pacific Coast, where most of them settled, they were despised and persecuted – giving rise to the expression "not a Chinaman's chance." The Chinese Exclusion Act of 1882 was not repealed until 1943. The Japanese – including American citizens – were uprooted and interned in concentration camps during World War II. Yet today, aided by a cultural tradition of hard work and respect for learning which did not disdain studying as "acting white," Asian-Americans are doing so well that they are among the most prosperous ethnic groups in the United States and disproportionately represented among those qualifying for the elite University of California at Berkeley. Promoters of racial preferences now confine their advocacy to what they call "underrepresented minorities," excluding the Chinese and Japanese.

CHAPTER VI

LEGAL, STATISTICAL, AND VERBAL CHICANERY

The racism-discovery industry, or more accurately the racism-concoction industry, is a formidable force. It includes racism-lawsuit specialists, academics anxious to demonstrate American bigotry, government departments (particularly under liberal administrations), race-advancement organizations and their leaders, specialized advocacy organizations (such as ACORN, which devotes itself to finding racism in housing and home finance), and would-be beneficiaries of "remedial" programs, working in cooperation with a sympathetic media ready to publicize accusations of racism to the fullest.

Finding racism in general minority underachievement in income and in higher-level employment, as discussed in the previous chapter, is a major thrust of this alliance. There are also a variety of additional ways in which supposed racism is targeted and exposed. Many of these involve demands for "corrective" wealth-redistribution in particular areas; some merely serve the important purpose of fostering the notion that there is a pervasive American racism that not only requires vigilant policing but also makes preferential treatment for minorities an appropriate counterbalance.

LAWSUITS
If one were to draw conclusions about conditions in the United States relative to the rest of the industrialized world from the prevalence of lawsuits, he would conclude that American employers are an incorrigibly racist lot. He would also conclude that American highways, airplanes, toys, playground and sports equipment, drugs and cars, to name a few

things, are uniquely dangerous. He would also conclude that American business enterprises are derelict in their duties to shareholders, employees, customers, and the public to an extent unknown anywhere else in the civilized world.

He would of course be dead wrong. The reason he would be dead wrong, and the reason in this country legal smoke does not mean the fire of wrongdoing, is that our legal system is quite unique. To a considerable extent, American law is now better described as an industry or a racket than as a profession. Opportunities for lawsuits have proliferated over the last few decades, created in part by legislation and in part by the same activist judiciary that during this period discovered in the Constitution so many previously unsuspected rights. More fundamentally, the United States, alone among the advanced countries, operates under the "American Rule" instead of the "English Rule": that is, nearly always the losing party in a lawsuit is *not* obligated to pay for the legal expenses he has forced the party in the right to incur.

Under the process known as "discovery," a party to a lawsuit has an almost unlimited right to demand documents from his adversary and to subject him, or his employees, to lengthy questioning in depositions. With a computer and the right software, a few minutes' effort can produce paperwork that will impose thousands of man-hours of work and hundreds of thousands of dollars of legal fees on his adversary. And there is no telling what a jury might do if the case goes to trial: for good measure, it might award punitive damages in an amount many times generously-calculated actual damages.

The temptation to cut one's losses and settle is consequently strong. That is why, although all scientific evidence indicates that there is absolutely no connection between silicone breast implants and any of the complaints from which women who had them subsequently suffered, billions of dollars were offered in settlement and a major corporation declared bankruptcy.

The number of lawsuits charging major corporations with racial discrimination has soared since 1991. Is this because American businesses were treating minorities fairly in 1991 but have since begun discriminating against them with a vengeance? Hardly. As was mentioned in Chap. IV, the 1991 Civil Rights Act made jury trials and large damage awards in such cases possible for the first time.

Another indication of the lack of connection between discrimination lawsuits and actual discrimination is the fact that federal employees are *seven times more likely* than private-sector employees to file such suits.[1] The obvious explanation is that the federal government is seen as an easy target, rather than that federal supervisors are exceptionally biased.

The situation is well summed up by the title of an article in the *San Francisco Daily Journal*, a legal newspaper, by San Mateo Deputy County Counsel Mary Mainland Ash: "Legalized Extortion." Noting that Texaco had agreed to pay $176 million to settle a racial discrimination suit although "blacks alone totaled 24 percent of those earning between $51,000 and $128,000" at the company, she concluded,

> Though ostensibly "civil rights" actions, current employment discrimination and harassment litigation is better classified as extortion. Plaintiffs' lawyers are well aware that employers are reluctant to take such cases to trial, no matter how weak the plaintiff's evidence, given the risk that juries may award damages vastly exceeding actual injuries, if any. The only real question is how large a settlement offer can be extracted from the employer. Having entered law school as a result of working in the civil rights movement I am profoundly disturbed by the extent to which my profession has perverted its ideals.[2]

An example of what she is talking about occurred when a Negro former associate at the Chicago-based law firm of Katten Muchin & Zavis sued the firm claiming racial discrimination. An obliging jury of seven Negroes and one white awarded the plaintiff $1 million in compensatory damages plus $1.5 million in punitive damages, even though, as the appellate court held in reversing the award, no evidence had been presented from which a reasonable juror could have concluded that the firm had intentionally discriminated against the employee.[3]

Statistics showing relatively slow progress by the minority group's members may cause the company to cave in to a multi-million-dollar class-action suit; if a manager expressed exasperation with disgruntled members of the minority group who were suing, as in the Texaco case

---

[1] *Wall Street Journal*, Jan. 19, 1999, p. 1.
[2] Jan. 29, 1997.
[3] "Court Reverses Bias Award Against Chicago Law Firm," *Wall Street Journal*, July 9, 1997.

(see "Finding Racism in Reaction to Unsatisfactory Conduct" below), that will make it all the more fearful of what a jury might do.

It is not even necessary to claim any tangible mistreatment by the employer, such as a promotion withheld because of race. The basis of the claim can be that the company was not sufficiently vigilant in protecting the employee against a "hostile environment" created by the conduct of one or more co-workers. For a lawsuit to succeed on this basis, the conduct is supposed to be so pervasive and serious as to make the employee unable to do his job normally. But, as in the case of analogous sex discrimination cases (see Chapter VIII), these employees turn out to be very sensitive. What one might expect grown men or women to take in their stride leaves them devastated. In their $30 million lawsuit against Morgan Stanley & Co. in 1997, two employees cited an e-mail "joke about the way some blacks speak."[4] (This suit was dismissed by the federal judge.[5] However, the plaintiffs were allowed to re-file some of their claims, including one that they had been retaliated against after complaining, and eventually won a settlement.[6]) An actual racial slur means a home run. According to a San Francisco employment plaintiffs' lawyer, employers "don't go near juries when there are racial epithets involved. They pay what you want."[7]

The resolution of the e-mail joke case calls attention to a current growth area in discrimination lawsuits, the retaliation claim. The law forbids retaliation for an employee's filing a discrimination complaint, and he can win on this basis *even when his underlying claim of discrimination proves false*. The number of such claims, not surprisingly, is soaring.[8] The more outrageous the initial claim, the more likely the employer will become angry and manifest this in some way; the watchful employee can then seize on that as evidence of retaliation.

Another reason for the capitulation of major corporations to discrimination suits is effective work by Negro organizations and the media. The

[4]Frances A. McMorris, "Morgan Stanley Employees File Suit, Charging Race Bias Over E-Mail Jokes," *Wall Street Journal*, Jan. 13, 1997.

[5]"Morgan Stanley Wins Dismissal of Bias Suit Over Racist E-Mail," *Wall Street Journal*, July 21, 1997.

[6] "Morgan Stanley Settles Suit by Two Black Employees," *Wall Street Journal*, March 2, 1998.

[7]"Court Watch," *San Francisco Recorder*, Jan. 26, 1999.

[8]"Flood of 'retaliation' cases surfacing in U.S. workplace,." *USA Today*, Feb. 10, 1999.

New York Times gave front-page coverage to news that a Texaco manager had used the word "nigger," and negligible coverage to the revelation that in fact he had not done so. Jesse Jackson was among those calling for a boycott of Texaco products, a call widely reported in the press. He and affiliated organizations also promoted a boycott against Mitsubishi which yielded a commitment to increase its quota of dealerships for women and minorities from 10 to 15% and to assist with their financing, and then moved on to a boycott of 207 United Dairy Farmers convenience stores.[9] In June, 1998, he targeted the Federal Home Loan Mortgage Corporation, "Freddie Mac," which a former employee was suing for $15 million charging a "hostile environment."[10]

These tactics do not always work. The United Dairy Farmers boycott effort was largely unsuccessful, and the company was also successful in defending itself in court: Maudie Williams and her son Michael had been fired for violating cash-handling procedures but sued for $17 million claiming the real reason was that they were black, prompting the boycott effort, but in October 1998 a federal jury rejected their claims.[11]

But such victories hardly ever repay legal expenses. The best that can generally be hoped for when a meritless suit is fought to the end is some reimbursement for court costs, as was provided in the case of a raid on Credit Lyonnais: "A federal race discrimination case in Manhattan has ended with the plaintiffs – and their lawyers – paying a $34,000 settlement to the defendant, an international investment bank." The law firm, "known primarily for its plaintiffs securities class action work," paid $20,000, and "the seven plaintiffs – African-American employees at the bank's North American headquarters in Manhattan" were to pay the rest. "Apparently acknowledging that their discrimination claims were baseless, three plaintiffs withdrew them with prejudice in August, after full discovery, as did the remaining four plaintiffs in October."[12]

In a particularly outrageous California case, Judge David Garcia awarded an employer $127,000 in attorney's fees after the plaintiff, Phillip Martinez, had failed to produce a single instance of discrimination in his race-

---

[9]"Jackson Calls Off 8-Month Boycott of Mitsubishi," *San Francisco Chronicle*, Jan. 16, 1997, p. A8.

[10]"Jesse Jackson Wants Big Shareholders of Freddie Mac to Disinvest From Firm," *Wall Street Journal*, June 2, 1998.

[11]"Store Chain Prevails in Bias Claims," *San Francisco Daily Journal*, Oct. 7, 1998.

[12] "Firm Must Pay $20K After Bias Suit Fails," *San Francisco Recorder*, Dec. 14, 1998.

discrimination suit; a local employment lawyer attributed this unusual action to courts' exasperation at being "inundated" with frivolous discrimination suits.[13] The prospects of collecting such a sum from a maintenance worker, however, seem doubtful.

Transforming The Facts Of Economic Life Into Racism

Advocates of preferential treatment for members of relatively unsuccessful ethnic groups like to talk about something they call "institutional racism." All this nonsense means is that the relatively unsuccessful are relatively unsuccessful: that is, they are relatively scarce at the top, which proves nothing whatsoever about racism. Similarly, a disproportionate number of Negroes and Hispanics are poor: for example, in early 1997, Negroes, 13% of the general population, accounted for 37% of the welfare rolls, and Hispanics, 11% of the population, for 22%; together, these two groups, representing 24% of the population, had twice as many welfare recipients as whites, who make up 73% of the population.[14] Anything at all that affects the rich and the poor differently, thus, can be expected to affect Negroes and Hispanics differently than whites. The game is to try to turn this commonplace fact of life into something sinister-looking in order to justify giving special privileges to members of these groups.

Typically, these discoveries of "racism" involve areas where the government has a major presence or influence, so that it can proceed to "remedy" the "problem" or "compensate" the "victims," or, better yet, to get the private sector to do so at its expense. Particularly under the Clinton administration, there appears to be a clear understanding between Democratic leaders and those of the relatively unsuccessful minorities that in exchange for their faithful support at the polls, the Democrats will do all they can to create a quota economy in which they are provided a larger "piece of the action" than they succeed in earning on their own.

In Chapter III, viewing the lower advertising rates of radio stations aimed at minority groups, as reported in a Federal Communications Com-

---

[13]"Worker Finds He Must Pay to Play," *San Francisco Recorder*, Dec. 16, 1998.

[14]Jason DeParle, "Shrinking Welfare Rolls Leave Record High Share of Minorities,"*New York Times*, July 27, 1998, p. A1.

mission study, as discrimination was cited as a January, 1999 example of the media's credulity. An observer waiting for the other shoe to drop did not have to wait long; the following month came news that the FCC and other agencies are "trying to prod the broadcast and advertising industry" to set up a "code of conduct" aimed at "ensuring equal opportunities for minority-owned ad agencies and stations," and that Vice President Gore was planning to establish an interagency working group to look into the "issue" of "diversity in advertising."[15]

"ENVIRONMENTAL RACISM"

Although there is no evidence that factories or incinerators generally represent a health hazard to those who work there all their lives, let alone to those living in the area, they are not a plus in terms of the ambience of a residential area. In the typical case, the facility was there first; the present residents knew it was there when they moved in. "In industrial area" is not high on home-buyers' wish lists. Those who can afford better do not move there, and it is the poor who make do with such low-cost housing.

And new plants or incinerators are located in appropriately zoned areas, where land is relatively cheap. The plant does not care whether it has lovely homes nearby, or attractive views; in fact, affluent neighbors would be likely to know how to keep it away, and the prospect of factory job opportunities will not weigh in its favor with them.

Either way, given the facts about income levels, it is a safe bet that a higher-than-average percentage of those living near industrial facilities will prove to be Negro or Hispanic.

These obvious facts of life have been ingeniously transformed into something sinister – "toxic racism" or "environmental racism." Bad people are singling out minorities for exposure to harmful or at any rate unwelcome substances. The charge is manifestly absurd in the typical case where people moved voluntarily near an existing facility and only slightly less so where a new facility is sited consistent with existing use and zoning. (If a county changed the zoning of a predominantly Negro or Hispanic suburban residential area to allow, for the first time, a factory, that would be different altogether, but that is not what this is all about.)

---

[15]Kathy Chen, "FCC Is Seeking Code of Conduct To Ensure Equal Opportunities," *Wall Street Journal*, Feb. 19, 1999.

In 1993, an "Environmental Justice Conference" was staged in Washington, in which Vice President Gore and then NAACP Executive Director Ben Chavis participated. The press dutifully reported dramatic performances. "Our babies are choking. Our children are sick. Our people are dying," declared the Rev. Charles Adams. Charlotte Keys, founder of Jesus People Against Pollution, who lived "near an old chemical plant," said, "My life has been cut in half because of toxic exposure." (The "old chemical plant" would seem clearly to have been there before her.) There was, as usual, no actual evidence of harm to employees or neighbors of plants, but Gore, author of a notoriously silly book on the environment, exhorted the participants to "rally people of conscience in black America and in all America to . . . environmental justice." At about the same time, the Environmental Protection Agency's office of civil rights reversed its previous policy and announced that it was going to look into whether the siting of incinerators violated the Civil Rights Act.[16]

The lunatic concept of "environmental racism" is now bearing fruit in the form of depriving poor Negroes of eagerly-sought employment opportunities. The EPA delayed approval of a $700 million Louisiana plastics plant certified as meeting exacting emissions standards. Local people would love to have the job opportunities the plant would offer as an alternative to labor in the sugar cane fields. All the local Negro elected officials are in favor of the plant, and 73% of the people in the communities near the plant site favor it, according to a NAACP poll. But because this is a predominantly Negro area, it represents "environmental racism," and Jesse Jackson and Greenpeace oppose its construction.[17]

In California, "community groups" filed complaints with the EPA claiming that racism against Latinos was behind the siting of toxic-waste dumps.[18] Remote rural sites, of course, had been chosen, and out there a high percentage of the few inhabitants are farm workers who, in California, are largely from south of the border.

In the 1960s, Gulf Oil Co. sold a developer a parcel of Texas land where in the 1920s it had stored crude oil underground in earthen pits.

[16]*Human Events*, Feb. 11, 1994, p. 18.

[17]Henry Payne, "'Environmental Justice' Kills Jobs for the Poor," *Wall Street Journal*, Sept. 16, 1997.

[18]Reynolds Holding, "Rural Residents Fight Toxic Dumps," *San Francisco Chronicle*, Dec. 10, 1994, p. A17.

Getting into the spirit of the times, the largely Negro residents of the subdivision recently filed a lawsuit against Chevron Corp., which bought out Gulf in 1985. $3.5 million worth of scientific tests by Chevron have shown no evidence of contamination or health risks, but shakedown specialist Jesse Jackson threatened a boycott of Chevron.[19]

"BIAS IN MORTGAGE LENDING"

A few years ago, stories about "bias in lending" began to appear prominently, and regularly, in the press. Judging from the headlines – "Bias in Home Lending Prevalent, Study Says"[20] is a representative example – lenders were foregoing good business opportunities so they could have the pleasure of rejecting Negro and Hispanic loan applicants. Delving a little more deeply, and simply reading the story itself through was often sufficient, one realized that this was just one more attempt to promote racial preferences by means of trumped-up charges of racism.

In the story cited, one learned that the study referred to (showing that Negroes and Hispanics were 2.7 times as likely to be rejected for a home loan as whites with the same income) was the work of the Association of Community Organizations for Reform Now ("ACORN"), an advocacy group, and that it was based on federal data that took no account of the credit histories of applicants. For, indeed, the data that lending institutions are required to report to regulatory authorities include neither credit histories nor debt-to-income levels at the time of the loan application. Determining creditworthiness without that information is obviously impossible. (Interestingly, Negro-owned banks had particularly "bad records" in minority lending, a rather clear indication that racism was not the reason.)[21]

Net worth is obviously an extremely important element in home loan creditworthiness; a borrower with minimal reserves is likely to default quickly if he loses his job, and lenders, and regulators, hate to see defaults. In 1996, according to the White House's Council of Economic Advisors, although the typical white family earned not quite twice the

---

[19]"Jackson to organize boycott of Chevron," *Contra Costa Times*, May 29, 1997.

[20]*San Francisco Chronicle*, Oct. 13, 1993, p. B2.

[21]It might be thought that location would play a part in loan rejection, since real estate in places such as South Central Los Angeles is not the obvious first choice for collateral. But exclusion of geographical areas is forbidden "redlining."

income of the typical black family, "the typical black household had a net worth of only about $4,500, a tenth of the white figure."[22] Lose nine-tenths of your net worth and your creditworthiness is a lot less.

Such facts are of course publicized for use only for such purposes as promoting the idea that racial preferences are "needed." They don't slow up the politicians, or the headline-writers, any. "Federal Data Detail Pervasive Racial Gap In Mortgage Lending." "Lenders Targeted for Bias." "U.S. Intensifies Its Investigation of Lending Bias."

When a study that included credit histories and other relevant variables was finally done, by the Boston Federal Reserve, it showed that 89% of white vs. 83% of Negro applicants similarly situated were approved, hardly a notable disparity; focusing on the hole rather than the doughnut, rejection rates, gave 11% vs. 17%, which was trumpeted as clear proof of bias.[23]

The "bias in lending" campaign was effective. By early 1994, according to a Gallup poll, 83% of Negro homeowners and 60% of Hispanic and white believed mortgage discrimination existed, even though only 16% of the Negroes and 7% of the Hispanics (and 3% of the whites) thought they themselves had experienced it: and that was with a definition of discrimination that "ranged from racial, ethnic or gender to age, economic status, location of property and the length of time it took to get a mortgage."[24]

Political and regulatory pressure to lend to minorities was strong. Regulators would judge banks by their minority lending, and merger applications could be held up if they had not done enough. An article in *Forbes* magazine, shortly before the 1994 Congressional elections, asked as a subhead, "Why is the Federal Reserve Board going along with racial lending quotas on banks?"[25] The Justice Department went a step further and accused Chevy Chase Federal Savings Bank of discrimination for having failing to locate branches in Negro areas, and the bank agreed to mend its ways.[26] The Clinton administration had, in March 1994, pro-

---

[22]"Black-White Income Inequalilties," *New York Times*, Feb. 17, 1998.
[23]Paulette Thomas, "Boston Fed Finds Racial Discrimination In Mortgage Lending Is Still Widespread," *Wall Street Journal*, Oct. 9, 1992, p. A3.
[24]Sonya Ross, "9% of home buyers felt bias in borrowing," *Contra Costa Times*, March 10, 1994, p. C2.
[25]Howard Banks, "Politics as usual," *Forbes*, Oct. 10, 1994.
[26]Jonathan R. Macey, "Banking by Quota," *Wall Street Journal*, Sept. 7, 1994.

mulgated a creative new definition of discrimination, including "the impact of unintentional bias as a result of bank policies or practices."[27]

There were indications of some change after the 1994 elections. A January, 1995 Federal Reserve Board study showed that default rates for successful white and Negro borrowers was the same, indicating that the latter were not being unfairly held to a higher standard,[28] and a study conducted under the auspices of the University of Texas management school found such flaws in the Boston study as to render it worthless to prove even modest bias.[29] Headline-writers were not convinced – "Federal Drive to Curb Mortgage-Loan Bias Stirs Strong Backlash" was a front-page headline[30] – but pressure to make questionable loans based on skin color eased somewhat.

It remains strong, however, and its consequences are particularly noticeable when regulated financial institutions seek to merge. Washington Mutual Inc., competing with Home Savings of America to acquire Great Western Financial Corp., countered Home's pledge to lend $70 billion to "inner-city residents and businesses" by pledging $75 billion.[31]

It is ironic that so soon after the bad-loan disasters banks should be competing to make questionable loans. "Mortgage Delinquencies Are Climbing" was a headline in June 1996.[32]

And the effort to find and proclaim bias goes on. "Real-Estate Bias Cited in Fed Survey" heads a recent story, which gives grasping at straws a bad name. "Documented cases of overt discrimination in home buying are difficult to find here," it begins, but not to worry: "subtle discrimination exists . . ."

And what is that? One example is that "the project found" – one waits with bated breath for the shocking discovery – "that some appraisers and insurance underwriters use Census-tract numbers or subjective assessments such as 'pride-of-ownership' in determining property value. This

---

[27]Sonya Ross, "9% of home buyers felt bias in borrowing," *Contra Costa Times*, March 10, 1994, p. C2.

[28]"Fed Study Challenges Notion of Bias Against Minorities in Mortgage Lending," *Wall Street Journal*, Jan. 26, 1995.

[29]Stan Liebowitz, "A Study That Deserves No Credit," *Wall Street Journal*, Sept. 1, 1993.

[30]Albert Karr, *Wall Street Journal*, Feb. 7, 1995.

[31]Don Clark, "Seattle Thrift Pledges $75 Billion Of Inner-City Loans," *Wall Street Journal*, April 11, 1997.

[32]Karen Blumenthal, *Wall Street Journal*, June 11, 1996.

works against minorities . . . because lower property values reduce the amount a mortgage lender will provide or an insurer will cover." How's that again? Lending less on shabby houses in poor neighborhoods is *racial bias*?

Exhibit 2 for the prosecution is that "some lending institutions . . . fail to take into account that recent immigrants often do not keep their money in banks, or that many families pool their funds to purchase property." Of course, Mr. Lopez; we'll be happy to go out and count the money in your mattress. And it's no problem that three families are going to live in this house.

Finally, of 100 mortgage and property-insurance offices around San Francisco, "only four" were in "predominantly minority and low-income neighborhoods in the southeastern part of the city." Actually, considering the opportunities for business in the San Francisco area as a whole, it is rather surprising that 4% of the offices *are* in that unpromising area. Somehow failure aggressively to pursue marginal business has become "subtle discrimination."[33]

One might think that calling reasonable lending practices "discrimination" is so transparently absurd that no one would take such nonsense seriously. But the object of such exercises is to provide a pretext for requiring racial preferences in lending, not to make sense. Thus, one reads, "Lending Guidelines Of 2 Mortgage Firms May Be Discriminatory." "Fannie Mae's and Freddie Mac's lending guidelines may be discriminatory, according to an independent report prepared for the Department of Housing and Urban Development. While the guidelines 'do not explicitly disqualify borrowers based on their race or ethnicity, they do disqualify borrowers with low incomes, limited wealth, and poor credit histories,' the report said. 'Borrowers with such characteristics are disproportionately minority.' "[34]

One wonders what HUD paid the Urban Institute for this gem, whose shocking findings would of course be acted on at once. "Assistant HUD Secretary William Apgar said, 'The report raises serious questions about [the firms'] lending practices and the department will look into these immediately."

Those whose job it is to decry bias in home loans, and the ever-cooperative press, will not be thwarted simply because the facts show no

---

[33]Sheila Muto, *Wall Street Journal*, Feb. 26, 1997, p. CA1.
[34]*Wall Street Journal*, April 30, 1999.

such thing. Hence bizarre stories with titles such as "Home Loans Discriminate, Study Shows" (Bill Dedman, *New York Times*, May 13, 1998) and "Racial Bias Seen in Federal Housing Loan Program" (*San Francisco Chronicle*, May 13, 1998), describing an effort of the Chicago Fair Housing Alliance financed by the MacArthur Foundation.

This is the sort of article one reads painstakingly, line by line, after first scanning, because he is sure he has somehow missed the key point. But all that emerges is this: Because of FHA loan guarantees, financial institutions under such programs lend freely to people with shaky credit, including minority-group members. Real estate agents frequently show minority buyers who express no preference as to neighborhood homes in neighborhoods popular with the same minority. Shaky borrowers often default and lose their homes in foreclosure. Consequently, "minority neighborhoods are pockmarked with the foreclosed homes of buyers who should never have been approved for the mortgage."

Now it is *making* loans instead of refusing to make them that is the basis of a charge of "bias." This is rather creative. Even the Housing Department called the charge "rather extreme." But, thanks to these headlines, there will no doubt be people who will say "Oh yes, racism is everywhere; I read in the paper that even the FHA is biased."

"DISCRIMINATION IN INSURANCE"

STUDY SHOWS BIAS AMONG INSURERS
Poor, minorities have more trouble getting coverage.[35]

Wouldn't you just love to write a fire-insurance policy in an area such as South Central Los Angeles? Well, you can't just exclude the whole area; the Fair Housing Act forbids "redlining" in insurance just as it does in mortgage lending.[36]

It is permissible to use some sense in writing property insurance, and that, according to the study, is the problem. "The problem stems from underwriting policies that restrict coverage based on property valuation, credit history of homeowners and subjective judgments about an applicant's 'lifestyle, stability and morals' . . ."

---

[35]*San Francisco Chronicle*, Dec. 23, 1994.
[36]"New Weapon in Battle Against Housing Bias," *San Francisco Chronicle*, Oct. 22, 1992, p. C3, reporting a Seventh Circuit decision.

This means people in poor areas with low incomes are at a disadvantage, and, in line with the reality of minority economic position, "the association looked at the concentration of minority populations within the zip code and concluded that there is a direct correlation between the price and availability of homeowner insurance and the presence of minorities." The study also showed "that the insurers charge higher premiums in these markets." One would think so, given the greater risk.

The study, by the National Association of Insurance Commissioners, was presented as "hard evidence . . . to prove that discrimination exists." Of course it proves no such thing. Reluctance to write high-risk insurance in low-income areas doesn't mean that racial bias, rather than reasonable recognition of the risks of insuring such properties, makes insurance companies reluctant to do such business.

But regulatory pressure can be expected to result in their doing so anyway. "Nationwide Insurance Enterprise, responding to accusations of discriminatory sales practices, said it will change its underwriting standards in order to sell more homeowners' policies in poor urban areas."[37]

That didn't help Nationwide in an October 1998 Richmond, Virginia case. This old Confederate capital has had a Negro majority for years; its city council's establishment of a racial spoils system in government contracting had prompted the Supreme Court's 1989 *Croson* decision outlawing such practices (see below). It is also headquarters of an advocacy organization called Housing Opportunities Made Equal Inc., which sued Nationwide claiming its local insurance-underwriting policies were discriminatory. Based on the results of seven pairs of requests for insurance quotations out of 15, a local jury composed of six Negroes and a white woman was pleased to award $500,000 in compensatory damages *plus $100,000,000 in punitive damages.*

Had the company in fact so outrageously been turning down desirable business because of applicants' skin color? One might have suspected that from the *Wall Street Journal's* headline, "Nationwide Mutual Insurance Found Guilty of Bias Against Blacks in Sales."[38] In fact, however, each "tester" was supposedly seeking insurance for a specific property,

---

[37]Leslie Scism, "Nationwide Insurance Plans to Sell More Homeowner Policies in Poor Areas," *Wall Street Journal*, Feb. 3, 1997, p. C15.

[38]Deborah Lohse, Oct. 27, 1998.

"saying alternatively that it was in a white neighborhood and then in a black one."[39] Given the well-known characteristics of the typical "black neighborhood," it is hardly surprising that an insurer would not be enthusiastic about underwriting such business. It may have run afoul of "redlining" laws, but there is no indication at all that it was guilty of racial bias.

"Bias in the Award of Contracts"

Government contracts, at the federal, state, and local levels, are a multibillion-dollar matter, and they are directly controlled by government, so here politicians have seen an opportunity to oblige minority groups directly rather than by coercing private businesses. But how is outright racial favoritism by government to be made to fit with the Equal Protection clause of the Constitution?

A few years ago I could not help noticing a front-page story in the Sunday Contra Costa Times. "County contract bias excludes minorities, women in business" was the headline. The lead stated, "Minority and women business owners are shut out of hundreds of thousands of dollars in . . . contracts . . . A new report also documents widespread discrimination against blacks, Hispanics, Asians and women in the public bidding process and by privately-owned businesses."

Finally something real, I remember naively thinking at the time. But all the report documented was the fact that minority contractors were not getting many contracts (2% of the dollar value was the percentage), and that many of them were blaming discrimination for their lack of success. I read the article a second time carefully, thinking I must have missed something; but not one single instance of actual discrimination was shown.

On the contrary, one gleaned some of the real reasons for their failure to get contracts. "Most large government contracts require construction bonds . . . Minorities are doubly disadvantaged . . . because many aren't properly educated or prepared for the stringent requirements. Others are turned down because they don't have the capital to back up the bonds."[40] It would be surprising indeed if contractors of an ethnic group, a dispro-

---

[39]Joseph B. Treaster, "Insurer Must Pay $100.5 Million in Redlining Case," New York Times, Oct. 27, 1998.

[40]Jan Ferris, Contra Costa Times, June 14, 1992.

portionate percentage of whose members are poor, and which has been particularly sparsely represented in business ownership, should win a proportionate share of contracts.

Furthermore, the county had actually set a goal of allocating up to 20% of its contracts to minority businesses. Far from discriminating against minority contractors, the county had a policy of favoring them; they still weren't getting the contracts because they weren't competitive. In fact the study was one of those commissioned in the wake of the Supreme Court's Croson[41] decision finding preferential treatment to violate the Equal Protection Clause unless designed to correct actual past discrimination, aimed at proving that the county had been guilty of nefarious conduct in the past so as to allow it to engage in what its politicians considered the virtuous or at least politically desirable course of giving preferences to minorities. Preparing these "Croson studies" had become a regular industry involving tens of millions of dollars. The problem was that the researchers (who had been forbidden by the county's affirmative action officer to talk to the paper) hadn't been able to find what hadn't been there. Theirs were the same "bald assertions and statistical comparisons" that the Supreme Court had rejected in Croson.

Courts are getting impatient with these phony studies. In the second half of 1996, those of Philadelphia, Miami and Columbus were emphatically rejected by federal courts. Columbus' "failed to measure up to any reasonable standard for a forensic investigation," the court found, excoriating Columbus for having put a minority-advocacy group in charge of collecting anecdotal evidence of discrimination. In the opinion, over 40 pages in length, the judge devastatingly analyzed, item by item, the extensive array of testimony and data with which the city was trying to justify the gravy train for Negro contractors it had established. Witness after witness solemnly declared that racial discrimination was pervasive in Columbus contracting without being able to cite a single instance; one Negro contractor, in fact, stated that he had seen none in 19 years in business in the area. The court threw out the Columbus set-aside program as "remedying" a purported discrimination of whose existence the most Herculean efforts had failed to find any evidence.[42]

---

[41]Richmond v. J.A. Croson Co., 488 U.S. 469 (1989).

[42]Associated General Contractors of America v. Columbus, 936 F. Supp. 1363 (S.D. Ohio 1996).

In the Miami case, the court pointed out that "statistical analyses purporting to show general trends or marketplace phenomena do not suffice to evince actual, identifiable discrimination." The Philadelphia study, produced by former Federal Reserve official Arthur Brimmer, was so unpersuasive that preference advocates urged the city not to appeal the decision.[43] (It appealed anyway and lost in the Supreme Court early in 1997.)

There is, of course, a very simple reason why it is so difficult for governments to prove themselves guilty of past racial discrimination in the award of contracts: historically, to prevent corruption and favoritism, stringent rules requiring competitive bidding were adopted.

FROM COMPUTERS TO KIDNEYS

"Blacks Found to Trail Whites in Cyberspace"[44]

The amazing news about the "sharp racial divide" in use of the Internet, which was front-page news from the *New York Times* to the *San Francisco Chronicle*, was of course the discovery of "a new study," this one by a Vanderbilt University professor. Given different average income levels, as noted above, anything at all that affects the better-off differently than the poor can be expected to affect Negroes and whites differently. Indeed, the study stated that among those with annual incomes of over $40,000, usage of the Internet is virtually identical among the two races. But that did not prevent the study's author from talking nonsense about "a significant segment of our society" being "denied equal access to the Internet," as if stores were refusing to sell modems to Negroes, or Internet service providers were rejecting their subscriptions.

"Blacks Found to Trail Whites in European Travel" or "Racial Divide in Accounts at Tiffany's" could also easily be demonstrated, but it would be hard to promote government subsidies, or mandatory subsidies by the private sector, in those areas.

"Disparities in Who Gets New Kidneys"

The relentless insistence of "advocacy organizations" on proclaiming discrimination everywhere was well demonstrated in reaction to a study

---

[43]*Wall Street Journal*, Sept. 26, 1996.
[44]Amy Harmon, *New York Times*, April 17, 1998, p. 1.

published in the Journal of the American Medical Association in October, 1998.

According to the study, four steps occur in getting a kidney transplant: first, a patient must be interested and medically suitable; second, he must seek a transplant; third, he must complete preparation work and get referred to the waiting list; and fourth, he must move up the list.

Poor people, the study found, are less likely than the rich to complete the first three steps, but then were just as likely to receive transplants. And "African Americans were 32 to 50 percent less likely than whites to complete the last three steps." The study did not look at why patients didn't complete the steps of the process, but a co-author speculated that they might not want transplants, they might worry about Medicare rules that might stop their coverage after three years, and they might have medical conditions such as high blood pressure requiring treatment first.

This seems pretty straightforward. Poor people do tend to be relatively less well-organized; that's one of the reasons they're poor. And Negroes not only are disproportionately poor, they also have more than their share of health problems, as noted in Chapter V. There is no reason to suspect racial hostility on the part of the professionals involved in the transplant process.

But that is no problem for professional accusers. "Public Citizen, a consumer advocacy group, said bias is to blame . . ." This study exposes just how discriminatory the U.S. health care system can be' said Public Citizen's Dr. Peter Lurie."[45]

Finding Racism in the Consequences of Conduct
Crime and Incarceration

An unusually stupid newspaper story appeared in 1994 headed "Grim Picture of Racism in the '90s." It began:

> American racism is alive and unwell from sea to shining sea, an international panel contended in a disturbing, detailed report unveiled . . . before a gathering of area lawmakers. The report ticked off a litany of abuses against people of color in the United States, from their over-representation in prison populations and toxic pollution of their neighborhoods to consistent trampling of

---

[45]"Disparities In Who Gets New Kidneys," *San Francisco Chronicle*, Oct. 7, 1998.

indigenous people's rights. Some of the information was generally familiar, such as the fact that 70 percent of America's prisoners are minorities . . . Other information was not, such as statistics showing that 80 percent of people with disabilities are minorities or that men living in Harlem have a shorter life expectancy than men in Bangladesh.[46]

Passing over the American Indian issue and the "toxic racism" nonsense (see above), what has any of this to do with racism? Are racists killing the men of Harlem, or the creators of minorities' disabilities?

Actually, this is rather a clever tactic: instead of hoping that facts that reflect no credit on the group are not noticed and acknowledging them with embarrassment if they are brought up, proclaim them with indignation, and many will take them as reproaches of society.

Although the disparity is not as great as in the case of professional sports teams, Negroes unquestionably are disproportionately represented in prisons. About a quarter of all Negro men between 20 and 29 are in prison or otherwise involved in the criminal justice system, and in California the proportion is one-third. In the case of one San Francisco Bay Area county, Contra Costa, whose population is 9% Negro and 76% white, 51% of its residents in state prison were Negro vs. 38% white. In the state prison system as a whole, 37% of the inmates in a recent year were Negro and 30% white.[47]

Statistics for the District of Columbia paint a picture of what can only be called pervasive criminality among its predominantly lower-class Negro residents. According to the National Center on Institutions and Alternatives, *half* the District's Negro men between 18 and 35 are in prison or jail, on probation or parole, or out on bond or a warrant. And that doesn't count those who have gone through the process or who haven't been caught yet. The Center's study says that over 80 *percent* of the District's Negro men will have been locked up at some point before they reach the age of 35.[48]

The common attempt to explain statistics of this sort as reflecting police racism is particularly implausible in the case of Marion Barry's

---

[46]Kevin Fagan, *San Francisco Chronicle*, Dec. 10, 1994, p. A17.
[47]Donna Wasiczko, "Scales of justice tilting by race," *Contra Costa Times*, May 12, 1991, p. 4A.
[48]"Half of D.C.'s Black Men In Trouble With the Law," *San Francisco Chronicle*, Aug. 26, 1997.

District of Columbia, whose political and police leadership, and police force as a whole, are predominantly Negro. The fact is that, just as a remarkably high percentage of the best athletes are of African heritage, so are a remarkably high percentage of those who commit crimes. According to a study by the Center for Equal Opportunity based on data compiled by the Bureau of Justice Statistics, the percentage of Negro defendants convicted was actually lower than that of white in 12 of 14 categories of crimes.[49] And a study of federal sentencing in the Western states by the U.S. Sentencing Commission, also released in 1996, found that, while Negroes typically received longer sentences than whites, this difference properly reflected factors such as prior crimes and the use of weapons.[50]

The reason so many Negroes are in prison, quite simply, is that so much of American crime is committed by Negroes. This criminal conduct is of course consistent with the disproportionate number of Negroes in the juvenile justice system and, before that, misbehaving in school.

MISCONDUCT ON THE JOB

One would not expect to find a more supportive environment for minorities than the federal government. In one area after another, from its own hiring practices to private employment, mortgage lending, insurance availability, "environmental equity," the drawing of Congressional and other district boundaries, and the awarding of contracts, it has zealously sought to advance the interests of "disadvantaged" minorities. It is hardly plausible that it would itself be guilty of pervasive discrimination against Negroes.

Yet that is the implication of articles such as "Black Federal Employees Twice As Likely to Be Fired, Report Says."[51] In 1994 a study was commissioned after the Office of Personnel Management, in the Clinton Administration, discovered what it called a "disturbing pattern" of dismissals. "These numbers were like a smoke detector," said the office's director: "They signaled the need for immediate action." During the 1992 fiscal year, 52% of the federal workers fired were Negro, although Negroes were only 28% of the total federal civilian work force.

---

[49]Linda Chavez and Robert Lerner, "Is the Justice System Rigged Against Blacks?" *Wall Street Journal*, Dec. 4, 1996, p. A19.

[50]William Carlsen, "Study on Sentences Finds No Racial Bias In Western Judges," *San Francisco Chronicle*, Aug. 21, 1996.

[51]Karen De Witt, *San Francisco Chronicle*, April 20, 1995.

Those figures accentuate the implausibility of claiming racism was at work, since, after all, 28% is more than double the percentage of Negroes in the work force. It would be a pretty peculiar type of racism that recruited Negroes so zealously and simultaneously subjected them to unfair disciplinary action.

The Brown University sociologist hired for the study wasn't slowed up by such an obvious point, however. "We should proceed as if there might be racial bias involved," she said. Various "possible explanations" for the firing were offered: "bias or lack of cultural awareness, poorly trained supervisors and managers or a general inability on the part of minorities to work the 'old boy' network."

But not the obvious one, that these firings, which were "primarily for 'misconduct,' a category that besides poor performance includes theft, embezzlement and insubordinate acts such as striking or throwing something at a supervisor," simply reflected bad behavior.

Along similar lines is "Black Leaders Allege Racism in Army Sex Case."[52] It turns out that all 13 non-commissioned officers facing charges in the Aberdeen Proving Ground sexual misconduct scandal are Negroes, a fact that had not previously appeared in press coverage. Again, since over half of the facility's drill instructors and faculty are minority-group members, the suggestion that the charges reflect Army racial prejudice seems implausible. More likely the drill instructors felt that their race exempted them from the rules, forgetting that women have victim-group status too and furthermore that some of them were minority-group members as well.

FINDING RACISM IN REACTION TO UNSATISFACTORY CONDUCT

If you joke about the peculiar speech of the ill-educated white hillbillies of Appalachia, or react to the manners and mores of lower-class whites with scorn or disgust, or make references to "trailer park trash," no one will accuse you of anti-white racism, although the determinedly egalitarian might accuse you of snobbery. If you are impatient with sullen and disgruntled white employees, no one will take that as indicative of racism and few would hold such a normal reaction against you. Race, obviously, is not the issue at all.

---

[52]*San Francisco Chronicle*, March 4, 1997.

Change the color of those to whom you have a negative reaction, however, and your reactions will be taken as examples of racism. This would seem obvious nonsense; and yet this game is regularly played, as in the case of the student at the University of Pennsylvania who was accused of racism for calling a group of Negro girls disturbing his studying by making noise late at night "water buffaloes."

It should be unnecessary to make the point that reacting with disapproval to unsatisfactory conduct does not become racism because the bad actors are Negroes. If someone yells "Jerk!" at a driver who runs a red light the remark is not transformed into an expression of racism because the offending driver has a dark skin. The case would of course be different if the individual habitually reacted with an understanding smile when a white driver ran a light, but this is not the sort of situation we are talking about. It was not suggested, for example, that the Pennsylvania student would have been perfectly content to have his studying disrupted by noisy white girls.

It should also be unnecessary to point out that aversion to lower-class mores, to types of conduct disproportionately present among the socio-economic lower class, from loudness to lack of self-discipline to criminality, does not become racism because a relatively high proportion of the lower class are of minority ethnic groups. It is not with the color of their skin but with the content of their character, or with their conduct, that other people have a problem.

Yet, even years ago, in a New York City mayoral campaign, a candidate attacking "crime in the streets" was accused of racism on the ground that everyone knew that most such crime was committed by Negroes and Puerto Ricans. The real target supposedly was the minorities, and their criminality merely a pretext; no doubt had they been prominent in ophthalmology, the racists would have been attacking eye doctors.

With this technique, racism can be found everywhere, since no one who is not infinitely tolerant of objectionable behavior, or at least possessed of superhuman control over how he expresses his disapproval of it, can possibly be innocent of it.

Becoming a direct victim of this "racism" may require some effort on the part of the supposed victims. Employees who are not as successful in their careers as they would like to be, for example, are to assume that this is due, not to any deficiency on their part, but to racism on their superiors' part, and to respond by becoming sullen, withdrawn, and angry.

In terms of specifics, as in the 1996 Texaco case, they may make a point of not standing for the National Anthem, celebrate Kwanzaa instead of Christmas, and file lawsuits charging racial discrimination and demanding millions of dollars in damages. Sooner or later, human nature being what it is, someone in management is bound to become impatient or exasperated at this behavior and say something less than deeply respectful about the disgruntled employees or their conduct, which will instantly be taken by the employees' lawyers and the media as conclusive proof of the racism that has been holding them back.

But no effort may be needed to trigger negative-reaction "racism." Hostile, resentful Negroes with offensive lower-class mores and behavior patterns can simply be themselves. Such people inspire a dislike that has nothing to do with their color and everything to do with they way they act, but nevertheless it is often taken as more proof of whites' ingrained racism, with no suggestion that it may instead reflect a perfectly human and understandable *reaction* to black conduct. There will be no hint that perhaps the chain of causation ran in *that* direction.

Laughter at foibles and idiosyncrasies may be seized on as evidence of racism, too, as in the case of the Morgan Stanley & Co. employees and the e-mail joke earlier in this chapter. Laugh at what is funny and you are a racist.

When *reaction* to *conduct* is called racism, we have come far, far indeed from its definition as adverse feeling based on race as such. With this preposterous definition, someone in the 1930s who found many Germans unappealing would have been guilty of racism. It says a great deal about the orientation of the media that such examples of "racism" as in the Texaco case are allowed to pass unchallenged.

When bad actors are of a particular ethnic group, or predominantly so, it is quite natural for someone to make a reference to it in a comment. An epithet may provide a means of blowing off steam. But if an American soldier, reacting to the Bataan Death March, had exclaimed, "Sadistic Japs!" it would be wrong to conclude that he was a racist hostile to all of Japanese ancestry, even if he failed to add "But of course I am referring only to the brutal rats who perpetrated this atrocity on helpless prisoners and not to the many fine and loyal citizens of Japanese ancestry."

Much the same applies, I think, to the use of "the N-word," "nigger." I remember an old Southern lady once telling me that this was the term for a *bad* Negro, meaning of a criminal or extremely lower-class type.

Much more recently, a white taxi driver drew a similar distinction in a conversation with author Dinesh D'Souza. "I never pick up niggers," said the driver. "You don't like blacks?" "Not blacks. Niggers." "That sounds like racism to me." "Hey, that's crap. I pick up older blacks all the time. I have no problem with giving black women a ride. My black buddies won't pick up no niggers. I ain't no more racist than they are."[53]

It does not follow from, say, a policeman's applying "nigger" to a street thug, or someone of the type Negro talk show host Ken Hamblin calls "black trash,"[54] that he would apply it to a law-abiding, hard-working, middle-class individual of African heritage, or that he is a racist who treats someone unfavorably solely on the basis of skin color. There presumably are policemen whose exposure to Negro criminals has disoriented them to that extent, as indeed there are real racists, but even Mark Fuhrman was said by Hispanic and Negro police officers who had worked with him to have shown no sign of racial antagonism or discrimination in his dealings with them.

MAKING RATIONALITY TANTAMOUNT TO RACISM

Another supposed demonstration of Americans' racism is, not negative reaction to unsatisfactory conduct or to the individuals guilty of it, but simply being in touch with reality: knowing that members of some racial groups are more likely than others to have certain characteristics, particularly if this knowledge is acted upon. A relatively high percentage of Negroes are in less-skilled occupations and relatively few are lawyers or bank presidents, and this is common knowledge, so guesses that one is a messenger or a doorman, as in the previous chapter, are inevitable. Similarly, known facts as to what is widespread among Negroes in terms of educational level, family and economic background, patterns of speech, and so forth, will create expectations in rational people, and sometimes they will express them, or express surprise when what they encounter is quite different, such as when someone meets in person a Negro whom, from his standard and completely unaccented English on the telephone, he has assumed to be white.

It is also common knowledge that an unusually high percentage of Negroes are inclined to commit crimes, and people react accordingly.

---

[53]*The End of Racism*, The Free Press, 1995, p. 252.
[54]See *Pick a Better Country*, Touchstone, 1996, Ch. 2.

Security guards in department stores tend to keep a particularly close eye on young black men, and pedestrians sometimes cross the street when they see groups of Negroes on the sidewalk ahead of them.

To those determined to convict Americans of racism, these are all examples of the ubiquitous evil. In an article entitled "Racism in America sometimes surprisingly subtle," a *Washington Post* writer described an experiment involving a group of "well-intentioned white liberals . . . who swore they would never deliberately discriminate against anyone on the basis of race." Telephone calls were made to them by someone who apparently had called their numbers by mistake. The caller said his car had broken down, he had no more change, and he needed to have a tow truck called. When the caller had "an identifiably black voice," the participants hung up prematurely six times more often than when the caller sounded white.[55]

This was supposed to be an example of "the phenomenon known within psychological circles as aversive racism," the racism of "people who would vote for a black president but might unconsciously steer away from sitting next to a black person on the bus."

Not very well put; passengers on a bus can see the other passengers and are not likely to avoid sitting next to a clean and respectable-looking person, as opposed to a thug type, of any race. The subjects of the experiment had only a voice on the telephone to go on. What the experiment shows is simply that these liberals were not out of touch with reality. They apparently had a sense of where a disproportionate amount of crime comes from and an inclination to avoid the risk of getting entangled in it.

If this is anti-black racism, then the Rev. Jesse Jackson is an anti-black racist, for in a 1994 speech he told of hearing footsteps behind him on a deserted street at night and being relieved to see a white face when he turned around. Given the statistics on Negro crime in the District of Columbia mentioned above, his reaction there is particularly understandable.

Similar manifestations of simple common sense on the part of whites, however, are commonly looked askance at, as if demonstrative of racism. At President Clinton's December, 1997 "town hall" on racial matters in Akron, according to the *New York Times'* account, a white student "confessed that when a poorly dressed black man walked toward him some-

---

[55]Malcolm Gladwell, *Sacramento Bee*, July 21, 1991, p. A12.

times, 'I may be a little bit scared.' " Questioned as to how he came by this apparently remarkable reaction, "he said that his feeling 'has nothing to do with my personal experience,' and that he might have learned to react that way from television and 'things that I have heard.' That is exactly the kind of sentiment that the White House has said it wants to unearth and discuss . . ." "That's a pretty gutsy thing for you to admit . . ." responded Mr. Clinton.[56]

"Confessed"? "Unearth"? "Gutsy"? "Admit"? That such terms, appropriate to the divulgence of a shameful secret, should be applied, by President and press, to a rational response to known facts – exactly as was Jesse Jackson's – is a striking demonstration of how far from reality and common sense discussion of these matters has moved.

Even a knowledgeable scholar opposed to racial preferences is not immune from falling into a trap in this area. At a White House conference in December, 1997, President Clinton called the tendency of the police to question blacks "a race-based public policy," apparently intending to argue that then racial preferences must also be appropriate in employment or in college admissions. Abigail Thernstrom responded by declaring that such police practices also were "unacceptable to me." When Mr. Clinton posed the question in terms of whom the police ought to stop to slow the flow of cocaine across the Mexican border, Mrs. Thernstrom was consistent: "Every third car and come up with some of the criminals that way . . . I think police departments have to be held to the same standard that I want to see employers and universities and everybody else . . ."[57]

But applicants to medical school are not admitted or rejected based on their appearance as they drive up. It is feasible to scrutinize their qualifications carefully before making a decision. The question whether objective standards should be applied on a race-neutral basis in making such a final determination is completely different from the question whether the police should be compelled to act mindlessly in determining who shall have the temporary inconvenience of having his car stopped and searched. If a victim describes her mugger as a tall black male, must the

---

[56]James Bennet, "Clinton, at Meeting on Race, Struggles to Sharpen Debate," *New York Times*, Dec. 4, 1997, p. 1.

[57]"Excerpts From Round Table With Opponents of Racial Preferences," *New York Times*, Dec. 22, 1997, p. A6.

police stop whites lest they be guilty of racism? Women lest they be guilty of sexism? Short people to avoid heightism? The only "public policy" here is that the police should use common sense in fighting crime. This is not race-based, or sex-based, or height-based.

The fact is that, while one cannot *accurately* judge a book by its cover, there are times when one cannot read the book and has to make a decision quickly with nothing to go on but the cover. If people know that an unusually high percentage of those who look a certain way have an important real characteristic, this will certainly affect their initial reaction. If racism is defined so that only the brainless can be innocent of it, the definition obviously is nonsensical.

It should be even more obvious that it is not racism to be aware that not everything is hunky-dory with an ethnic group. Yet respected academics can find it here.

A new book by a Stanford professor of political science, Paul Sniderman, and Indiana University Professor Edward Carmines, *Reaching Beyond Race*,[58] has some good features. It makes clear that the great majority of Americans, from all parts of the political spectrum, find racial preferences repugnant. Its authors also set out to see, using some sophisticated techniques, whether white Americans are actually as fair-minded toward Negroes as they say they are, and they found that, by and large, they are. (That they were quite surprised at these findings is of course quite consistent with the academic world's mind-set.)

But they also concluded that there is still plenty of bigotry around, although less than 50 years ago: "But because there are fewer bigots does not mean that there are only a few."[59]

How did they determine this? When it sinks in, one is incredulous. Their study asked whites whether they thought certain descriptions of blacks were generally apt. These were: "hard-working," "friendly," "intelligent at school," "dependable," "law-abiding," "determined to succeed," and "keep up their property." "Friendly" got a 75% yes vote, but the rest, shockingly, only around 50 to 60%, and "keep up their property" only 41%. How many the respondent chose as apt determined whether he was classified as a bigot or not!

---

[58]Harvard University Press, 1997.
[59]*Ibid.*, p. 70.

It is not hard to see how someone with some familiarity with the real world might doubt the aptness of these descriptions. How does committing about half the crimes, although constituting only about a tenth of the population, fit with "law-abiding"? Disproportionate representation on welfare and unemployment rolls with "hard-working," "dependable," and "determined to succeed"? Consistent relatively poor academic performance with "intelligent at school"? The Negro slum with "keep up their property"? No matter. These professors solemnly declare, "Hostility to blacks can show itself in two ways – by agreement that blacks have negative characteristics, or alternatively, by denial that they have positive ones."[60]

The authors use "hostility" interchangeably with "prejudice" and "bigotry," which is sloppy enough. What is really ridiculous is equating them all with unwillingness to apply favorable adjectives of questionable appropriateness. I don't think I'd pick "enthusiastic athletes" as an apt description of Jews or of Chinese-Americans, but that doesn't make me an anti-Semite or an anti-Chinese bigot.

The professors' nonsensical definition of bigotry leads, not surprisingly, to some peculiar conclusions. They find that liberals are nearly as prejudiced against blacks as conservatives, and that nearly as high a percentage of the non-prejudiced as of the prejudiced are opposed to preferences for them. Findings such as these should set off alarm bells immediately. Any definition of anti-Negro bigots that has any at all, let alone 20%, supporting preferential treatment for Negroes obviously has something radically wrong with it. The professors' survey tests not freedom from bigotry but possession of an unrealistically rosy view of Negroes, and it would appear that the incidence of this affliction is not dramatically greater among liberals than conservatives in the country as a whole: as the "car breakdown" experiment above suggested.

"RACIST HUMOR"

If all else fails, there is humor to fall back on. And it will be sufficient if someone laughs at a joke rather than tells it; says Patricia Digh of the Society of Human Resource Management, whites may not even know they have prejudices. "I may not have told a racist joke, but I may have laughed at some. Racism is not always an overt act."[61]

---

[60]*Ibid.* p. 61.
[61]Maggie Jackson, "Texaco Scandal No Surprise," *San Francisco Chronicle*, Nov. 22, 1996.

The only solution is to be totally devoid of a sense of humor. But not only is this a condition not achievable voluntarily, it is one from which few would wish to suffer.

Is it really true that ethnic humor constitutes objectionable racism? Not long ago the very idea that it did would have been considered laughable. Ethnic humor has been a staple of American humor throughout the country's history. I am not sure whether the Triple I Society, or whatever its exact name is or was, still exists in San Francisco, but it used to have jolly banquets where those of Irish, Italian, and Jewish heritage (the third I stood for Israel) would joke about their nationalities' foibles in a spirit of laughter and camaraderie.

The essence of ethnic humor is to make a joke out of some characteristic more common in a particular ethnic group than in others. As in the case of the Scotsman on the train. He dragged a large and heavy trunk and then got into a heated argument with the conductor as to the proper fare. Finally the conductor got so exasperated and angry that, as the train passed over a river on a bridge, he threw the trunk off. The Scotsman was beside himself. "First you try to rob me, and now you have drowned my boy!"

No one, of course thinks that *all* Scots are parsimonious, or that *all* Irishmen are drunks, or that *all* Frenchmen are amorous. Nor does telling jokes mean that the teller hates the ethnic group that is the subject. Someone who says that in Heaven the cooks are French, the police are English, the mechanics are German, the lovers are Italian, and everything is organized by Swiss, whereas in Hell the cooks are English, the police are German, the mechanics are French, the lovers are Swiss, and everything is organized by Italians, does not hate all these nationalities.

Not that long ago the notion that ethnic jokes indicated race hatred would have been considered conclusively refuted by the fact that they were told of all ethnic groups. Only a childishly oversensitive, whining sorehead, "unable to take a joke," would fail to see the humor in them or take offense, was the general view.

With the "discovery" of general American oppression and victimhood, it is no longer that simple. To those with this outlook, the universality of ethnic humor does not prove that it cannot represent racism but instead demonstrates the ubiquitousness of racism: just as jokes about men and women, fat people, morons, and homosexuals demonstrate America's sexism, ableism, and heterosexism. Any finding of humor in differences among groups is a sign of bigotry that should be combated by strident denunciation and ultimately stamped out by re-education.

Nuts like this cannot be argued with, but they should not be taken seriously.

Complete Nonsense

A skilled professional whiner can find racism in any ethnic reference at all. Taco Bell, a Mexican-food chain, ran commercials in which a Chihuahua says, "Yo quiero Taco Bell," which means "I want Taco Bell." The president of the League of United Latin American Citizens denounced this as – favorite word again – "very demeaning." "It is definitely a hate crime that leads to the kind of immigrant bashing that Hispanics are now up against."[62]

If the Wienerschnitzel chain had a dachshund saying, "Ich moechte Wienerschnitzel haben," would that be demeaning to Germans? A poodle, "Je desire Marcel & Henri pate"? What is supposed to be the rationale for this complaint? Is it suggested that the commercial implies that Spanish-speaking people are dogs? That they are undignifiedly small? Would it be all right if the dog were a Great Dane speaking in a deep voice? Is it thought that the commercial suggests that Spanish is the language of choice for dogs? Are all the talking animals who speak English, including Donald Duck and Porky Pig, demeaning to English-speaking Americans?

Some people apparently spend their time on the prowl for anything that, with enough determination and ingenuity, can be attacked as racism. Two fine examples appeared the same day in the *San Francisco Examiner*.[63] One story was headed "Memorial plaque seen as racist." In an old Mother Lode town dating back to gold rush days, a plaque in the Pioneer Cemetery commemorated the resting place of "the first white settler's child" born in the town.

The other began, "Skin bleach coupon seen as offensive," "Drugstore's ad targets blacks." In honor of Black History Month, Walgreen's had distributed a coupon book which included a coupon for a popular brand of product designed to even skin tone. This was attacked as an "insult" implying "that it's not acceptable to be black." More sensibly, an assis-

---

[62]"Hispanic civil rights group wants Taco Bell ad muzzled," *Contra Costa Times*, March 3, 1998.
[63]Feb. 24, 1997.

tant dean at Stanford commented, "It's not an attempt to be white. It's for evening out our skin . . . It's just crazy. You can really go crazy with it unless you think for yourself."

That's a good word for the goings-on in New York City in November 1998. According to the New York Times, "School officials reassigned [teacher Ruth Sherman] after a raucous public meeting Monday at Public School 75 in the Bushwick section of Brooklyn in which parents denounced her for assigning a book called "Nappy Hair" by Carolivia Herron, a black writer and scholar."[64] The critically-acclaimed book, recommended to hundreds of teachers at training institutes at the Columbia University Teachers College Reading and Writing Project by its research and development director (also a Negro), dealt with a little girl with "the nappiest hair in the world." According to its author, the teacher was using the book "exactly as she had intended: to celebrate racial diversity and teach children to be proud of who they are."[65]

Vigilant grievance-scroungers had distributed photocopies of selected pages from the book to parents and "community organizers." This way, said the local school board president, "it looks like pictures to degrade African-Americans." The teacher (who was white) was reassigned after parents and "leaders of community groups" told her at the meeting, "You better watch out," and "We're going to get you."

Even an obvious compliment can be turned into a racist insult by those determined enough, as with the hardy perennial complaint about athletic teams called "Indians." Manifestly the name reflects the image of the brave and determined warrior, along the same lines as "Vikings," a name never complained about by those of Scandinavian heritage.

Indeed, any manifestation of awareness (on the part of a white person, that is) that there is such a thing as race or ethnicity will suffice to support the charge of racism, as in the case of the state senator in Chap. III. And of course not even complete silence or ignorance will save someone from the "unconscious racism" that the Harvard speaker in Chap. II attributed to all whites not guilty of the overt variety.

Some kind of prize should go to the District of Columbia employees who accused a white district official of using a racial slur, causing him to

---

[64]Lynette Holloway, "School Officials Support Teacher on Book that Parents Call Racially Insensitive," New York Times, Nov. 25, 1998, p. A24.
[65]"Teacher in Book Dispute Mulls Return Amid Threats," New York Times, Nov. 27, 1998.

apologize and resign. He had used the word "niggardly" to refer to his administration of a fund.[66]

Of course, this is all nonsense. None of what has been discussed in this chapter is actually racism, which in case one has forgotten means having hostility toward others or deliberately discriminating against them solely because of their race. Amidst all the din, it is easy to lose sight of that fundamental fact.

---

[66]Melinda Henneberger, "Race Mix-Up Raises Havoc For Capital," New York Times, Jan. 29, 1999, p. A8.

CHAPTER VII

A REVIEW OF
"AFFIRMATIVE ACTION" AND PREFERENCES

When "affirmative action" is seen for what it is – racial preferences, deliberate racial discrimination – it is widely rejected, both by judges based on the Equal Protection Clause of the Constitution and by the general public based on elementary fairness. And for good reason.

COLLECTIVE GUILT

A system of racial preferences is tantamount, in terms of the civil law, to mass tort liability in combination with mass restitution. If the preferred group is Negroes, then it means that every non-Negro is subjected to a penalty by being put at a disadvantage in securing employment, being promoted, receiving a contract, whatever; and every Negro shares in this massive award of damages by being given a leg up in all these areas. The system of preferences can also be analogized to mass punishment on the one hand and mass punitive damages on the other.

The analogy to the law is appropriate whether what is involved is governmentally-administered quotas and set-asides, in various programs by federal and state governmental entities which are now being regularly struck down by the courts, or similar programs in the private sector put into effect in response to the civil rights laws. Mass penalization and mass restitution are what is involved.

It should be obvious that such a thing can only be justified by pervasive guilt or blame on the part of those to be penalized which caused pervasive harm to those now to be compensated.

"War guilt" is an example. The theory of imposing reparations on Germany after World War I was that Germany as a whole was guilty of bringing the sufferings of the war on the Allies and ought to compensate them. Less controversial is the case of what the Germans did to the Jews in the 1930s and 1940s. West Germany paid reparations to the state of Israel by way of compensating Jews for Nazi crimes against them. Few would quarrel with the justice of that remedy, even though some Germans did all they could to oppose Hitler's murderous policies.

The imaginative definitions of racism that have been developed, from "aversive racism" to "unconscious racism" and "toxic racism," and the creativity with which examples of "racism" are discovered and decried, suggest at least a subconscious recognition on the part of advocates of racial favoritism that justifying what they want requires general guilt. But to suggest that the rest of the American population stands in relation to Negroes as Germans of the 1930s and 1940s to Jews is obviously absurd. Not only are such Americans living today virtually unanimous in expressing opposition to discrimination against those of African ancestry, they have for decades now been engaging in heroic efforts to be fair, from passing Civil Rights acts and providing preferential treatment to desperately trying to avoid "insensitive" speech.

What results from racial preferences is an arbitrary and capricious apportionment of burdens and benefits bearing no relation to any rational concept of justice. "Affirmative action" does not seek out individual Negroes who have demonstrably been penalized because of their race and advance them at the expense of those guilty of it or unfairly preferred because of it. Somewhere in New York a Negro is passed over for promotion in favor of a less-qualified white, and somewhere in California a Chinese-American from a poor immigrant family, who never discriminated against anybody, loses out to the son of a Negro lawyer who may very well himself owe his position to preferences.

ANCESTRAL GUILT

Preferences make even less sense as a remedy for past rather than present injustice. Here the injustice of collective guilt is compounded with that of ancestral guilt. We have warm relations with Germany and Japan and do not reproach today's Germans and Japanese for what their parents and grandparents did or expect them to atone for their truly atrocious misdeeds; why then should non-Negro Americans of today be expected to suffer for the sins of past discrimination and ancient slavery?

And how many of today's Americans are descended from people who benefitted from the unfair treatment of Negroes? If we are talking about slavery, rather few. Many of them didn't get here until slavery had been long gone. Indo-Chinese, Chinese, Japanese, Armenians, Hitler-era and post-World War II refugees, obviously. But also those in the great wave of late-19th and early-20th century immigration: Eastern European Jews, Italians. Few of the Irish and the Germans who arrived in the middle of the 19th century settled in slave states or had anything to do with slavery.

Even among Southern whites, only a minority were slaveowners.

Many more of today's Americans had ancestors who were in the United States and might have had contact with Negroes in the years after slavery was abolished. But it would be wrong to attribute some sort of unjust enrichment to non-Negro Americans in general, north or south, because of discrimination in the post-slavery era. Many, for example the Chinese and the Japanese on the West Coast, were consistently discriminated against themselves.

When all is said and done, there is obviously no more rational basis for lumping all non-Negro Americans together for penalizing on the basis of ancestral guilt than there is on the basis of collective guilt for such racial discrimination as occurs at the present time.

Nor should the point made by Booker T. Washington around the turn of the century be lost sight of, ". . . the . . . Negroes inhabiting this country, who themselves or whose ancestors went through the school of American slavery, are in a stronger and more hopeful condition, materially, intellectually, morally, and religiously, than is true of an equal number of black people in any other portion of the globe."[1]

Those originally brought here as slaves were not wrenched away from an idyllic existence in an advanced tropical Utopia. And sub-Sahara Africa is still not an advanced tropical Utopia. The names of its countries continually thrust themselves at us in the news in connection with misery, corruption, and barbaric violence. In his recent book, *Out of America: A Black Man Confronts Africa*, Keith Richburg, a former African bureau chief for the Washington Post, described the horrors he encoun-

---

[1]Booker T. Washington, *Up from Slavery*, Pocket Books, 1940 (1900), p. 11.

tered during his three years' stay on his ancestral continent and reflected on the course of events that brought his ancestor here as a slave 400 years ago: "Thank God my ancestor got out, because, now, I am not one of them . . . In short, thank God I am an American."[2]

OTHER RATIONALES FOR PREFERENCES

Those without African ancestry are on the whole not receptive to the idea that they should be discriminated against in order to atone for someone else's unfairness to Negroes, and preference advocates have been ingenious in developing other justifications for such policies.

Playing games with words is a common approach. As discussed in Chap. III, the most popular word in this regard is "diversity," meaning, in the racial context, "If you've seen one white or Asian, you've seen 'em all, but every black enriches a workplace/academic community." Reduced to its essence, this argument refutes itself.

Sometimes the answer to one question is presented as though it proved something else entirely. The 1998 book *The Shape of the River*, by Derek Bok, former president of Harvard University, and William G. Bowen, former president of Princeton,[3] received wide press coverage as demonstrating that "affirmative action works." A Seattle newspaper (see below) cited it as a reason to vote against eliminating State of Washington race and sex preferences.

Whether the detailed survey of thousands of Negro college graduates (the book's appendix is over 150 pages) on which the book is based demonstrates that affirmative action works depends on – to use an expression made famous by President Clinton – how you define "affirmative action" and "works." As to the first, it deals solely with graduates of 28 selective institutions of higher learning, all of which give preference to Negroes in undergraduate admissions. Its research does not cover any other kind of racial preferences, whether in employment, the award of contracts, or admission to graduate schools.

What about "works"? Well, if you have read that underqualified Negro students at elite universities often get frustrated and resentful and that many of them fail to graduate, and you therefore fear that perhaps the intended beneficiaries of "affirmative action" all drop out or are crippled by their experience even if they graduate, this massive work will reassure

---

[2]Reviewed in *Wall Street Journal*, Feb. 6, 1997.
[3]Princeton University Press, 1998.

you. Yes, the dropout rate is high, but most graduate, and, while their subsequent earnings are well below those of the better-qualified, they are higher than in the case of those who did not graduate from top schools.

But it is hardly news that a Yale or Princeton degree, coupled with the contacts made in four years there, gives someone a significant advantage in later life. That is why generations of parents have pulled every string they could to get their children into prestigious colleges even when their grades and SAT scores were less than impressive. A Mississippian in years past could equally meaningfully have cited the successes of all-white Ole Miss's less-promising graduates as proof that "segregation works."

The book's authors appear to understand that all the exhaustive research they discuss doesn't really get to the heart of the matter. "Would society have been better off if additional numbers of whites and Asian Americans had been substituted for minority students [by color-blind admissions]? That is the central question, and it cannot be answered by data alone."[4] They recognize that "on the basis of the evidence in this study, the excluded white male students might have done at least as well as their retrospectively rejected black classmates, and probably even better in terms of average earnings."[5]

So why is racial discrimination the right thing? Relatively little of the book is devoted to this $64 question. One argument is that it's like handicapped spaces in a parking lot: they do the handicapped a lot of good, and the effect on everybody else is minimal. This is sophistry. In the first place, whether the favoritism is in college admissions, or in employment, or in government contracts, specific non-blacks lose opportunities once and for all, while the parkers face only a tiny enhancement in the remote possibility that they will have no place to park (unless they are habitually late and the lot often filled to capacity). In the second place, something that is unjust cannot be justified on the ground that the likelihood that any particular person will be a victim is slight. Could a city sell a limited number of licenses entitling their holders to one purse-snatch a month?

Bok and Bowen speak of the desirability of building up the black middle class. Such an approach might be justified if we anticipated a racially-segregated society in which the white and black communities largely kept to themselves. But wasn't the whole civil rights revolution

---

[4]Ibid., pp. 282-283.
[5]Ibid., p. 282.

about getting away from dividing people by race? At bottom, the book's attempt to justify racial preferences on the basis of building up the "black middle class" reflects a preoccupation with race that deserves to be buried rather than given validation. Do we still assume that people will separate themselves, in their business and social lives, based on whether they have African ancestry or not? Do we want them to? If not, policies that assume they will and encourage them to do so by proclaiming race to be extremely important have no place.

And are there not other groups, both ethnically and non-ethnically defined, that would benefit from having the standing of their middle-class members enhanced? There are geographical areas of the country that are relatively poor. A poor state such as Mississippi or Arkansas would surely benefit from a stronger middle class. There are differing degrees of affluence among *white* ethnic groups. And among religious groups. Should Episcopalians be discriminated against in order to build up the "fundamentalist middle class"? What about Jews, whose percentage at elite universities is at present close to ten times that in the population as whole: should they be discriminated against, perhaps with their numbers be kept down by quotas as in times past, to enhance the "Christian middle class"?

The idea that advancing a particular ethnic group at the expense of others by preferential treatment, whether in college admissions, graduate school admissions, employment, or contracts, is somehow a unique, overriding national interest, transforming racial discrimination from something indefensible into something noble, does not bear scrutiny.

Nor does the claim that preferential hiring is needed so that minorities will feel welcome or have "role models." Again this assumes an obsession with race that hardly ought to be encouraged, let alone used to justify racial discrimination. Do short students need to be inspired by short teachers, and stutterers by stuttering instructors? Preposterously, the new director of the National Park Service, a Negro, discovering yet another "diversity" problem in the relatively few minority-group visitors to national parks, has suggested that they are not comfortable in the parks because they do not see enough black park rangers there.[6]

---

[6]Mary Curtius, "Park service tries to draw minorities," *Contra Costa Times*, Jan. 18, 1999.

Individual Guilt

While it is clear that racial discrimination against minorities in the United States today is not sufficiently common to constitute a national problem or to justify preferential treatment for Negroes generally, that does not mean that penalization of discrimination on an individual, proven basis, which is what the 1964 Civil Rights Act was originally thought to be all about, may not be appropriate. It is, indeed, self-defeating, self-penalizing, to reject the best-qualified because of race, but many other things that tend to be self-defeating (at least in the long run) but harm specific innocent people, such as cheating customers or employees, expose those who do them to civil or criminal penalties.

To take a recent example, H. DeWayne Whittington was valedictorian of his high school in Maryland and subsequently a teacher, a principal, and finally, 40 years later, superintendent of schools in Somerset County. The school board voted 3-2 in 1992 not to renew his contract, and one of the members told a reporter that he "did not want a nigger running the schools," according to Mr. Whittington's lawsuit. He was awarded $920,000.[7]

This is an appropriate result, the wrongdoer compensating the person wronged. Justice would hardly have been served if instead Mr. Whittington had been left without his job while a Negro was selected over a better-qualified white to head a Montana school district.

But is it possible, as a practical matter, to provide for the one without getting the other, and moreover without doing society as a whole more harm than good, as everyone understands outlawing unfairness in general would do?

Consequences

Presumably some of those who passed the 1964 Civil Rights Act thought the result would be a relatively small number of individual cases of racial discrimination, clearly demonstrated by the facts of each case, whose number would become progressively smaller as the word spread that there was a new law and it was being enforced; and we would enter a new era of racial harmony and good will.

---

[7]"School Named After Fired Superintendent," *San Francisco Chronicle*, Jan. 16, 1997.

Perhaps such a result might have been achieved had the Act been written differently, for example as a criminal statute providing for fines and requiring that there be intent to discriminate. Such a statute would have brought into play the standard rules of the criminal law, including requiring proof of all elements of the crime beyond reasonable doubt. There would have been no need to accuse Americans of continuing pervasive racism – after all that ought anyway to have been an implausible accusation since the law was passed – if all it did was address provable instances of deliberate discrimination.

But what was passed, as interpreted by administrative agencies and the courts and amended most recently in 1991, is instead an invitation to massive redistribution of wealth and position based on creating "discrimination" by statistical legerdemain. For the alienated egalitarian intellectual establishment, it is a wonderful opportunity to overthrow injustice and oppression. For members of minority groups, it holds out tantalizing possibilities of a proportional sharing in the good things of life: proportional to their numbers, not according to their deserts or qualifications. Why should they not enthusiastically accept what respected professors and lawyers say is only their due, of which they have long been cheated? The presumption that inequality means inequity now affects everything from employment law to college and graduate school admissions to the awarding of contracts and the extending of credit, as discussed in the previous chapter. The real-world result is preferential treatment for those belonging to racial groups of below-average qualification: the same thing, and as indefensible as, outright "affirmative action" preferences.

Promoting preferences on this basis means a steady diet of media coverage of accusations of racial discrimination, often in connection with lawsuits. The message, endlessly repeated, is always basically the same: anti-black racism is everywhere.

Being inundated with this message can be expected to make those without African ancestry more receptive to the various forms of preference presented as combating or compensating for this pervasive evil, exactly as those who proclaim it often intend. But inevitably the purported victims are also inundated with the message. And it has had – also inevitably – a poisonous effect on them.

As Los Angeles Police Chief Parker observed at the time of the 1965 Watts riots, "You cannot keep telling [people] that they are being abused and mistreated without expecting them to react."[8] One ought to take with a grain of salt the idea that rampaging lower-class hoodlums and looters are necessarily motivated to any significant extent by political issues: to paraphrase Sigmund Freud, sometimes a rampaging looter is simply a rampaging looter, even though the press invariably attributes a Negro looting spree to profound grievances stemming from white racism. Even so, the timing is interesting: this outbreak occurred the year *after* the passage of the landmark Civil Rights Act. The rioters certainly could not have been angry about the Act's passage; but perhaps they had been affected by the day-in, day-out barrage of talk about racism that had been so important in getting it passed.

It is more than 30 years now since its passage, and, down in the slums, for example South Central Los Angeles, "rage" seems even greater. A significant percentage of lower-class Negroes have dropped out of the work force altogether. Whereas in the 50s Negro and white men participated equally in the work force, by the late 70s 7.7% fewer Negro men than white were employed or looking for work; while in 1952 59% of Negroes between the ages of 16 and 24 were employed, only 44% are now. One doubts that more generous welfare payments are the whole reason.

Nathan McCall, a Negro reporter with the *Washington Post*, wrote a few years ago about a visit to his old once-segregated neighborhood in Portsmouth, Virginia. It had been "middle class by black standards . . . There are sprawling homes, manicured lawns and two-car garages. A scenic lake winds through part of the neighborhood." Residents when he was growing up included "role models . . . teachers, postal workers and a smattering of professionals."

But, tragically, after the civil rights revolution, "most of the guys I hung out with are either in prison, dead, drug zombies or nickel-and-dime street hustlers." What happened? "We came to regard the establishment as the ubiquitous, all powerful 'white man' who controlled our parents' lives and, we believed, determined our fates as well. I think once we resigned ourselves to that notion, we became a lost and angry lot." As McCall puts it, "rage" was "one of the many things a young black could die from." Preferences and quotas are no help to those incapable of availing themselves of them.

---

[8]*Time,* Aug. 20, 1965, p. 19.

The devastated state of the Negro slum today is in part a consequence of acceptance of the endlessly-repeated accusation of pervasive racism. "Gangsta rap," full of hostility to American society and the police, defiantly flaunts destructive lower-class attitudes. Accepting the discipline of the lawful workplace is seen as "selling out" to the racist enemy.

In these areas, one is no longer in civilization. *Time* magazine described life in a Chicago housing project:

> Every school day . . . Diana Brooks turns to the window of her apartment . . . She stares at the bleak concrete landscape . . . until she spots [her children] picking their way past the broken glass, rusty cars and trash. Only when the boys are safely inside . . . can the . . . mother relax. The window . . . has been pierced by a bullet, and there is another bullet hole in the wall. [The families] live in a cross fire between rival gangs, who have turned the project into an American version of Belfast or Beirut . . . During the summer, someone gets shot on the average of every other day . . . Sonja, who has childhood friends in the gangs, cannot remember how many funerals she has attended. On a hot July night . . . Laketa awaited her turn in a . . . jump-rope game . . . Suddenly, the taunting chants of warring gangs filled the air, and gunfire broke out. A bullet pierced Laketa's chest, and . . . she died on the hospital operating table. Laketa was nine years old.[9]

One reason these areas are jungles is the general hostility to the "racist" police. "Police brutality" is constantly charged. If a drug-crazed criminal meets his death at the hands of the police, the neighborhood is likely to erupt. According to a San Francisco police officer, the police do not dare crack down on crime in Negro areas for fear of accusations of racism.[10] Homicide is now the leading cause of death among young Negroes of both sexes.

Resentment and anger, rather than delight at their educational opportunities, are common among Negro students at major universities. As the well-known scholar Thomas Sowell has pointed out, when these students fail to cope with the work at these elite institutions to which

---

[9]"In Chicago: Raising Children in a Battle Zone," Dec. 15, 1986.
[10]*San Francisco Examiner*, Oct. 11, 1992, p. B-4.

"affirmative action" has recruited them, they have two alternatives. The first is to accept the prevailing standards and confront their own failure to meet them. The second is to "retain their self-respect by continually attacking, undermining, and trying to discredit the standards that they do not meet, scavenging for grievances and issuing a never-ending stream of demands and manifestoes. Given the alternatives, it is hardly surprising that so many choose the second."

A somewhat analogous situation commonly arises in companies that have recruited by quota rather than qualifications. "Managing diversity" is the pretentious jargon term for what basically amounts to coping with the presence in the company of the underqualified and resentment-prone workers such "affirmative action" guarantees.

Whether constant talk about racism reflects hostility toward Americans in general, sincere if not well-reasoned conviction, an effort to promote preferences, or a well-meaning effort to concoct some rationale for Negro underachievement that does not reflect on a group whose members have experienced real injustice, it does Negroes no favor. Anger doesn't make people happier or more effective in their work. And if people are relentlessly against you because of the color of your skin, you have no need to improve what you are doing, and it would be pointless anyway.

There is an obvious connection between this preoccupation with racism and the spread of the self-defeating view of learning as "selling out" or "acting white," which Booker T. Washington and the founders of the United Negro College Fund would have considered idiocy; as well as with the similarly self-defeating embrace of lower-class manners and mores, from bad English to bad behavior, as "authentic black culture."

The conviction that they are permanently excluded from full participation in America by their skin color encourages some Negroes to withdraw into black separatism. A local news article dealt with Stanford University's first Negro graduate, now a judge, back for his 40th reunion. He had not felt himself to be a victim of racism in that long-ago time: "Things were pretty good for me. I was encouraged to think I was a member of a fraternity and something special. Fellow-students . . . were willing to be friends . . . Socially, I was quite accepted."

But he had caught on to the spirit of the new times. He was glad that now "young blacks . . . are demanding that the campus be free of 'cultural racism' . . . When I was here, it was enough to learn white man's education and play white man's games, then go practice white man's law and become white man's judge."[11] So much for the great English common law tradition. What sort of "black man's law" or "black man's games" does he have in mind?

Racially segregated dormitories have become common at colleges and universities, demanded by Negroes and some other ethnic groups so that they can escape the white racism they have learned to see all around them.

As was noted above, even many successful Negro professionals seethe with anger at what they now perceive as racist slights. Some years ago simple cases of mistaken identity, long the source of much humor, seem to have been taken more in stride. Carl Rowan liked to tell of being asked by a white motorist, as he was mowing his lawn in Washington, how much he charged, and responding that he didn't get any money but the lady of the house let him sleep with her.

Some Negroes turn away to an imaginary African heritage. A San Francisco couple called their child "Zaire" after consulting a map of Africa. Many celebrate "Kwanzaa," a 1966 invention of a Long Beach State professor of black studies, instead of Christmas. Some of its supposedly African principles, honored by the lighting of candles on successive days, have a distinctly 60s-socialist air: *ujima* is "collective work and responsibility," and *ujumaa* is "cooperative economics." *Kujichagulia* is "self-determination," whatever that is supposed to mean to present-day Americans, and *umoja* is "unity."

Ah, unity! Happy Africa! How free from the ethnic divisions and hostilities of less-fortunate areas. "Hutu soldiers, who have participated in the slaughter of up to 500,000 Rwandans, most of them from the minority Tutsi tribe, not only show no remorse but can't wait to repeat their acts," wrote *USA Today* reporter Jack Kelley in 1995.[12]

If German-Americans were doing relatively poorly in this country, one doubts that it would be a constructive step for them to give their children names such as "Friedrich," "Wolfgang," and "Adelhaid," wear lederhosen, and celebrate festivals in honor of Thor and Wotan instead of Christmas.

---

[11]Bill Workman, "Stanford's 1st Black Grad Tells How It Was in 1949," *San Francisco Chronicle*, Oct. 7, 1989.

[12]Aug. 5, 1995.

The pervasive-racism message is separating Negroes from the American mainstream in a variety of unfortunate ways. In a front-page story entitled "A Racial Divide Widens on Network TV," the *New York Times* described the increasing tendency of blacks to concentrate their television viewing on "black" programs, in contrast to the situation in the 1970s and 1980s when a program such as the "Cosby Show," featuring a cast of normal, middle-class people who happened to be Negroes, was highly popular with both races.[13]

For a long time, lamentably, white America forced definition by skin color on those with African ancestry, but it gradually outgrew this foolishness and recognized it as such. Now, ironically, it is Negroes who are doing it to themselves.

Rage and withdrawal don't make people more effective in the workplace, as was noted in an earlier chapter. And they prompt adverse reactions in others, helping get a vicious circle going. This is a particularly likely outcome in view of the widespread recognition that Negroes are being artificially advanced over others because of racial preferences. Anger over anger and favoritism in turn is seen by Negroes as further proof of intractable white racism, and racial disharmony increases further.

There is much more than anecdotal evidence of what decades of beating the drum of "racism" have done to Negroes' attitudes toward other Americans. In 1963, the year before the Civil Rights Act was passed, 70% of Negroes asked whether they thought "relations between blacks and whites [would] always be a problem" or that "a solution [would] eventually be worked out" expected a solution; by 1993, the percentage had dropped to 44%. Between 1983 and 1994, the proportion of Negroes who thought "most white people" wanted to see them "get a better break" dropped from a third to a quarter, while those who thought most whites wanted to "keep blacks down" or didn't care either way rose from half to two thirds.[14] Going to college appears to worsen Negroes' view of white people; among those with only a high school education, 18% believe it is "true" that "the government deliberately makes sure that drugs are easily available in poor black neighborhoods in order to harm black people,"

---

[13]James Sterngold, Dec. 29, 1998.
[14]Stephan and Abigail Thernstrom, *America in Black and White*, Simon & Schuster, 1997, p. 506.

and 24% believe it "might be true," but among the college-educated the percentages are 29% "true" and 38% "might be true."[15]

This sort of thing does not just happen, without causes. What's the likely cause here? To suggest that since 1963 whites have become more opposed to fair treatment for Negroes is preposterous. Back then no one dreamed of proposing actual preferential treatment for minorities; now many whites are advocates of it (if not volunteering to turn their own positions over to minority-group members, enthusiastically in favor of other whites' receiving second-class status in order to further what they believe to be racial justice). Efforts to be fair to minorities, from rewriting history to suppressing ethnic humor to adulation of prominent Negroes to obediently using whatever the latest term for Negroes is, have been heroic. No, the only plausible explanation for the increasingly negative Negro view of whites is the steady diet of accusations of "racism" in the battle for preferment.

When after 30 years of heroic efforts to combat racism as a top national priority Negroes appear more convinced that they are its victims than they were at the beginning, and racial disharmony is also greater, it stands to reason that something is radically wrong.

All this hasn't come cheap. One study estimates the cost of government enforcement mechanisms and private sector coping mechanisms at over $100 billion a year. Then there is the cost of litigation. Then there is the effect of the inevitable hiring of the less-qualified, which Peter Brimelow and Leslie Spencer estimate at $236 billion a year.[16] Another study, by Michigan State University industrial psychologist John Hunter and Frank Schmidt at the University of Iowa, estimates that GNP would be $150 billion a year higher if hiring were done solely on merit.[17] These figures make it pretty clear that the laws have forced a great deal *more* racial discrimination: even in terms of basic fairness, the cure is worse than the disease.

One indication of the effect of preferences in filling well-paying jobs with minority-group members can be found in a recent University of California report, which found that "the average black student in a California family earning more than $60,000 in 1985 scored lower on SAT

---

[15]*Ibid.*, p. 515.

[16]"When quotas replace merit, everybody suffers," *Forbes*, Feb. 15, 1993.

[17] J. Edward Pawlick, *Freedom Will Conquer Racism and Sexism*, Mustard Seeds, Inc., 1998, p. 240.

tests than the average for white and Asian students from families earning below $20,000." This, noted *San Francisco Chronicle* columnist Debra Saunders, is consistent with nationwide statistics cited by Andrew Hacker in *Two Nations: Black, White, Separate, Hostile, Unequal*: Asian students from $10,000 – $20,000 income per year families scored 860 and Negro students whose parents earned $50,000 – $60,000 scored 798.[18]

What is one to make of this? Ms. Saunders' suggestion is that "millions of minority kids are being deprived of a quality education." This isn't at all convincing, since people who earn over $60,000 a year (*a fortiori* people who earned it in 1985) generally live in neighborhoods where the public schools are good and also can afford private schools.

Two suggestions of UC Regent Ward Connerly that Ms. Saunders mentions ring truer: that these parents haven't "embraced the educational culture," and that the youngsters believe that they are doomed without racial preferences. It's true that many children of prosperous Negro professionals are drawn to the "authentic blackness" of the slum culture, where application to studies is regarded as "acting white," and neither that idea nor a belief that study is useless will help. Still, one is skeptical that such deficiency in attitude by itself could produce such a dramatic relative deficiency.

What is the likely cause? The reason that there is normally a strong correlation between family income and SAT scores is that there is a correlation between wealth and *each* of the determinants of intelligence, nature and nurture, or IQ and upbringing. People with high incomes tend to be smart, and smart, affluent people tend to provide their children with both a good education and good genes. Can these children have picked up such bad attitudes as to make the good schools they presumably attend count for nothing and cause them to score, in aptitude, below white and Asian children of poor and presumably not-so-smart parents from presumably comparatively poor schools?

One suspects that the real explanation is that their parents have been earning such high incomes not because they are smart but because of racial preferences. Thus, given the importance of heredity in intelligence, the kids are not that smart either, and that is the main reason their SAT scores are so low.

---

[18]"Preferences For Middle-Class Minorities," *San Francisco Chronicle*, Aug. 27, 1997, p. A19.

LOOKING AHEAD

A tide is now running against open preferences. They are generally rejected by the population – the passage of Prop. 209 in California reflects that rejection – and a majority of the present Supreme Court consistently rejects governmental discrimination in favor of minorities as barred by the Equal Protection Clause (except in the exceptional case where the governmental entity is narrowly compensating for its own past discrimination against them). However, preferential treatment for minorities is an important part of the religion of the intellectual community, a high percentage of Negroes themselves, a faithful Democratic voting bloc, not surprisingly favor it, and the Clinton administration continues to promote it zealously, even intervening unsuccessfully against Prop. 209 in the courts. "Affirmative action" in the government sector will not die quietly.

It was widely suggested in the media that Houston voters' November 1997 rejection of a ban on affirmative action, by a 54-46 margin, suggested that the tide was turning or that opposition to preferences might have been largely a California phenomenon. The facts of the matter make clear that this was wishful thinking by the proponents of preferences who dominate the media.

In the first place, thanks to the intervention of the mayor and city council, the proposal's wording was changed from that of the California proposition, forbidding governmental discrimination or preferential treatment on the basis of race or sex, to asking whether to "end the use of affirmative action for women and minorities." The focus was thus changed from the simple and straightforward issue of preferential treatment and discrimination to the nebulous "affirmative action," which many people think means something like friendly openness or encouragement rather than outright preferences and discrimination.

Not only that, women and minorities appeared to be – and indeed specifically were – singled out. Vote for this and you are voting to take away affirmative action from women and minorities only. Indeed, an underlying purpose of this wording may have been to provide a basis for challenging the measure as unconstitutional if it passed, on the grounds that it restricted programs to help women and minorities but not programs to help white males. Under the Supreme Court's Croson and Adarand decisions, preferential treatment by a state or city of a racial group may be constitutional where narrowly tailored to remedy past discrimination by that governmental entity. (Such treatment is never constitutionally *required*, however, which is why California could forbid it.) No group in fact is better-situated to demonstrate precisely that discrimination, at least over the last couple of decades, than white males who have been penalized by systems of open preference for women and minorities. As a matter of political reality, it is hard to imagine a city council voting to establish a compensatory white male preference system, but the fact that the Houston proposition would have allowed such a system while forbidding one for women and minorities might well have caused it to be thrown out as unconstitutionally discriminatory.

Another reason the defeat of the proposal was not a straw in the wind is that the population of Houston is about two-thirds Negro and Hispanic. That of course is reflected in the orientation of the city council and mayor who intervened to change the language of the proposition, as well as in its subsequent election of a Negro mayor.

Note should be made of the fact that the major corporations based in Houston funded a major drive in opposition to the proposed measure.[19] Their position is an example of big business' commitment to preferential treatment for minorities, which was cited in the introductory chapter as among the reasons for doubting the plausibility of the claim that anti-minority discrimination is actually a widespread problem in the United States.

In any case, Houston's city government remains subject to the U.S. Constitution, and barely a week after the vote a federal judge threw out the preferential contracting policies of Houston's county transit authority as unconstitutional.[20]

Far more significant is the November 1998 vote in Washington State on an initiative using the same language as California's 209. Determined to avoid another setback, preference advocates raised $4 million, largely from major corporations, and out-spent proponents 4-to-1, blanketing

---

[19]G. Pascal Zachary, "Big Business Helps Fund Fight in Texas To Defeat Bill to Ban Affirmative Action," *Wall Street Journal*, Oct. 30, 1997.

[20]Sam Howe Verhovek, "At Odds With Voters, Federal Judge in Houston Halts Affirmative Action Plan," *New York Times*, Nov. 14, 1997. Putting his finger on the fundamental injustice of such programs, the judge wrote, "To correct an injury to a historic black by a historic white, the program allows Metro to take current opportunities from a nonoffending white and allocate them to an uninjured black."

the heavily Democratic state with advertising portraying Proposition 200 as a threat to women and as sure to lead to litigation (they certainly knew whereof they spoke there, being the ones ready to create it). The state's popular governor and its leading newspaper crusaded against the measure. The press beat the drums against it; the *Seattle Times*, for example, ran a lengthy editorial entitled "Affirmative action works," citing *The Shape of the River*,[21] but 200 won by a vote of 58% to 42%.

When voters get a chance to reject preferences, they can generally be expected to do so. It is quite clear to the great majority of Americans that race and sex discrimination is wrong, regardless of which groups are discriminated against, and that in general unless efforts to confuse them about measures to forbid them are successful they will vote for non-discrimination and against "affirmative action." They know that they are not racists or sexists and in any case have no fear that they will be called that for casting their secret ballot.

It is different with politicians. The basic dynamic underlying all pork-barrel and special-interest politics is to reward those with a strong interest in something at the expense of the rest, for whom the cost is insignificant, as an effective way to buy support. In the case of race, preferences are dear to the hearts of those who benefit from them, and minorities are an important part of the Democratic coalition. And even though in the 1998 election Negroes were only 10% and Hispanics 5% of those voting, Republicans have long been tantalized by the dream of garnering significant numbers of minority votes. Voting against preferences will certainly antagonize many members of these groups, and will it make much difference as regards white voters, what with so many other issues concerning them? Besides, they would doubtless be denounced as racist and mean-spirited. Efforts in legislatures and Congress to eliminate preferences, even ones clearly unconstitutional under Supreme Court rulings, have gone nowhere.

Thus, paradoxically, it is the most democratic governmental mechanism – direct popular vote – and the least – the courts – that offer the best prospect for removal of explicit preferences by government. Ward Connerly, the University of California regent who spearheaded the California and Washington campaigns, intends to carry the effort to other states with initiative provisions; in early 1999, he indicated that Florida would be next.

---

[21] *The Seattle Times*, Sept. 20, 1998.

The laws principally relevant to private sector preferences are not subject to change by state electorates. They include various federal laws, including the Civil Rights Act, as amended. And under the 1991 amendments, the burden is on the employer to demonstrate that any "employment practice" that disproportionately rejects members of a particular race is "job related for the position in question and consistent with business necessity." So long as this is the law, racial preferences, by whatever name, will be prevalent in private sector employment.[22]

They are also encouraged by government pressure, as the Clinton administration has engaged in with a vengeance. In Senate hearings in 1995, the Labor Department's Office of Contract Compliance was accused of turning its mandate to ensure equal employment opportunity in companies with federal contracts into promoting "a disguised system of quotas."[23] Totally undeterred, at the end of 1998 the Labor Department was preparing to demand that thousands of companies begin providing its auditors with the name, race, age, sex, and salary of each of their employees.[24] As noted earlier, it is not only in employment that quotas are being actively promoted by this administration: it is particularly aggressive in using its leverage with regulated industries to promote them in areas such as lending and insurance.

De facto preferences will continue to be common so long as the antidiscrimination laws and the incentives to litigation they contain are in force, although a change in administration that led to an end to the government's aggressive campaign to compel minority hiring and promotion would reduce the pressure for them.

Excessive race-consciousness is obviously encouraged when membership in a race is an entitlement to special consideration. Sometimes the results are rather funny. A San Francisco fireman who always had been

---

[22]The Supreme Court's United Steelworkers v. Weber decision, 443 U.S. 193 (1979), held that Title VII's prohibition of discrimination did not apply to preferences in favor of minorities that an employer voluntarily adopted. This principle was applied to pro-woman preferences by a 5-4 majority in Johnson v. Transportation Agency, 480 U.S. 616 (1987). This remains the law; fearful that the Supreme Court would make a change if it revisited the issue, civil rights groups contributed over $300,000 in late 1997 to fund a settlement for a white New Jersey teacher who had brought a suit under Title VII.

[23]Asra Q. Nomani, "Affirmative-Action Agency Is Assailed For Pushing Quotas, Preferential Hiring," Wall Street Journal, June 16, 1995, p. B10.

[24]"Affirmative Dishonesty," The Weekly Standard, Jan. 25, 1999, p. 2.

thought to be of Italian heritage discovered a grandmother born in Mexico in order to take advantage of preferences for Hispanics; others groused that they ought not to have to share their preferences with someone of such marginal Hispanicity.[25] A socially-prominent state judge, of an old Spanish family, who had graduated from a prestigious law school, turned out to have profited through the preferences accorded a family business on the basis of "disadvantaged minority" status. For purposes of these state contracts, Hispanic ancestry pretty much amounted to a conclusive demonstration of disadvantaged condition, regardless of the circumstances of the particular individual. When race is your ticket to advancement, you become very race-conscious.

But race consciousness is also encouraged merely by the forbidding of discrimination. Someone of a different race than his supervisor has a basis for challenging his firing or non-promotion that someone of the same race does not. Race matters.

Our anti-discrimination laws thus have the effect of keeping alive and meaningful the extreme and artificial "one-drop rule" of racial definition. If this had been done in reverse, with equal logic defining as black only those with no European ancestry at all and calling all those with any "Blancoes," then we would all be Blancoes except for the estimated one-quarter of Negroes who are purely African. Everyone from George Washington to W.E.B. DuBois, from Theodore Bilbo to Louis Farrakhan, from Strom Thurmond to Colin Powell and Thurgood Marshall would be a member of the same race.

This discussion is rather fanciful, but it is certainly devoutly to be wished that color of skin would come to matter as little as color of hair in how people regard themselves and each other. This happy state of affairs is less likely, even if formal racial preferences went away completely, so long as race allows someone to bring an anti-discrimination complaint.

That is another good reason to get rid of anti-discrimination laws entirely, as proposed by Richard A. Epstein, James Parker Hall Distinguished Service Professor of Law at the University of Chicago, in his fine

---

[25]And of course they had a point. What are called "Hispanics" are actually basically mixed-race people from south of the border, originating in Mexico and Central America. Some in fact are pure Indian with no Spanish blood at all. If France instead of Spain had colonized that area they would be called something like "Franconics," but their predominant ethnicity would be the same.

1992 book, *Forbidden Grounds: The Case Against Employment Discrimination Laws* (Harvard University Press). In fact, the December, 1997 *New York Times*/CBS News Poll shows that 27% of Americans overall believe it is "not necessary to have laws to protect minorities against discrimination in hiring and promotion," vs. 69% believing it is (among whites the percentages were 31% and 65%).[26] This is actually a surprisingly high "not necessary" percentage, considering that virtually all public discussion of the matter for decades has taken for granted the need for such laws, and suggests that the possibility of achieving their repeal ought not to be dismissed out of hand.

Eliminating formal racial preferences, "affirmative action," which is built on a false view of how the free enterprise system works in America today, is an important first step toward a free, sane and color-blind society, where race doesn't matter. But we won't get far in that direction so long as laws are in place that make race a matter of critical importance and create racial preferences in practice.

---

[26]Sam Howe Verhovek, "In Poll, Americans Reject Means But Not Ends of Racial Diversity," *New York Times*, Dec. 14, 1997, p. 1.

CHAPTER VIII

SEX DISCRIMINATION

Women are another group now widely thought to be victims of bigoted attitudes and in need of both anti-discrimination law and formal preferences. Discrimination in the workplace is the common complaint.

Working permanently outside the home was the goal of very few women thirty or so years ago. "She has to work," women would often say pityingly of a married woman who held a job; it was understood that her husband was a "poor provider." Many women worked after school or college until they found husbands or until the children came, but few chose to make a career of it. Home and family were understood to be the norm for a woman's focus, as had generally been the case since the dawn of recorded history in East as well as West.

There was no general perception that discrimination against women was a national problem nor any mass movement to outlaw such a thing when Congress addressed proposed civil rights legislation in 1964. Sex discrimination was added to the 1964 Civil Rights bill as a tactical move by its opponents, who hoped that this extra baggage would tip the balance against the legislation. But if, as was widely believed at the time, such legislation did no more than assure fair treatment, without creating pressure for quotas or preferences or a flood of litigation, it was hard to see why women should not have the same protections as members of racial minorities, and the legislation passed.

The results, once administrative and judicial interpretations of the law occurred, have been similar to those with respect to race: the concept of discrimination has grown like Topsy, leading to the discovery that the country is permeated with sexism as well as racism, and thence to quotas, preferences, and enticing opportunities for lawsuits. As in the case of race, this view is promoted by an alliance of those seeking preferential treatment, a grievance industry including advocates, lawyers, and consultants, politicians eager to gain political advantage, and of course those always eager to do battle against oppressive America and the rights of private property that facilitate oppression.

Some of the same reasons for skepticism as to the existence of pervasive discrimination exist in the case of women as in the case of Negroes. Practically everybody insists that he does not hold women's sex against them, laws against sex discrimination have received overwhelming support from both sexes, and it would make no economic sense to hire less-qualified men instead of more-qualified women.

But there are also other reasons. It is one thing to oppress a tenth of the population who are predominantly poor and uneducated to begin with. It is a task of a far higher order to oppress the majority of the population, who in fact are the majority because they have a greater life expectancy than the supposed oppressors, and who in fact control the great majority of the personal wealth in the country (a recent figure is 86%[1]). Depriving this group of its just due is no mean feat.

And why would the men of the country want to do such a thing, in the first place? The speed and ease with which sex discrimination was outlawed itself says a lot about the absence of sexual animosity. There is no history of widespread aversion to women or to association with women comparable to racial segregation. Men have, on the contrary, consistently had the most intimate relations with "the fair sex." They have fallen in love with them, married them, entrusted the management of their homes and children to them, and treated them protectively. No man suggested that women should fight and die on the battlefields to save our country or make the world safe for democracy. In time of disaster, the rule for rescue or safety was "women and children first."

Not only that, an all-male electorate, and all-male legislatures, voluntarily gave women the right to vote and enacted laws recognizing women's rights in their husbands' earnings. In community property states, half of

---

[1]*Republican National Committee Women's Wire*, April 1996 (Source: Women and their Money, by Paul Sheldon, Prudential Securities).

everything a man earns belongs to his wife as community property, and women's interests are protected through other mechanisms in other states. When these laws were passed, they were as a practical matter a one-way street in the wives' favor; although they might speak of each spouse's rights in the other's earnings, it was almost always the husband who earned money outside the home.

If women face significant discrimination in the workplace, it must be for some reason other than that men generally dislike women. Could it be that men dislike seeing women work outside the home, or are not comfortable with them there earning an independent income? The idea that men have been trying to force women to remain in the home, in what some feminists view as a dependent relationship despite the wife's entitlement to her husband's earnings under community property and similar laws, by discriminating against women in employment, makes very little sense. There is no evidence that employers see themselves as enforcers of traditional mores in this area, and in any case an individual employer could have only a minuscule effect on the overall situation.

Nor is the idea that men yearn to keep women out of jobs for which they are qualified given plausibility by the extensive employment of women long before there were any laws against sex discrimination. Retail establishments, the telephone company, schools, offices, nursing, hotels, and factories, to name a few, provided employment to millions of women, and of course when the country was largely agricultural many a farm wife worked alongside her husband on the chores of the farm. And many of these jobs involved positions of respect and responsibility – schoolteacher is an example – rather than subservient status. Women did not get these jobs because government enforcers or threatened lawsuits compelled it; they got them through the choices made by individuals in a market economy. Indeed, as readers of Victorian novels such as Emile Zola's *Germinal* know, women had the opportunity, a century and a half ago, to toil right alongside men at hard and dangerous work in mines and factories. Advocates for women strove mightily to free them from such opportunities.

Normally, particularly for the unmarried, a "coed" workplace is a plus, and hiring only men or only women would not only limit the pool of potential employees to one sex, hardly desirable in itself, but also make the jobs less attractive to its members. Sometimes, as noted in Chap. III, when the best-qualified employees are predominantly of one sex and there is no shortage of them, a single-sex workplace may nevertheless seem desirable because of simplifying arrangements and reducing distractions. But this is not a major problem for women: these cases are unusual, they rarely involve high-level or professional jobs, often they involve physical strength requirements which very few women can meet, and when they do not, it might well be women rather than men the employer would choose to hire, as demonstrated by airlines' former practice of staffing their planes with stewardesses (as opposed to the Pullman Company's all-male corps of sleeping-car porters).

More likely to be a problem, because it is particularly relevant at the professional level, is the perception of managers that a woman is less likely than a man to have, and to continue to have, complete commitment to the career, and not to interrupt it (perhaps at a very inopportune time for the employer) or terminate it for reasons related to pregnancy and child-rearing. And, on the basis of averages and the odds, they are right in that perception, although it may not apply in the case of a particular candidate.

It would be rational and profit-maximizing for them to act on that perception. Is it desirable to forbid it? Much business is conducted on the basis of averages and probabilities. The whole insurance industry, for example, is based on them. A 70-year-old cannot buy life insurance at the same price as a 30-year-old. He may in fact outlive the 30-year-old, but the rates are set on the basis of overall life expectancies. If the law required that life insurance rates be the same regardless of age, it would be unfair to the average younger person. Analogously, requiring employers to operate on the assumption that the probability of uninterrupted availability is identical for men and women amounts to unfairness to the average man.

Now that the anti-discrimination laws are in place, major corporations are so eager to be on the right side of the law-as-interpreted-and-enforced that they "are dropping their 'last hired, first fired' rules in order to preserve their carefully cultivated ranks of women and minorities, typically the newest hires. Employers don't want to risk job-bias suits . . . nor jeopardize government contracts tied to affirmative-action efforts."[2] In hiring, companies sometime tell recruiters, "We will interview men, but we are only going to hire women."[3]

---

[2]Julia Amparano Lopez, "Companies Alter Layoff Policies to Keep Recently Hired Women and Minorities," *Wall Street Journal*, Sept 18, 1992.

[3]Joann S. Lublin, "Firms Designate Some Openings for Women Only," *Wall Street Journal*, Feb. 7, 1996.

What is going on with these laws in place of course says nothing in itself about what would be occurring without them. But when 30 years after the passage of the Civil Rights Act, after so much strenuous effort, including preferential treatment ("affirmative action"), to employ and promote enough women, unfair discrimination is blamed for the fact that they do not have a proportionate share of some jobs, including some of the most desirable jobs,[4] it seems particularly obvious that the charge must be taken with a grain of salt. In fact, a quantity more like that represented by Lot's wife is appropriate.

DIFFERENCES BETWEEN THE SEXES

"Women and minorities" has become a commonly-used term. The linkage suggests a common victimhood at the hands of unfriendly white males. Sex apparently is as irrelevant a characteristic as skin color. But this is nonsense. There are real differences between men and women, and they will necessarily produce significant differences in the sexes' representation in various segments of the work force regardless of the presence or absence of discrimination.

Some scholars are convinced that because of physiological differences men are more inclined than women toward aggressiveness and leadership. Steven Goldberg, chairman of the City University of New York department of sociology, author of *Why Men Rule*, is of this view.[5] Certainly such would be consistent with the historic pattern of male domination in human societies as well as with the general rule throughout the animal world. In any case, there are unquestionably other real differences between the sexes.

PHYSICAL DIFFERENCES

It would seem a rather tall order to explain the standard division of responsibilities between men and women over thousands of years of recorded history as due solely to oppression. Division of labor and comparative advantage are economic terms of comparatively recent origin, but the concepts are not. The necessary work is divided up on the basis of who can do what best. A woman might be able to be every bit as good

---

[4]For example, 95 percent of the senior-level managers in the Fortune 1000 industrial and Fortune 500 companies are men, according to the Congressionally-created Glass Ceiling Commission.
[5]Steven Goldberg, "Is Patriarchy Inevitable?" *National Review*, Nov. 11, 1996, p. 32.

at ploughing as her husband. She might even be better. But there is absolutely no way her husband can bear children. So the wife's chief responsibility is what only she can do, having children and what goes naturally with that.

Even today in the United States, a large minority of women choose the traditional wife-and-mother path, planning to work, if at all, only until marriage or until the first child comes. As many of such women do work on that basis, a portion of the women in the work place is made up of non-career-oriented workers whose motivation and orientation are quite different from those intending to work until they retire. There is obviously no comparable group of men planning to work only until they get married or their wife becomes pregnant.

It is intriguing to speculate as to the further effects of this opting out of the workplace on the extent to which working women are representative of the women of the country as whole. The traditional wife-and-mother women are absent from the workplace, either right from the start or once husband or child comes along. Does this eliminate the best and the brightest, who realize that the most fulfilling thing they can do is marry a promising man and further their community interests? Studies in fact show that, other things being equal, husbands in such families earn 20-25% more than those whose wives also work.[6] The lucky wife can enjoy home, motherhood, social life, and community involvement, and very possibly end up a rich widow.

Or does it eliminate those without the intellect and drive to make their way in a challenging career, ready instead to settle for what many feminists consider the stifling suburban world of kiddies and gossip, so that it is the best and brightest who remain in the work force? Do a significant number of women who choose work instead of traditional marriage do so because they have hostile feelings toward men? Are there many women who remain at work only because they failed to get a husband and whose deficiencies are now accentuated by their disappointment?

Working women, unlike working men, are not a cross-section of the sex's population in the working years. I will not speculate, however, as to

---

[6]Tamar Lewin, *New York Times*, "Husbands who are sole breadwinners get better pay, raises," *Contra Costa Times*, Aug. 12, 1994, p. l, citing several studies presented at the Academy of Management annual meeting.

whether on balance those in the workplace are more or less likely to deserve career success than the cross-section.

We do know, however, that a significant number of women workers – those intending to work only until marriage or children – are not career-oriented. Many women, too, just want to add a few dollars to the family income on a periodic basis.

The fact that women and not men bear children has other effects in the workplace as well. The great majority of career women intend to have children and do have children. Having a child is not as easy as having a haircut. Pregnancy produces stress and strain. Birth and its aftermath require absence from work for some time.

Children can be the occasion for more extended absence from the workplace. According to a U.S. Bureau of the Census study, while only 1.6% of the average male worker's work years were spent away from work, 14.7% of the average female worker's were.[7] It hardly needs to be pointed out that significant interruptions of work are a hindrance to career progress.

Not uncommonly, women who had decided on careers decide that they want the traditional wife-and-mother role instead. "More women decide their job is at home" heads a news story about the choices of several women, including Lotus Development's No. 1 software salesperson, who left their careers for the home.[8] A contestant on Jeopardy! identifies herself as a former lawyer, now a mother with a young child. A study of mothers with MBA degrees from Harvard Business School finds that 25% of them have left the workplace entirely.[9] According to a Wall Street Journal article entitled "Stay-at-Home Moms Are Fashionable Again In Many Communities," Yankelovich's Monitor, an annual survey, reported that the percentage of women workers who said they would quit their jobs if they didn't need the money rose from about 30% previously to 38% in 1989 and 56% in 1991.[10] According to the article, there is nearly universal agreement among the former career women that their children turn out better than those of mothers who work outside the home.

---

[7] *Free Markets, Free Choices: Women in the Workforce*, Pacific Research Institute, Dec. 1995.
[8] Joyce Routson, *Contra Costa Times*, July 31, 1994, p. 1.
[9] *Sacramento Bee*, April 24, 1994.
[10] Vol. CXXIX no. 16, p. 1.

These facts suggest three things: that a relatively high percentage of women workers are not happy in their work; that some women do not reach high positions because they leave before they get there; and that it is not irrational for employers to suspect women, at least women of a certain age, of being less likely than their male counterparts to be available to the company until normal retirement age. It may be illegal to take the last into account in making employment decisions, even to break a tie, but it is hard to see reasonably considering probabilities in one particular area as objectionable discrimination that ought to be forbidden.

Childbearing and maternal instincts do not represent the only physical differences general between the sexes that are relevant to the workplace. *San Francisco Chronicle* columnist Adair Lara wrote of another:

> Sylvia, one of the calmest people I know, says she gets massively bad headaches . . . and bursts into tears if she drops a bag of groceries . . . She knows a woman who forgets her ATM number and just stands in front of the machine, crying . . . Robin, a waitress, feels that strangling would be too good for the man who wants another glass of iced tea . . . Not every woman gets PMS, but every woman understands it. If anything sets us apart from men, it's the way our reproductive systems rule us, upset us, derail us.[11]

Indeed, women have been acquitted of crimes with premenstrual syndrome as an extenuating circumstance.

Liza Minnelli recently spoke of another occurrence peculiar to women, menopause: "It gives you enormous mood swings, which nobody told me about. You start out loving somebody at the beginning of a sentence, and by the end you're going, 'You son-of-a-b-communist bastard!' You really don't know what's happening to you."[12]

Certainly those with these difficulties deserve sympathy and understanding, but they do not enhance job performance. Perhaps there is some connection between them and a recent Gallup Poll finding that most women in most countries prefer working for men, the percentage in the United States being 54%.[13]

---

[11] Adair Lara, "The Periods of Women's Discontent," *San Francisco Chronicle*, Sept. 12, 1991, p. E8.

[12] "Liza Explains: Girls Will Be Girls," *San Francisco Chronicle*, Aug. 27, 1996.

[13] "Send her to Congress, elect her president, but don't make her my boss," *Wall Street Journal*, March 26, 1996, p. 1.

Another difference between men and women relates to the old term "weaker sex." One manifestation is illness and disability; women on average are disabled for longer periods than their male counterparts. A 1985 report showed that 35-year-old men on average filed 10.71 disability claims per 1,000 vs. 30.96 for women of the same age, and that the discrepancy in disability periods occurred even after taking pregnancy into account.[14]

Of more significance, "weakness" affects the percentages of the sexes who meet qualifications for jobs requiring physical size or strength. This has a bearing beyond those jobs themselves, many of which are lower-level, since they can be the first rung of the ladder leading to top positions.

The fact is that women on average are smaller, lighter, and weaker than men. Where size, strength, and stamina are required to do a job well and there are reasonable standards for qualification, a disproportionate number of women will fail to qualify. According to the 1992 report of a commission on women in the military, only 7 of 100 women scored 60 on a push-up test, while 78% of men exceeded that standard; 77% of women failed a Navy test for shipboard hose-dragging, vs. one-half of one percent of the men who took it. The commission, however, unanimously recommended the same standards for all. As Commissioner Elaine Donnelly put it, "Equal opportunity is not the primary purpose of the military. The purpose of the military is to defend the country."[15] She might also have noted that equal opportunity sensibly understood does not mean equal opportunity regardless of qualification.

But some are so infected with the egalitarian mania as to ignore the fact that in a rational society jobs are created to get work done. Physical standards for police and fire departments have been reduced so that more women can be hired, apparently in the belief that giving women these relatively high-paying jobs is more important than, say, having firefighters (there is a good reason the term was "firemen" until recently) capable of carrying someone down a ladder. Since 1974, the Los Angeles fire department has sought to have 50% of recruits be women or minority-group members, and the City Council has ordered strong steps to ensure a "work force which is representative of the community it serves."[16] Pre-

[14]Leslie Scism, "Insurers End Unisex Rates on Disability," *Wall Street Journal*, March 28, 1994.
[15]"Combat Panel Cuts No Slack For Women," *San Francisco Chronicle*, Nov. 3, 1992.
[16]"Sex, Fires, and Videotape," *National Review*, Jan. 23, 1995, p. 8.

sumably the blind, the halt, and the lame, to say nothing of the aged, should be proportionately represented in the firehouses too.

Charges of sex discrimination are made as freely as charges of racial discrimination. The South Eastern Pennsylvania Transportation Authority requires applicants for its police positions to be able to run 1.5 miles in 12 minutes; on one day, 27 women took the test and failed; one filed a complaint with the state Human Rights Commission claiming that the test discriminated against women.[17] Women who failed an FBI trigger-pulling test complained that it constituted discrimination against women.[18] A colonel, a veteran of two wars, was run out of West Point in part, at least, because his emphasis on the importance of combat forces was considered bias against women (because women do not serve in combat).[19]

If, of course, fire departments and the like had cheerfully hired 110-pound male weaklings all along and only established physical requirements when women began to apply, one might suspect an ulterior motive for the standards. But in fact such standards were general long before having women in such positions had crossed anyone's mind.

OTHER DIFFERENCES

Not only do average physical differences provide the obvious explanation for why there are few women in many occupations – it is not because of discrimination that there are so few women lumberjacks (lumberjills?) – but there is substantial evidence that there are more than physical differences between the sexes.

Such is certainly suggested by success in the exact sciences. For example, in 1993, it was reported that 75% of the scholarships in a new federal program intended to encourage students to go into mathematics, science or engineering had been awarded to males.[20] In a study of more than 10,000 medical students published in 1994 in the Journal of the American Medical Association, the passing rate on the science examination required for a medical student to become a licensed doctor was 89.9% for white men and

---

[17]"Running Dispute: A female transit-police candidate sees bias in a fitness test." *Wall Street Journal*, April 26, 1994, p 1.

[18]"FBI Accused of Bias in Gun Test," *San Francisco Chronicle*, Oct. 5, 1995.

[19]Thomas E. Ricks, "Army at Odds: West Point Posting Becomes a Minefield For 'Warrior' Officer," *Wall Street Journal*, March 13, 1997, p. 1.

[20]"Males Get Lion's Share of Science Scholarships," *San Francisco Chronicle*, Nov. 17, 1993.

84.1% for white women, with comparable differences within other races (53.9% and 44%, respectively, for Negroes).[21]

In terms of increasingly important computer skills, women lag, with the percentage of degrees in computer sciences awarded to women nationally declining from 37% in 1984 to 30% in 1990.[22]

Boys also consistently do better than girls in qualifying for National Merit Scholarships, to take another indication of aptitude. In 1992, it was reported that "for the fifth year in a row, fewer high school girls than boys qualified for National Merit Scholarship," with 59% of the semi-finalists boys vs. 37% girls, "according to the National Center for Fair and Open Testing, known as FairTest."[23] (As to the apparent mystery group, the reason the percentages do not add up to 100 is that FairTest made its study based on names and some were ambiguous as to sex.) Things were basically the same the next year: "Merit Scholarship Test Called Unfair to Girls" headed the article about FairTest's annual complaint.[24] This time only about 35% of the winners were girls. Next year, the ACLU filed a complaint with the Department of Education on FairTest's behalf.[25]

FairTest unintentionally undercut its own claim that unfairness rather than differing abilities underlay the different results by complaining that the standardized tests on the basis of which the scholarships are awarded "are biased against females because they require the ability to guess and decide quickly on answers, skills that favor boys." As Elaine Detweiler of the National Merit Scholarship Corp. put it, "to blame the test for the difference between how boys and girls perform is like blaming a yardstick that boys are taller than girls."

But ideology is impervious to common sense. If your starting point is the certitude, as from religious revelation, that there must be total equality, all tests that indicate otherwise are fatally flawed. So the Scholastic Aptitude Test is no good either. "S.A.T.'s Are Biased Against Girls, Re-

---

[21]"White Men Top All Women on Med School Test," *San Francisco Chronicle*, Sept. 7, 1994.

[22]Ellen Hale, "The next gender gap: Girls lag in computer skills," *Contra Costa Times*, March 5, 1995, p. 5C.

[23]"Fewer Girls Qualify For Scholarships," *San Francisco Chronicle*, May 6, 1992.

[24]*San Francisco Chronicle*, May 26, 1993.

[25]"ACLU Says Boys Get Too Many National Merit Scholarships," *San Francisco Chronicle*, Feb. 16, 1994, p. A3.

port by Advocacy Group Says." "High school girls get lower scores than boys on the Scholastic Aptitude Test because the tests are biased against girls, according to a report released . . . by a private group . . . The study offers no analysis of the standardized tests and gives no examples of biased questions," according to the *New York Times* story. Indeed, "At a news conference . . . representatives of the group said that they did not know why girls, who make up 52 percent of the test takers, received lower scores than boys. 'We don't really know why girls are scoring lower,' said Phyllis Rosser, the main author of the report." Only in an area like this can you get away with charging bias while admitting that you have nothing with which to back up your charges.

A new effort by the equalizers, breathtaking in its simplicity and in its transparent intellectual bankruptcy, was announced at a Washington press conference by Leslie Wolfe, the president of the Center for Women Policy Studies. "To pressure the College Board to equalize the results by eliminating questions on which boys regularly score better than girls, Wolfe announced a toll-free number – (888) SEX-BIAS – to call for an 'action kit' on urging Congress to investigate."[26]

If the supposed flaws on the tests cannot be identified, the next step, as in the Negro case, is to blame the schools. "Schools Unfair to Girls, Study Says." This is the American Association of University Women's contribution to logical analysis. Among the shocking "findings" in this widely publicized study were that boys score much higher than girls on the mathematics and science section of the SAT and that only 18% of girls taking high school physics and calculus plan to major in science or engineering in college, vs. 64% in the case of boys; neither of which has any apparent bearing at all on whether schools are being unfair to girls.

Ah, but "teachers call on boys 80% more often than they call on girls"! We are supposed to assume, apparently, that this reflects not teachers' desire to get worthwhile answers or reluctance to embarrass the poorly-prepared, but rather their dogged desire to suppress girls. Since the great majority of teachers are women and it would be hard to imagine a more liberal or consciousness-raised group, the implausibility of this accusation is obvious. Indeed, in her article, "The Myth of Schoolgirls' Low Self-Esteem" (*Wall Street Journal*, Oct. 3, 1994), Christina Hoff Sommers debunked the whole AAUW study as fundamentally worthless.

---

[26]"SAT Changes Sought to Raise Girls' Scores," *San Francisco Chronicle*, March 15, 1997, p. A7.

"The problems are real subtle," says Judith Christensen, a physics (not English, fortunately) teacher at a high school "in the progressive Bay Area." She describes bringing in flashlights for her class to take apart, working in groups of three; and "when she stopped them in the midst of their investigations, it emerged that the pupils holding the flashlight were almost invariably boys. 'In one class, 100 percent of the kids holding the flashlights were boys,' she said. 'It was frightening.' "[27] Where does this horror begin?

In fact, studies consistently suggest a real difference in the way the typical male and female brains work. In an article entitled "The science that isn't politically correct," Washington Post writers Anne Moir and David Jessel explained,

> In the past 10 years there has been an explosion of research into what makes the sexes different. Doctors, scientists, psychologists and sociologists, working apart, have produced a body of findings which, taken together, paints a remarkably consistent picture of startling sexual asymmetry. The sexes are different because the brain, the chief administrative and emotional organ in life, is differently constructed in men and in women. It processes information in a different way, which results in different perceptions, priorities and behavior. The truth is that virtually every professional scientist and researcher into the subject has reached that conclusion.

As the article notes, "from school age onwards, boys will generally outperform girls in areas of mathematics involving abstract concepts of space, relationships and theory . . . This male advantage . . . perhaps explains the male dominance of chess, even in a country like the Soviet Union, where the game is a national sport played by both sexes." Psychologist Camilla Benbow is quoted: "After 15 years looking for an environmental explanation [of male superiority in mathematically gifted children] and getting zero results, I gave up."[28]

A recent study by University of Chicago researchers reported in the journal Science found that, while men and women are roughly equal in

---

[27]Nanette Asimov, "Schools Unfair to Girls, Study Says," *San Francisco Chronicle*, Feb. 12, 1992, p. 1.
[28]"Thinking About the Real Differences Between Men and Women," *Washington Post*, May 5, 1991, p. K03.

average intelligence, seven of every eight people in the top 10 percent on IQ tests are men (with men also accounting for a disproportionate number of the mentally deficient, particularly in terms of reading and writing skills).[29] Of 343 Nobel Prize winners in science and economics in the last 50 years, only eight were women; of the total of 563 Nobel laureates in the natural sciences, economics and literature between 1901 and 1995, only 19 were women.[30]

When you think about it, the political "gender gap" in relative support of Republican and Democratic candidates that has been much commented on around election times is indicative of differences in the ways the sexes see things. A post-election survey commissioned by the Republican National Committee in 1996 indicated that Clinton lost to Dole among men by 49 to 39 percent but beat Dole 59 to 35 percent among women.[31] (Interestingly, although not surprisingly given the orientation of the media, the thrust of commentary on this subject is almost invariably on the failure of the Republican candidate to make himself more acceptable to women rather than on the Democrat's deficiency in appeal to men.) It can hardly be entirely due to positions on abortion; women do have other things on their minds as well, and in the 1996 elections pro-choice Gov. Weld in Massachusetts lost the women's vote to his Democratic opponent by a wide margin while pro-life Sen. Jesse Helms had nearly half the women's vote in his race.

Perhaps the gap arises because women do not inform themselves about political issues as much as men do. A Gallup Poll in mid-1996 indicated that 62% of men but only 44% of women knew the name of the Speaker of the House and 55% of men vs. 35% of women that of the attorney general.[32] According to the Media Studies Center, women were less likely than men to listen to news on the radio, or to read newspapers, news magazines, or books about politics or government.[33]

And that may be because they think differently or form their conclusions differently. A "gender gap" has been observed on a variety of issues.

---

[29] Thomas H. Maugh II, "More Men Are Dumber Than Was Believed," *San Francisco Chronicle*, July 7, 1995.

[30] Gosta Wranglen, "No Belles: The Second Sex," *National Review*, Nov. 11, 1996, p. 34.

[31] Dan Balz, "GOP Seeks to Bridge Gender Gap," *San Francisco Chronicle*, Nov. 27, 1996.

[32] "For the Record," *National Review*, Feb. 24, 1997, p. 6.

[33] *The American Spectator*, Dec. 1996, p.59.

For example, in the case of the young American vandal caned by Singapore authorities in 1994, a Los Angeles Times poll found that 61% of men but only 39% of women surveyed favored the punishment, while 58% of women and 36% of men opposed it.[34]

Feminist lawyers in fact have attacked traditional legal reasoning as unfair to women on the grounds that they think differently and criticized law schools' teaching and grading methods on similar grounds. Law professor Lani Guinier, whose unusual ideas about enhancing Negro political strength led to the withdrawal of her nomination to a Department of Justice position, publicized a study that took note of the fact that men are three times more likely than women to be in the top 10% of their law school classes. The reason apparently was that women find the law school environment "alienating," because it "forces women to be more like men and focuses on a 'winner-take-all' mentality . . . It does not value people who are either helping the losers or are perceived as losers."[35]

Queen Victoria had the view that "we women were not made for governing,"[36] but more recently women have often suggested that they should be elected to office or placed in certain positions because they have insights or ways of looking at things peculiar to their sex. This was particularly noticeable in the 1992 "Year of the Woman" hullabaloo. Rules against "sexism" and "stereotypes" apparently do not apply to the attribution of unique strengths to women. "Women are much more open to works that involve the whole body," explains Carla DeSola, an adjunct faculty member at the Pacific School of Religion, as students in her "liturgical dance class" carry a large wooden cross across the floor "improvising a fluid meditation on the theme of Good Friday" while "wailing, mournful music" pours from two large speakers.[37]

But women cannot be just the same and yet different at the same time, any more than skin color can be both meaningless and an important qualification. In the case of men and women, there are certainly differences more profound than skin color. It is not hard to see how thinking differently could

---

[34]Ronald Brownstein, "Singapore's Caning Sentence Divides Americans, Poll Finds," *Los Angeles Times*, April 21, 1994, home ed. Part A.

[35]"Ex-Nominee Focuses on Gender Gap in Law School," *San Francisco Journal*, March 30, 1995.

[36]"The Consummate Consort," *Wall Street Journal*, May 23 1997, reviewing *Uncrowned King* by Stanley Weintraub.

[37]*San Francisco Chronicle*, March 30, 1997.

have an effect on women's representation in various positions without any invidious discrimination being involved at all.

Examples of how this sort of thing works, and of how the media treat it, are plentiful, when one looks beyond the headlines. Take a recent front-page article in a San Francisco Bay Area newspaper, headlined "Bias still handcuffing female police officers."[38] Policewomen are unhappy about their career progress and are suing their employers. Penny Harrington, former police chief of Portland, Ore. (who clearly was not prevented by her sex from holding the top position in that city), now directing the National Center for Women in Policing in Los Angeles, opines that things are "not getting better."

One gleans what is going on from remarks by the police chief in the Bay Area suburb of Livermore, Ron Scott. Scott clearly is someone who has "gotten it," having dismissed and refused to rehire a male officer dismissed over allegations of sexual harassment despite an outside arbitrator's opinion that he should be reinstated. He says there is a "cultural" problem, "as police move to a community policing philosophy centered on problem-solving, tighter community bonds and prevention. The 'strong, male-dominated' police culture that fought crime and left the social work to civilians, dies hard, he said."

Former chief Harrington seems to have a similar concept of police work. "Women naturally have the skills needed for community policing. They don't want to go around shooting people and racing around in cars." Note the sweeping generalizations about women; if a man said something similar in a critical way, such as "women want to be social workers, not police officers," it would be denounced as sexist stereotyping. Note also the disdain for the hard, life-threatening part of police work.

The real problem with the unhappy policewomen, one suspects, is not that they are victims of sex discrimination, but that they want to be social workers while being paid police officers' salaries.

APPLES AND ORANGES

Certainly women's presence in the workplace is different from men's. Women are largely absent from physical-strength occupations. (Indeed, 23 of the 25 "worst jobs," from The Jobs Related Almanac, are over 90%

---

[38]Renita Sandosham and John Simerman, Contra Costa Times, Feb. 15, 1998.

male, with men accounting for 92% of all job-related deaths, although they are only 54% of the workforce.)[39] They are also relatively scarce at the upper levels of the business world and the professions. Between 1970 and 1995, the percentage of women between 25 and 54 years of age working outside the home rose from 50% to 76% and they now constitute 40% of the work force, but they are only 5% of senior managers and 10% of the members of Fortune 500 boards of directors. A San Francisco newspaper in 1998 ran photographs of the 102 San Francisco Bay Area business executives paid $1 million or more in 1997; all but four were men.[40] The average pay of women is about 73% that of men, and the difference is general, from business to medicine to the academic world.

Yet, considering the numerous differences between the sexes discussed above, from the consequences of motherhood for the pursuit of careers to other physical differences to mental and attitudinal differences, it hardly follows that men are taking leave of their economic senses and irrationally discriminating against women in the workplace.

There are many indications that this is not a significant problem. A straw in the wind is the fact that, after decades of consciousness-raising about sex discrimination, only 8% of working women surveyed believed that they personally had been shortchanged by bias, according to a survey by psychologists Diana Cordova of the University of Michigan and Faye Crosby and Karen Jaskar of Smith College reported in January 1994. (They were nevertheless convinced that sex bias was prevalent in the American workplace.)[41]

In the case of women entrepreneurs, a study released in November 1995 concluded that "contrary to common belief, women entrepreneurs looking for help have as much access to the 'old-boy network' as the old boys themselves." It studied 217 entrepreneurs of both sexes in North

---

[39]Linda Chavez, "Feminists Abuse Statistics to Hype 'Equal Pay Day,'" *Human Events*, April 23, 1999, p.10.

[40]"The Million-Dollar Club," *San Francisco Chronicle*, June 1, 1998, p. E2. This sort of thing is not an exclusively American phenomenon; in March 1997, the French prime minister lamented the fact that none of France's 200 top firms was headed by a woman ("French Push for Quotas On Women in Politics," *San Francisco Chronicle*, March 12, 1997).

[41]"Sex discrimination? It happens only to others, many women say," *Wall Street Journal*, Jan. 25, 1994, p. 1. It should be noted that a Department of Labor survey later in the year achieved a 14% figure.

Carolina's Research Triangle Park and found that "the view that many women entrepreneurs are excluded from circles of men who serve as important sources of financial, legal and other kinds of business assistance" was, one may say, an old wives' tale.[42] Nationwide, among small businesses, the number of women-owned businesses grew by 43% between 1987 and 1992 and employment by such firms doubled.[43]

As to the supposed difference in pay between men and women, a recent study, *Women's Figures: The Economic Progress of Women in America*, by Diana Furchtgott-Rott of the American Enterprise Institute and Christine Stolba, a women's history professor at Emory University, found that it resulted from comparing apples with oranges. For example, in the case of men and women between 27 and 33 without children, the women earned 98% of the men's pay.[44] This is consistent with what was found decades ago; Thomas Sowell, in his *The Vision of the Anointed*, cites a 1973 government study showing that single women who worked continuously and full-time actually earned slightly more than their male counterparts.[45]

Recently, a Stanford researcher found that the reason young male doctors earn more than their female counterparts – $155,000 a year on average vs. $110,000 – is that they work longer hours and are more likely to have special training: the gap "virtually vanishes" when they work the same hours, in the same field, with similar training."[46]

That differences in average pay between women and men have a straightforward rather than a sinister origin is also suggested by Census Bureau demographer Suzanne Bianchi's explanation for the rise in the "women's pay as a percentage of men's" figure from 60% in 1979 to 72% in 1992: succeeding groups of women entering the work force had more education and a greater proportion remained single and working throughout their 20s and early 30s.[47]

Of particular significance is a study completed in late 1995 by Katherine Post and Michael Lynch of the Pacific Research Institute in San Fran-

[42]Michael Selz, "New Study Finds Female Entrepreneurs Aren't Locked Out of 'Old-Boy Network'," *Wall Street Journal*, Nov. 14, 1995, p. A7B.

[43]"Women's Worth," *Harvard Business School Bulletin*, Feb. 1997, p. 49.

[44]"Wage Gap is Farce Says New Study," *Human Events*, Dec. 27, 1996, p. 23.

[45]"The Economic Role of Women," *The Economic Report of the President, 1973*, p. 103, cited at p. 188 of Mr. Sowell's book.

[46]Sabin Russell, "Stanford Studies Gender Gap in Doctors' Pay," *San Francisco Chronicle*, April 11, 1996.

[47]*Wall Street Journal*, April 15, 1994.

cisco entitled *Free Markets, Free Choices: Women in the Workforce*. It points out that the "women only earn 72 percent as much as men" claim is based on dividing the median annual earnings for all full-time working women by those for all full-time working men, taking no account of age, educational attainment, or continuous time spent in the work force; and that when these *are* factored in as wage determinants, "the gender pay gap virtually disappears."

For example, analysis of relative earnings of men and women by highest educational degree earned brings the percentage of average men's earnings represented by women's up to 76% for those with bachelor's, 79% for those with master's, and 85% for those with doctoral degrees. And that is not the end of the story either, for all degrees are not equal in terms of their implications for earnings. And those who pursue college and advanced degrees in fields associated with relatively high levels of compensation are disproportionately male (in physical and earth sciences, 74%; in engineering, 91%; in mathematics and statistics, 67%; and in business, 70%), while women account for most degrees in English and journalism (74%), liberal arts and humanities (61%), and education (72%).[48]

And, degrees aside, men also disproportionately gravitate toward relatively high-paying areas, often with scientific or mathematical requirements: in 1993, for example, 94% of those choosing careers in mathematical and computer science were men, while 75% of those choosing teaching were women.

The idea that a significant proportion of American men in supervisory positions have an irrational hostility toward women that surfaces only in the workplace (and only in connection with certain positions and areas of work), causing them to reject qualified women to their own cost, ought to provoke strong skepticism in anyone with common sense, *a fortiori* if he has an elementary understanding of economics. A little thought and attention to the facts about differences between the sexes suggests obvious non-discriminatory reasons for differing workplace representation, and, indeed, honest research using sound methodology confirms that causation.

This overall situation does not mean, of course, that there can not be individual cases of real discrimination. But charges of it are not always convincing.

---

[48]Citing 1990 Bureau of the Census statistics.

183

Take, for example, a piece of front-page news in the *New York Times* in March 1999: "M.I.T. Acknowledges Bias Against Female Professors."[49] The bias was "pervasive"; but, oddly, according to the School of Science's dean, "in no case was this discrimination conscious or deliberate. Indeed, it was usually totally unconscious and unknowing."

That seems remarkable, that such a thing would go on in the consciousness-raised halls of Academe, of all places. How was this evil, unsuspected by its perpetrators, detected?

As summarized in MIT's *A Study on the Status of Women Faculty in Science at MIT*,[50] the study was prompted by three tenured woman professors who felt they were not getting the recognition and support they deserved; polling the other women in the School of Science (15 out of 209 tenured faculty), they found that they had similar feelings that they were being held back by sex discrimination, and in 1994 the Dean "became a strong champion of the women's cause"[51] and a committee, predominantly of women, to study the situation was formed.

Review of data on distribution of resources and rewards to men and women was done "by senior women faculty." They "revealed" that "in some departments men and women faculty appeared to share equally," but "in others they did not. Inequitable distributions were found involving space, amount of 9-month salary paid from individual research grants, teaching assignments, awards and distinctions, inclusion on important committees and assignments within the department."[52]

The report, apparently, equates inequality with inequity. But might it not be that the women were getting less because they deserved less, and there was no sex discrimination? This is apparently not a question one is supposed to ask. "First and foremost it is essential to set aside the issue of whether these women were treated badly because they were simply not good enough . . . Once and for all we must recognize that the heart and soul of discrimination, the last refuge of the bigot, is to say that those who are discriminated against deserve it because they are less good."[53] Well, this is more than a little muddled. In the first place, it's not bigotry

---

[49]Carey Goldberg, March 23, 1999.
[50]*The MIT Faculty Newsletter*, Special Edition, Vol. XI No. 4, March 1999.
[51]*Ibid.*, p. 5.
[52]*Ibid.*, p. 7.
[53]*Ibid.*, p. 9.

to be open to the possibility that differing rewards may reflect differing merits rather than discrimination, and, in the second place, if in fact they do, then no one is being "treated badly" or "discriminated against."

Circular reasoning and emphatic language don't really work. "Despite discrimination, most of these women achieved at an outstanding level within their professions . . . Only people above the average MIT faculty could have succeeded at this level despite the many obstacles the senior women faculty encountered in their careers. Indeed, it should almost be obvious that the first women, the first blacks, the pioneers who break through despite enormous barriers must be exceptional." Well, it could also be that someone said, "We've just *got* to have *some* tenured women professors," and they were really beyond their depth from the beginning. And the logical flaw in "We know these women's lack of greater recognition proves discrimination, because they had to be truly outstanding to have done what they did despite discrimination" is not hard to find.

The female professors are not happy with their small numbers, either, although the situation at Harvard and Cal Tech is similar: "But to be as bad as these unenlightened institutions is not a defense we should take!"

Perhaps some of the MIT women have been held back by sex discrimination, but neither the rhetoric nor the reasoning of the report, nor the peculiar concept of unknowing and unconscious discrimination, is very convincing.

LAWSUIT OPPORTUNITIES, "HOSTILE ENVIRONMENT," AND "SEXUAL HARASSMENT"

Lack of proportional representation, however, even in parts of a workplace, is likely to be taken as indicative of hostility to women, and this can have very costly results. The 1991 Civil Rights Act made jury trials and compensatory and punitive damages available in sex and race discrimination suits. People respond to economic incentives (which was one reason, right at the outset, for being skeptical about the claim that profit-oriented companies reject the best-qualified because of their race or sex), and they have certainly responded here: a quarter of a century after sex discrimination was outlawed, major sex-discrimination lawsuits began proliferating, with some law firms specializing in this new opportunity. As Max Boot put it in his *Wall Street Journal* column, "Rule of Law," ". . . well-intentioned discrimination law has degenerated into nothing more than a shakedown scheme to enrich a handful of lawyers."[54] And provide bonuses to women not above taking part in the game, he might have added.

One boost to such lawsuits is that there are real differences between men and woman, as noted above, as to typical interests, physical strength, and need for flexibility to accommodate childbearing and mothering. This naturally results in differing representations of men and women in different parts of many companies, facilitating charges of discrimination. For example, at Home Depot, recently the target of a lawsuit, sales personnel, who sell lumber, electrical supplies, hardware, and the like, are about 70% male, while the operations people, including cashiers and back-office employees, are 70% female. According to the company, this was because most women job applicants have experience as cashiers while men are more interested in carpentry, plumbing and other crafts. (According to some women employees, the regular hours of cashiering fit their child-rearing needs better, and they turned down promotions to sales work.)[55]

But this, according to the lawsuit, made the company guilty of reinforcing "gender stereotypes." A federal judge, a former class-action lawyer herself, certified a class action on behalf of 22,000 Home Depot employees, and a class-action suit was also filed in California on behalf of all the company's female employees in 10 western states. The company insisted it would not settle the upcoming California case and that many of its women employees had urged it not to settle.[56] It would have been the first such case taken to trial since the 1991 change in the law, but Home Depot changed its mind and settled the case for $65 million.

It seems clear that under the Clinton administration the mission of the federal agencies involved is not to act against discrimination pursuant to the law but rather to use the law as a tool to maximize the hiring and promotion of women, at least so long as their proportions fall short of the mathematical equality so beloved of simple-minded egalitarians and professional feminists.

---

[54]"For Plaintiffs' Lawyers, There's No Place Like Home Depot," Feb. 12, 1997, p. A19.

[55]Max Boot, "For Plaintiffs' Lawyers, There's No Place Like Home Depot," Wall Street Journal, Feb. 12, 1997, p. A19.

[56]Oscar Suris and Barbara Martinez, "EEOC to Join Suit Against Home Depot Alleging Bias Against Female Workers," Wall Street Journal, March 25, 1997.

For example, in 1993 Ford Motor Co. needed to add 800 workers to its truck-assembly line in Louisville. In that area, women hold 23.8% of durable-goods manufacturing jobs; and a full 26.4% of Ford's new hires were women. No problem here, surely? On the contrary, the Labor Department's Office of Federal Contract Compliance Programs filed a complaint charging Ford with discrimination in this hiring. Apparently Ford thought it had figured out how to keep the fairness-enforcers happy and still hire the best-qualified workers: it rounded up a lot of suitable women to interview. They were, in fact, 37% of the qualified-applicant pool. So Ford's failure to hire women for 37% of the openings is now being construed as sex discrimination.[57]

Not only may not having enough women employees cost the employer big bucks, so may not being sufficiently vigilant in protecting them from fellow-employees' bad manners, even in places typically considered "no place for a lady." There are cases where perfectly qualified women workers in what had been all-male workplaces encounter abusive treatment from co-workers simply because they are resented as intruding into what the workers had come to regard as something of a macho club. This sort of behavior seems most common in working-class environments where the job involves physical labor; it would appear that the basis of these men's feelings of self-esteem may be threatened when it is shown that a woman can do the work.

It is of course not only women who encounter this sort of thing. College students with summer jobs on ships or on Forest Service fire crews have been known to be less than cordially received by the regular workers. But that does not make the unpleasantness any less deplorable. Still, unless it is encouraged by the employer, it is hardly a sign of discrimination on its part against either women or college students. Nevertheless, while the college students are out of luck, the women have a discrimination claim based on the "hostile environment."

The innocent employer whose lack of proportional representation of the sexes reflected the use of legitimate standards is caught between Scylla and Charybdis, for, if it tries to fend off lawsuits based on not having enough women employees by lowering standards to hire women, it will create resentment among its male employees that may expose it to

---

[57]"U.S. Accuses Ford of Sex-Bias in Hiring At Kentucky Facility," *Wall Street Journal*, May 12, 1997.

hostile-environment lawsuits. Men who are passed over for hiring or promotion because of their sex, those forced to work with under-quali- fied women, those told they must take down pinups from their lockers because the newly-hired woman welder says they offend her, or to stop reading *Playboy* in the firehouse because a firewoman says this creates a hostile atmosphere, quite understandably will get angry.

And women's attitudes are not improved by hearing constantly that they are the victims of oppression. A recent Roper Organization poll showed "growing numbers of women expressing anger over sexism and unhappiness with men" compared to 20 years earlier. While in 1970 67% of women agreed that "most men are basically kind, gentle and thought- ful," only 50% agreed in 1990. 54%, up from 41%, now felt that "most men look at a woman and immediately think how it would be to go to bed with her."[58] Seething resentment does not seem to have anything like the incidence found among Negro professionals (see Chap. V), perhaps be- cause most working women are kept in touch with reality by going home to their husbands at the end of the work day, but it is to be assumed that more than a few women are impaired in their work by the anger that all the talk about "sexism" has generated.

Thus far the "hostile environment" situation as to sex discrimination is parallel to that as to racial discrimination. But there is another dimen- sion in the case of sex. There is an important element between men and women, celebrated in the expression, *vive la difference!* Women and men are sexually attracted to each other. And here in somewhat tortured manner arises a unique opportunity for suing employers for sex discrimi- nation, the "sexual harassment" lawsuit.

In the world as a whole, men and women who are not married to each other generally manage their relationships without recourse to the courts. In the extreme case of rape, criminal penalties are imposed on a perpe- trator found guilty according to the usual standard of the criminal law, beyond reasonable doubt. Short of that, the criminal law recognizes of- fensive touching as a type of battery, but practically no one, male or female, goes to the district attorney seeking a criminal prosecution for a stolen kiss or unwelcome touch. Such a thing is as a practical matter also

---

[58]"Women's opinions of men take turn for worse," *Contra Costa Times*, April 26, 1990.

very hard to prove beyond reasonable doubt without witnesses. And verbal or written expressions of attraction are not illegal.

Civil lawsuits for offensive-touching battery are also rare. Even though in civil suits only a preponderance of the evidence, rather than the absence of reasonable doubt, is required (as in the O.J. Simpson wrongful-death case), the absence of witnesses is still commonly a great obstacle. And how much is the offense worth, in terms of damages, unless it was so outrageous as to inspire punitive damages? And how much can be gotten out of the offender without driving him into bankruptcy? The offense will have to be great indeed and the offender very rich before a lawyer will take such a case on a contingent-fee basis. The normal response to unwelcome attentions is simply to avoid further contact with the offending party.

And life goes on. Women in this liberated age manage to cope with compliments, winks, leers, whistles, suggestive remarks, and outright propositions (men seem generally to take such attention from women as a compliment) on the street, in restaurants and bars, in their apartment building or neighborhood, at parties, in museums, wherever, in their stride, without emotional devastation.

But it is different at the workplace. Congress passed a law against discrimination on the basis of sex, not against "sexual harassment." But the courts concluded that if an employer or his representative insisted on sex as the price for a job or a promotion, this constituted discrimination – the so-called *quid pro quo* discrimination. The woman (presumably) was being treated discriminatorily. So far, so good. The employer has engaged in obvious significant misconduct; the employer is liable.

The courts also recognized "hostile environment" as a type of discrimination. This is not unreasonable either. If someone says he does not discriminate against Jews but decorates the office with swastikas and pictures of Adolf Hitler, he has obviously created an environment in which a Jew could work, if at all, only under a severe handicap. A hostile environment is also obvious if the employer encourages his male employees to insult the female workers. The employer is at fault and is responsible. But what has happened, as court decisions have broadened the meaning of "hostile environment" (of which "sexual harassment" is a part), is that the employer is now liable for unwelcome attentions of a sexual nature paid by one employee to another, even if he does not know about them, unless he can show that he has been sufficiently vigilant in attempting to shield his employees from such poor manners; *and* he may also be liable on account of offense an employee takes over anything in the workplace that relates to sex, even if it was not directed at the complaining party at all.

In other words, in the workplace the woman employee now has recourse to the employer's deep pockets when offended at work in a way she would not have been had she been a man, if the source of the offense was within the employer's control.[59]

In theory, the sexual harassment has to be a pretty serious matter, seriously upsetting to a reasonable person (or, according to some courts, a "reasonable woman.") Courts use the term, "sufficiently severe or pervasive to alter the conditions of the victim's employment and create an abusive working environment." But it is truly remarkable how sensitive women in the workplace have now become. "We're rough! We're tough! Anything you can do, we can do better! We're not little stay-at-home-with-hubby-and-babies women. We're out in the workplace, competing as equals! We're sexually liberated, and we insist on reproductive freedom. We're not the stereotypical shrinking violet who bursts into tears when there's a little stress on the job: we're aggressive career women." But – "He winked at me! And he asked me out several times! And he talked of – gross things!" The poor dear deserves a substantial sum from her employer for failing to shield her from this demeaning and humiliating experience.

---

[59]The ramifications of the principle that any offense that would not have occurred had the offended person been of the opposite sex constitutes sex discrimination if the employer failed to take adequate steps against such behavior go on and on, to the point of threatening brain fever. "When Ribaldry Among Men Is Sex Harassment" is the title of a June 5, 1997 Wall Street Journal article. The target of a homosexual advance has been held to have been discriminated against because of his sex; presumably, had he been a woman, the advance would not have been made. But then logically a bisexual's non-discriminatory advances to both men and women should not constitute sex discrimination. What about a man who is bothered by crude behavior by fellow *heterosexual* men employees? Whether this constitutes sex discrimination will have to be determined by the Supreme Court, as lower courts are divided on the question. Is it perhaps discrimination if the vulgar co-workers had better manners than to subject a woman to equal crudity, but not discrimination if they lacked that restraint? And why should sexual content enter into it at all? If male employees regularly invite other men at the shop, but not female employees, to go deer hunting with them, may not this constitute discriminatory treatment on the basis of sex? But, on the other hand, might not an invitation to go deer hunting with a group of men be taken as sexual harassment?

Offensive touching at work, although not on a date, can be extremely lucrative. A secretary who worked briefly for the large Baker & McKenzie law firm sued the firm and was awarded $7 million by a San Francisco jury (reduced to $3.5 million by the judge) because of a partner's roaming hands. That is far more than the typical judgment for wrongful death.

Gifts can constitute harassment. One woman sued Title Search Co. saying she resigned "because one of the owners harassed her, partly by giving her a scarf on Valentine's Day. A Federal jury awarded her $82,000. The company, saying it acted to protect her against any further such conduct, has appealed." An employee of the New Jersey Turnpike Authority sued for harassment "that included a gift from supervisors of a 'baby doll' nightgown at a Christmas luncheon."[60]

Pinups on workers' lockers have qualified as constituting "sexual harassment" or a "hostile environment."[61] Perhaps with this in mind, the Los Angeles County Fire Department banned the reading of *Playboy* magazine in firehouses, even on employees' own time. Patricia Vaughan, a department employee who helped draft this policy, testified that "the county feared the magazines would create an atmosphere of women as sex objects and create a hostile environment," and the president of Los Angeles NOW praised the policy as a "model for the nation."[62] But a fire captain, at a remote station in the Mojave Desert at which no women worked, successfully challenged the policy as a violation of his First Amendment rights.

Ordinary language without any sexual implications may constitute sexual harassment; specifically, according to a federal trial court, using a "sexist" job title such as "draftsman" instead of "draftsperson." A Kentucky state agency made a company change its "Men Working" signs, at a cost of over $35,000, on the theory that they "perpetuat[e] a discriminatory work environment and [are] unlawful."[63]

Keep those eyes under control. The secretary to a Japanese executive whose duties included serving tea to visiting Japanese sued because they

---

[60]"Some office giving helps spur sexual-harassment litigation," *Wall Street Journal*, Feb. 11, 1997, p. 1.

[61]*Robinson v. Jacksonville Shipyards*, 760 F. Supp. 1486 (M.D. Fla. 1991).

[62]Jeff Wilson, "Firefighter, county in court over cheesecake magazines," *Contra Costa Times*, June 8, 1994, p. 14A.

[63]Eugene Volokh, "Harassment Law Flirts With Speech Suppression," *Wall Street Journal*, June 28, 1995, p. A19.

looked at her legs while being served. Also, there were nude pictures in the magazines they brought with them.[64]

And beware any jocular familiarity. A Los Angeles police commander was suspended for five days after he allegedly greeted two policewomen with "Hi, babe."[65] A jury, in 1995, awarded $50 million in punitive damages against the Wal-Mart Stores chain to a woman who charged that her supervisor liked to joke about her figure.[66] A training film designed to raise people's consciousness about "sexual harassment" has a woman at a photocopying machine saying, "Sorry, I'll be out of your way in a second," to which a man, leaning on the counter, replies, "Take your time. I'm enjoying the view." Asked writer Barbara Amiel in a *National Review* article, "Who, but disturbed human beings, would see this as sexual harassment? . . . the response of the pathologically neurotic woman has become the standard."[67]

Federal and state courts have grappled with the definition of crimes and torts for centuries. Did what occurred meet the definition, say, of rape? But for the courts to be addressing questions of manners – involving neither touching (battery) nor the threat of touching (assault) – and attempting to draw the line between what a normal and reasonable woman could be sufficiently seriously disturbed by to provide the basis for a lawsuit against the employer and what could trouble only a nut case – this is new.

Indeed, not too long ago, if a law led the courts to engage in such exercises, the consensus would have been that that conclusively proved that either it was being incorrectly interpreted or it should be repealed immediately.

Some rationality along this line came through at oral argument at the U.S. Supreme Court in January 1999 case in a suit against a school district because a fifth-grade girl had been teased by a boy. Asked Justice Sandra Day O'Connor: "Little boys tease little girls through their years in school. Is every incident going to lead to a lawsuit?" Justice Anthony Kennedy

---

[64]Valerie Reitman, "Cramming for the Exotic U.S. Workplace," *Wall Street Journal*, July 9, 1996, p. A8.

[65]"L.A. police official faces sexism charges," *Contra Costa Times*, Feb. 22, 1997, p. 13A.

[66]Elizabeth Larson, "Flirting With Dangerous Precedents," *Wall Street Journal*, June 7, 1996.

[67]"Guest Editorial: Feminist Harassment," Nov. 4, 1991, p. 14.

warned that a "necessary consequence" of the plaintiff's argument was "a Federal code of conduct in every classroom in the country."[68]

The lawyer for the little girl's parents couldn't see why not, reasoning from the situation in the workplace. And she had a point; the little girl had indeed been subjected to outrageous abuse from a little terror, far worse than has supported successful hostile-environment lawsuits against employers, with no effective action whatsoever by the school. But the reasoning runs better in the reverse direction: in a workplace sexual-harassment case, a justice ought to have said, "Men and women flirt at work all the time. Is every incident going to lead to a lawsuit?" and another to have ridiculed the idea of "a Federal code of conduct in every workplace in the country."

Thanks to the lawsuit industry, the law against sex discrimination has brought about a national sexual harassment mania. This started developing around the time of Clarence Thomas' nomination to the Supreme Court. The hope of the Left was that Anita Hill's charges would derail the nomination of the conservative jurist, which they certainly could not be expected to do if they were shrugged off as of no great importance. After all, as struck me when the charges were first publicized, even if everything Thomas' former subordinate said was true, he had done no more than make some boorish remarks and be overly persistent in asking her out; he was not alleged to have touched her or done anything remotely as serious as what Paula Jones accused Bill Clinton of doing. Those opposed to Thomas' nomination and the media, however, carried on – rather implausibly in view of the content of prime-time television – as though a little tastelessness were an unspeakable crime.

Supposedly Anita Hill had awakened the country to a terrible evil which had somehow long gone unnoticed. Another significant thing that happened around this time is that, shortly after the Thomas confirmation, Pres. Bush signed the 1991 Civil Rights Act, with its jury trial and punitive damages provisions, into law.

Soon "sexual harassment" became all the rage in the general press, the business press, and trade publications. "How to Guard Against Sexual Harassment" (*Hotel & Resort Industry*, August 1993). "Sexual Harassment Is Topping Agenda In Many Executive Education Programs" (*Wall Street*

---

[68]"Court Is Asked Not to Extend Harassment Law in Schools," *New York Times*, Jan. 13, 1999.

Journal, Dec. 2, 1991). "Horror Stories of Harassment On the Job" (*San Francisco Chronicle*, Nov. 15, 1991). "Male, Female Doctors Report Sex Harassment During Training" (*San Francisco Chronicle*, Feb. 4, 1993). "Sexual Harassment of Women Doctors By Patients Is Common, Study Suggests "(*Wall Street Journal*, Dec. 23, 1993). "Sexual-Harassment Cases Trip Up Foreign Companies" (*Wall Street Journal*, May 9, 1996). One observer estimates that American companies are spending hundreds of millions of dollars on sexual-harassment seminars and specialists.[69]

Matters have actually reached the point that a six-year-old boy was recently separated from his classmates for "sexual harassment" for giving a girl who, he said, asked him, a kiss on the cheek[70] (school districts, too, are "deep pockets," and frightened of lawsuits).

What is so absurd about this hysteria is the total lack of common sense and of a sense of proportion that it involves. Women do not generally go straight from the convent to the workplace, and they are unlikely to encounter anything offensive to them as women there that they have not already had to deal with frequently in their non-work everyday lives. And in the work place itself, among all of its various stresses, strains, frustrations, and disappointments, what now commonly goes by the name of sexual harassment hardly stands out as the priority problem.

A side-effect of the new preoccupation is that accusations of sexual harassment are a potent weapon for the unscrupulous. A *Wall Street Journal* article entitled "Control the Damage of a False Accusation of Sexual Harassment" tells of a woman who told her boss that she would accuse him of sexual harassment if she didn't get a certain promotion. He shrugged the matter off and told no one. The next thing he knew, he heard rumors that he was a "harasser." Confronting the woman in the hall, he attempted to break the ice with a fatherly pat on the back. The woman yelled, "Don't you ever touch me!" The man lost his job.[71] The fact is that now an employer is better off with an unjust-termination suit, with back pay the limit of his exposure, than with a sexual harassment suit where its exposure is greater.

---

[69]Elizabeth Larson, "Flirting With Dangerous Precedents," *Wall Street Journal*, June 7, 1996.

[70]"A First-Grade Kiss Gets Boy Banished," *San Francisco Chronicle*, Sept. 25, 1996, p. C1.

[71]Julie Amparano Lopez, *Wall Street Journal*, Jan. 12, 1994.

"BONA FIDE OCCUPATIONAL QUALIFICATIONS"

Not only does the employer now need constant legal advice rather than its own judgment and common sense as to the sexual composition of its work force and the policing of its manners, it can never decide to fill certain jobs exclusively with women, or with men, without a successful exercise in metaphysics. The law recognizes sex as a "bona fide occupational qualification" only when it relates to the "essence," or the "central mission of the employer's business."

A company thought it would be a good idea not to employ women of child-bearing age in work where they came into contact with lead, lest damage to fetuses (and perhaps resulting lawsuits) occur. Illegal discrimination, said the Supreme Court.[72]

The biddies of the new egalitarianism even frown on preference for women when it is based on attractiveness to men. Thus the term "stewardess" has gone out of use: men must be hired as flight attendants since feminine attractiveness did not go to the "central mission of the employer's business." Similarly, the EEOC attracted a good deal of ridicule in demanding that the Hooters restaurant chain, whose T-shirt-clad, attractive waitresses were a major part of its appeal, hire men waiters,[73] and eventually agreed to a settlement allowing the practice to continue. It is now, however, attacking the practice of Las Vegas casinos of moving pregnant cocktail waitresses to other duties when their pregnancies reach the point that they can no longer fit into their skimpy costumes. This is "an all too common Las Vegas practice, said Pamela Thomason, regional attorney for the agency. 'These women are there to serve drinks, not to be sexpots,' Thomason contends."[74] Sure: retired firemen could do this work just as well.

It took extensive litigation in the federal courts before it was decided that it was permissible not to hire a janitress to service the men's rest rooms in an office building. So far, at least, Nevada brothels have not been charged with sex discrimination for hiring women prostitutes.

---

[72]*International Union, UAW v. Johnson Controls, Inc.*, 111 S.Ct. 1196 (1991).

[73]James Bovard, "The EEOC's War on Hooters," *Wall Street Journal*, Nov. 17, 1995.

[74]"U.S. agency sues to aid pregnant waitresses," *Contra Costa Times*, Dec. 28, 1997.

"SEXISM"

Just as those who crave levelling among the races combine spurious statistical "evidence" of racial discrimination with discoveries of racism in all sorts of things, as discussed in previous chapters, those who crave levelling between the sexes (which of course includes many of the racial-equality zealots, the troubled souls who see oppression everywhere in America being a major component of all the "struggles for equality") find ubiquitous sexism to supplement their statistical chicanery as justification for preferential treatment for women.

Most of the concoctions of "racism" designed to justify specific types of preferential treatment have no practical equivalent in the area of sex. Women do not congregate in low-income neighborhoods, so "toxic sexism" will not fly. "Sexual discrimination in mortgage lending and insurance" does not have great promise, since relatively few single women (or single men, for that matter) are interested in applying for mortgages and buying houses, the number of same-sex couples doing so is very small, and it has not been shown that those consisting of females get less favorable treatment from lenders and insurers than male couples. (For that matter, given prevailing attitudes, it would not be the easiest thing to arouse national indignation against "discrimination against lesbian couples," which presumably is what a high percentage of home-buying female couples are.) Lumping women-owned companies in with minority-owned as supposed victims of racist/sexist contracting practices is all that advocates of female preference have been able to accomplish in these areas.

Nor can sexism be found in the rate of incarceration or execution of women; on the contrary, if one were to apply the reasoning – using the term loosely – of those who attribute Negroes' problems with the law to racism, the far higher rate of men's criminal convictions than women's would demonstrate anti-male bias in the criminal justice system. Similarly, women cannot complain that department store security guards persistently watch them suspiciously.

There are types of women that men tend to dislike. There are also types of men that women tend to dislike, and types of each sex that members of the same sex typically do not like. Aversion to angry feminist scolds no more demonstrates sexism than does aversion to hostile and paranoid Negroes demonstrate racism.

Feminists have done their best to find sexism in the English language. A new Random House dictionary suggests that the spelling "womyn" avoids the unfortunate sequence of letters that spells "men." Manholes no longer officially exist in Los Angeles, being known, pursuant to a 1990 directive from then-mayor Tom Bradley, as "maintenance holes." Sacramento's woman mayor was apparently the pioneer in calling attention to this objectionable piece of sexism.

Everyone seems to have understood perfectly well for hundreds of years that "mankind" included both sexes – and children too – and that "everyone must bring his own lunch" was not an insult to females but the only grammatical way to express the idea without wasting time with "his or her." "Chairman" was a longstanding piece of the language, and no one had any problem with the standard Robert's Rules of Order form of address for a woman in this office, "Madam Chairman."

No matter. These commonplaces have all been attacked as "sexist" – as "marginalizing" women, in the pretentious gibberish of which many of those obsessed with supposed oppressions are so fond. And this crusade has been widely successful. One's ears and sensibilities are continually assaulted by pathetic concoctions like "chairs," "everyone does their job," "fishers," and the like. Those on the cutting edge of correctness, like Stanford University's president at a recent talk, will say "a professor in her or his laboratory": for "his or her," don't you see, is sexist in placing "her" behind "his."

Even old David Brower, lifelong environmental warrior, ran afoul of the sexism patrol. His organization, Friends of the Earth, published a monthly magazine entitled, from a passage in poet Robinson Jeffers' *The Answer, Not Man Apart.* Staffers on the magazine rebelled. "This title alienates women," said a woman editorial board member unhappy at the organization's board's decision to retain the name after Brower had pleaded, "It's too late to edit Jeffers or the Bible." Clearly she was not single-mindedly focused on the environment, for she lamented, "We want to reach out and make connections with other parts of the movement, the women's, and disarmament, but now we're saying we're not ready to make connections."[75]

---

[75]"Friends of Earth publication will keep 'Not Man Apart' name," *San Francisco Sunday Examiner & Chronicle*, Dec. 18, 1983.

Brower was soon proven wrong about the Bible. True to their real religion, many churches have not hesitated to purge the Bible. The National Council of Churches' *Inclusive Language Lectionary* eliminates such offensive wordings as "The Lord is my shepherd," and the "Son of God" is now the "Child" instead. "Much hurt is caused by oppressive speech," declared a woman Methodist minister on the revising committee.

Q.: How many feminists does it take to screw in a light bulb?

A.: That's not funny!

Humor is also out where the sexes are involved. "Scrippsie" is a common nickname for students at all-woman Scripps College, and at nearby Harvey Mudd College, in 1990, students put out a humorous freshman handbook which defined "Scrippsie" as "generally a cross between Miss America and a begonia . . . often armed with cute red subcompacts and a Nordstrom card." The Scripps student body president was outraged and pronounced the humor "demeaning to women" – "demeaning" just has to be feminists' favorite word – and Harvey Mudd's judicial board ruled that the handbook's editors must retract the humorous definition "because it perpetuates a negative stereotype."[76]

Esquire magazine published a humorous piece at about the same time entitled "Your Wife: An Owner's Manual." The president of the Los Angeles chapter of NOW held a press conference at which she protested, "It puts us into a subhuman level, places women into a thing mode."

The absurdities of language scolds and humorless soreheads prove nothing about the existence of unfairness based on sex and probably mislead rather few as to its existence. Their successes, however, point in precisely the opposite direction: that people accede to ridiculous demands lest they be called sexist is indicative of a strong national consensus in favor of fairness to women. This is of course consistent with the research discussed above.

COSTS VS. BENEFITS

Not least in importance, preferential treatment for women has meant unfair treatment for many men, particularly white men, who lack either a race or a sex credential. A San Francisco legal newspaper proclaimed a triumph in the crusade for "diversity": of 26 faculty hired for tenure-track

---

[76]"Nickname's no joke, student argues," *Sacramento Bee*, Oct. 21, 1990.

positions at Bay Area law schools, only three were white males. It can safely be assumed that few of the men now being rejected because of their sex have ever been in a position to discriminate against women in employment, even had they had a mind to do so.

A plague of litigation has been created by the various laws against discrimination. Federal bias actions as a whole grew twenty-fold between 1970 and 1989.[77] (In a saner age, the very idea of having the federal courts occupied with issues involving manners on the job would have been considered preposterous and a conclusive argument against laws that brought that absurdity about.) Organizations' efficiency has been impaired by the hiring of less-qualified personnel, and huge sums have been spent by government in enforcing and by the private sector on coping with the law as applied. A 1993 study by Peter Brimelow and Leslie Spencer estimated that in 1991 the federal government spent $425 million on civil-rights oversight overall (and state and local government $120 million) and that this imposed $5-8 billion in compliance costs and $95 billion in indirect costs on the private sector. They estimated the additional cost of bad hiring, effects on morale, and misallocation of financial resources at $236 billion, for a total cost of 4 per cent of GNP.[78] (These figures include the anti-discrimination effort in its entirety rather than strictly that part devoted to sex discrimination, which of course represents a major part of the total, with race the other main part.)

It is one thing in terms of economic significance when the "sex discrimination" averted by the law involves unreasonable rejection, perhaps out of ill-will, of those who, taking all relevant factors into account, are unquestionably the best-qualified. It is another when the "best-qualified" is so only if considering the probabilities of such things as career interruption for family-related reasons is ruled out. It is also another matter when what is averted is acting on a feeling that despite objective qualifications the employer's interest in efficiency will be better served by not introducing a woman into a predominantly or wholly male environment, or a male into a predominantly female one.

This may be because the employer believes the men (or women) would resent what they would consider an intrusion. This sort of situation is analo-

---

[77]"The New Shakedown Artists," *Wall Street Journal*, May 20, 1997, citing *The Excuse Factory* by Walter Olson.
[78]*Forbes*, February 15, 1993.

gous to fearing that white workers will resent a Negro co-worker. In the case of a traditionally all-male or all-female workplace, such a reaction may be a real possibility. The employer who rejects an applicant for this reason is giving effect to genuine sexism. When the law prevents sexism from depriving the best-qualified applicant of the job, it is achieving a real benefit.

The employer's reluctance may arise, however, not because the men or women are sexists but because they are men or women, and the disruptive effect on the workplace of sexual crosscurrents is not desired. This is not sexism, nor is it irrational. In fact, is the candidate, under the circumstances, really the "best-qualified," if qualification includes, as it should, ability to function in a non-disruptive way in the workplace, where it is not sexist attitudes but human nature that is the problem? It can certainly be argued that it is better to leave such decisions to the discretion of the employer on the scene – a fishing vessel or a fire-fighting crew is not an office – than to require the hiring regardless of the cost. And certainly negative effects of sexual crosscurrents on workplace efficiency deserve to be taken into account in adding up the pluses and minuses of this rigorous "non-discrimination."

The benefit side also includes reducing the unpleasantness of sexual harassment. This benefit would look more impressive if the reality were what lawsuit allegations and news stories suggest, the protection of sensitive, virginal young ladies from the rude and lewd attentions that boorish men insist on inflicting upon them despite their modest dress and demeanor, with devastating effects on these innocents' psyches. But in reality women employees are part of a society that practically glorifies sex and sexual freedom; extra- and premarital sex, and obscene language, leap out at the television viewer and the moviegoer. In their personal lives, too, surveys show, the women of America are predominantly quite cavalier about sexual activity; a recent issue of *Bride* magazine stated that only 4% of brides are virgins. Presumably there are working women who have lived such sheltered lives that matters of a sexual nature genuinely shock them, and even the most promiscuous swinger, of course, can find certain remarks or advances offensive. Reducing offensiveness must still be considered a plus, but what we are talking about here is rather far removed from averting the rape of cloistered nuns.

Whether someone is punished as the result of a false accusation or severely penalized for a minor "insensitivity," an injustice has been done that has to be weighed against the benefits from reducing women's exposure to offensive words or touches. Another cost is the chilling effect on speech and interaction generally that fear of "sexual harassment" has brought to the workplace. These are not minor costs.

All in all, there is much less reason in the first place to suspect discrimination as the cause of women's position in the work force than in the case of Negroes, and here too analysis indicates that there are nondiscriminatory reasons. Here too, the law has resulted in the application of a ham-handed quota mentality, and the price for averting relatively few instances of real discrimination has been a disproportionate one, in both dollars and cents and equity.

And, as in the case of race, while outright preferences are unpopular and being eliminated, much of the mischief is the result of the antidiscrimination laws.

Chapter IX

Age Discrimination

Three years after the Civil Rights Act forbade discrimination on the basis of race, color, national origin, or sex (or religion), government's new supervisory authority to police the fairness of the American workplace was broadened to include unfair treatment due to age by the Age Discrimination in Employment Act of 1967.

Someone alert for signs of oppression in recent history and current status might have fairly easily found some here. Just as Negroes had had to sit at the back of the bus and experienced other discriminatory treatment and real hostility, and women had not been able to vote until well into the 20th century and been automatically rejected for many jobs, so oppression along age lines was easy to document.

Among analysts of World War I, the theme of old European politicians, generals and admirals, their attention often still fixed on the previous conflict, sending young men to their deaths in war was popular. Roosevelt decried what he called the "nine old men," the U.S. Supreme Court that for years rejected key parts of his New Deal, reflecting the predominance of gray hair among those who ran the country. Rich old men, and rich old women too, patriarchs and matriarchs, controlled a disproportionate share of the nation's wealth, controlling corporations through electing directors and their progeny through the power of inheritance.

And of course. Respect for maturity and experience, respect for one's elders, was an ingrained part of the culture; it went back to the Biblical patriarchs and beyond. And the old by definition had a head start on the young. They had had longer to accumulate experience, and wealth, and power, and if they had a mind to hang on to it, as they often did, they were hard to dislodge, even if their powers were no longer what they had been.

Young people had long chafed under the domination of entrenched age, whether they were the Prince of Wales during Queen Victoria's endless reign or a young executive in a company all of whose important decisions were made by a domineering old tycoon wont to dismiss his juniors with demeaning terms such as "young whippersnappers." In the age of the modern corporation, it became common to establish mandatory retirement ages in order to ease the problem to some extent, but still seniority counted for a great deal indeed everywhere from Congress to the executive suite.

But this is of course not the "age discrimination" that the 1967 Act addressed. Quite the contrary. The laws against race and sex discrimination outlaw discrimination against *any* race and *either* sex, but not the 1967 Act: by its terms it applies *only* to discrimination *against those 40 years old and older.* One suspects that this is because of the unusual strength of America's old-people's – or, rather, to use their preferred term, "senior-citizens'" – lobby: which unusual strength is of course one more indication that older people are anything but an oppressed group.

If "discrimination against older people" really meant unfair treatment of people purely on the basis of chronological age with no reference to ability or effectiveness, it is hard to see how senior executives and stock-holders, older people themselves, would countenance it so that a law was needed to prevent it.

But of course the practical effects of this legislation are very much in line with laws against sex and race discrimination. The law compels preferential treatment of the protected group (in the case of race and sex discrimination, the group presumed to need protection) in order to avert lawsuits, gives employees who do not measure up to the employers' standards another chance at the brass ring, and gives the lawsuit industry another boost.

It is eminently rational and conducive to wise use of resources for an employer to take into account how long a trainee will be available for work when selecting from among available applicants. But in 1992 Los Angeles dropped its upper age limit of 34 for police recruits and admitted a 64-year-old man to its police academy, despite some grumbling by sane people about the absurdity of spending $100,000 to train someone with such limited potential for future service. The city's training expenses turned out to be even a poorer investment than might have been expected: the elderly recruit, apparently quite young at heart, was fired at age 65 for allegedly touching female trainees inappropriately. He then charged that he was the victim of age discrimination.[1]

Why not give it a try? Remember, under the "American rule," there is no real penalty, in the form of having to pay your opponent's legal expenses should you lose, for unreasonably pursuing a lawsuit. Women often file sex *and* age bias lawsuits and, according to a Women's Legal Defense Fund study, win 41% of the time.[2]

In a country of 300 million people, it is of course always possible to find someone who dislikes older people as such. Indeed, in the 60s, "Don't trust anyone over 30" was a popular left-wing slogan, reflecting the idea that older people were stodgy and conservative. But the idea that government action is needed to combat widespread unreasonable discrimination against relatively respected and powerful people is particularly ridiculous.

It is a fact of human life that people's physical and mental powers typically wane as they get past a certain age. Experience and skill are countervailing factors, and there is a great deal to be said for the making of personnel decisions on a strictly individual basis, without regard to age and without any arbitrary cut-off point. Even on that basis, however, as the age group becomes older and older, a disproportionate number of its members will not measure up in efficiency, and even fewer in terms of cost-effectiveness where compensation depends significantly on years on the job. To prohibit appropriate response, whether in the form of adjustment of compensation and duties or in the form of termination, is to prohibit intelligent personnel management and economically-sound human-resource use.

One California appellate court recently held that when the employer is motivated by cost cutting, it is not guilty of age discrimination just because it is primarily older workers who are laid off.[3] Protested a lawyer specializing in discrimination lawsuits, rather letting the cat out of the bag as to what "age discrimination" tends to be all about in reality:

---

[1]"Police recruit claims dismissal due to age bias," *Contra Costa Times*, March 21, 1996.
[2]"The Checkoff," *Wall Street Journal*, March 11, 1997, p. 1.
[3]*Marks v. Loral Corp.*, 57 Cal. App. 4th 30 (1997).

"There's always an economic advantage to employing younger people. That's the basis of age discrimination."[4] The sensible decision was appealed to the state supreme court, without success, whereupon the obliging Democrat-controlled state legislature passed a law that would have exempted older workers from the need to be cost-effective. Fortunately, it was vetoed by Gov. Wilson.

The federal courts, also, to the disappointment of plaintiff's lawyers, have held that the law was not intended to exempt those over 40 from the need to be cost-effective.[5]

One would think that a business enterprise of consenting adults, which exists to make a profit for its owners through serving its customers' needs, would be able to decide by itself how best to manage its personnel affairs to that end. It might well decide that a mandatory retirement age made sense: while it is true that Sophocles wrote splendid tragedies in his 90s and that many people are tremendously productive at a very advanced age, they are not the rule, and employers who do not wish to analyze each employee individually may wish to set a mandatory retirement age even at the expense of losing some exceptional employees. The problem becomes particularly difficult for the corporation when it is those who head it who are no longer up to their jobs. Stockholders like to avoid such problems, and promising younger people, critical to long-run success of the enterprise, are more easily attracted when they can look forward to progress toward the top jobs rather than the frustration of endless years of waiting.

As do Negroes and women, a disproportionate number of old people have real, not imaginary, weaknesses in qualifications for many jobs. And their position in the community, in terms of both respect and power, makes attributing their disappointments in the workplace to hostility or prejudice particularly implausible.

---

[4]Eric Brazil, "Court decision could be bad news to older workers," *San Francisco Examiner*, July 31, 1997, p. A-10.

[5]"Courts make age-discrimination cases harder to win, plaintiffs lawyers say," *Wall Street Journal*, May 18, 1999, p. 1.

CHAPTER X

MAKING THE SERIOUSLY IMPAIRED A PRIVILEGED CLASS

As was discussed above, the Civil Rights and Age Discrimination acts resulted in *de facto* preferences for minority-group members, women, and older persons. Under this system, able members of these categories might be expected to do particularly well and the less-qualified to be spared the normal penalties for their failings. But what about people who were simply poorly-qualified, but not in any of these groups? For some time, they were generally out of luck. Those anxious to get more Hispanics, or women, or whatever, into particular jobs tried to avoid simply lowering standards so that ordinary poorly-qualified people would share in the opportunities (although inevitably this did occur to some extent) but would try to set different standards or establish preferential "goals" or quotas to benefit the selected groups.

This injustice was corrected through a *reductio ad absurdum* of mindless egalitarianism: making disabilities themselves the basis for membership in a group presumed to be another victim of oppression and discrimination and therefore deserving of governmental protection and artificial advancement. The Americans with Disabilities Act ("ADA") conferred this status on 43 million Americans, to use the figure then-President George Bush proudly proclaimed to the 1992 Republican convention.

All these people, supposedly, had needed protection against being rejected or poorly treated on account of irrelevant disabilities by employers who either knew no better (not realizing, for example, that a crippled person could still be a perfectly good bookkeeper) or had it in for the unfortunate, and also deserved a leg up in being entitled to have employers accommodate to their disability; all of which could be effectively managed by bureaucrats, lawyers, juries, and judges. (There is also another dimension, which will be gone into below: providing special treatment for the irresponsible and obnoxious through the magic of defining them as "suffering from disabilities.")

At least in the case of the Civil Rights Act one did not have to be a socialist or an economic illiterate to defend the legislation; the idea of the 1964 Act was not so much that bureaucrats and the courts were better-equipped than the private sector to assess employees' abilities as that they were in a position to avoid giving effect to racial animosity. But it would have been hard to make a case that animosity toward such disabled people as the crippled or the blind was common.

Also, it is hard to believe that those who passed this law could have been unaware, from over a quarter of a century's experience with the Civil Rights Act of 1964, that seemingly-innocuous laws against unfair discrimination turn into something very different, and that they were creating yet another costly burden and wave of litigation. But who would want to be pilloried as a hard-hearted enemy of the unfortunate?

Part of the problem with this incredible piece of legislation is the same inability to distinguish reasonable from unfair discrimination that has plagued the field of race and sex discrimination, and part is the unusual, and in the nature of things inevitably very expansive, definition of what constitutes a "disability." Everything from physical problems to feeble-mindedness to mental disorders to alcohol and drug problems is covered.[1]

In the language of the statute, a disability is any "physical or mental impairment that substantially limits one or more of the major life activities" of an individual; *or*, "a record of such an impairment;" *or*, "being regarded as having such an impairment."

Not only may the employer not "discriminate against" an individual on such a basis, "discriminate against" is defined to include "not making

---

[1] The undiscriminating sweep of the Act is indicated by the perceived need to specifically exclude a few conditions from its coverage. These are, in the language of the Act, compulsive gambling, kleptomania, pyromania, psychoactive substance use disorders resulting from current illegal use of drugs, transvestism, transsexualism, pedophilia, exhibitionism, voyeurism, gender identity disorders not resulting from physical impairments, and other sexual behavior disorders. (The Act also provides that homosexuality and bisexuality are not impairments and thus not disabilities.)

reasonable accommodations" for the individual's limitations (unless that involves "undue hardship," in determining which "the overall financial resources" of the employer are to be taken into account!) It also includes using any qualification standards that tend to disqualify people with disabilities unless they can be shown to be "job-related for the position in question[2] and consistent with business necessity." Furthermore, the employer is prohibited from initially conducting a medical examination of a job applicant or asking him questions to determine whether he has a disability or as to its nature or severity.

Only after the applicant has been offered a job may a medical examination be required, and then only if all entering employees are subjected to such an examination; nor, after employment, may a medical examination be required or the employee asked about a disability unless the employer can show it is "job-related and consistent with business necessity."

These draconian provisions suggest a history of relentless animus toward the handicapped that must be zealously combatted. But had it been shown that Americans consistently harbored nasty feelings toward, say, cripples, akin to those of racists toward Negroes? Hardly. Far from persecuting cripples, Americans elected one to an unprecedented four terms as President. People with all sorts of serious disabilities had been holding responsible positions all along. There had been a blind governor of Texas. "Hire the Handicapped" campaigns had been around forever. The general attitude toward those with problems that were not their fault was supportive and sympathetic. The plucky crippled newsboy was a common fictional character.

Nor was there evidence that handicapped people had been getting the short end of the stick in the marketplace. Obviously people whose effectiveness is impaired can be expected to earn less, in a rational economy. But it by no means follows that they are not getting what they deserve, or that the market is not capable of assessing what their services are worth but government is. By definition, they have less to offer. They also are more likely to impose additional costs by getting hurt on the job; blind workers are three times as likely and deaf workers twice as likely to be injured, with disabled workers overall 36% more likely than their

---

[2]Note that this forbids taking into account the applicant's flexibility, or ability to do *other jobs* for the employer, either now or in the future.

able-bodied co-workers, according to a recent study by University of Iowa College of Medicine researchers.[3]

All human beings are flawed. This law means that those with sufficiently minor flaws can be held to as high a standard as the employer wishes, with no fear of a disability-rights lawsuit; but seriously-flawed individuals, or those thought to be seriously-flawed, are legally entitled to force the employer to bear part of the burden of the disability. We have finally openly achieved what Tom Lehrer used to joke about, forbidding "discrimination on the basis of ability." The mandate of this law is, not to avoid discriminating *against* members of a group, but rather to discriminate *in favor of* members of the group. Unlike Jesus, Congress could not make the lame man walk, but it could and did force employers to treat him, to some extent, as if he could.

What are "reasonable accommodations"? A 1992 news story told of a man with cerebral palsy whose employers had "denied him the accommodations – such as a clerical assistant – that he needs to work."[4] Hire two to do the work of one: something that may not be an "undue burden" to a large and prosperous employer.

With the expansive definitions of "reasonable accommodations" and "disability," it is hardly surprising that people who have trouble doing their jobs well are tempted to claim that this is because they have a disability, and that they are illegally being deprived of their rights under the ADA, and that they are entitled to compensation through a lawsuit. Playing the lawsuit lottery must be a particularly attractive alternative to honest work for those with limited ability.

And, indeed, litigation has exploded in this newly-created growth area. In the first year after ADA was passed, over 9,000 lawsuits were filed. In 1994, ADA-related complaints to the EEOC totalled nearly 19,000, up 23.5% from the previous year. Between 1992 and 1997, over 90,000 disability-discrimination complaints were received.[5] Examples of what this new frontier of government regulation of human-resource allocation has brought on the country make interesting reading.

---

[3]"Disabled more likely to be hurt on the job," *Contra Costa Times*, Dec. 24, 1997.
[4]Teresa Moore, "Confusion About Disabilities Act," *San Francisco Chronicle*, July 18, 1992, p. 1.
[5]Carolyn Lochhead, "How Law to Help Disabled Now Works Against Them," *San Francisco Chronicle*, Jan. 3, 1999.

The EEOC's first ADA case, filed two days after the act went into effect, had to do with a man with cancer which had metastasized to his brain: he was given six months to live. His employer felt that he was "not functioning," and asked him to retire. This "discrimination" cost the employer over $500,000 in a federal court suit.[6]

The New York State Bar was ordered by a federal judge, in a ruling upheld by the Second Circuit, to give a would-be lawyer who claimed a "reading disorder" extra time to finish the bar examination, even though an outside expert said she had no disability. (This was her fifth attempt; despite the additional time, she failed again.)[7]

A lawyer with a utility in San Francisco became depressed and stopped working effectively, and he was asked to resign. An arbitrator awarded him $1 million on the grounds that "reasonable accommodation" to his problem had not been made.

A student who uses a wheelchair sued the College of Marin because, she said, she was barred from full participation in a theatre dance class.[8]

United Parcel Service does not allow people without good vision in both eyes to be delivery drivers. This, contends the EEOC, violates the ADA, and it has sued UPS for back pay and punitive damages for such persons.[9]

On the other hand, a waitress in Alabama who claimed that expecting her to cope with the stress of busy dinner-times and learning menu changes constituted discrimination lost her case.[10] Sometimes sanity prevails, although not without legal fees.

One of the quirks of the theatre of the absurd created by the ADA is that on the one hand a problem has to be pretty severe to qualify as a disability and trigger application of the Act, while on the other hand, if it is too severe, the complaining employee is out of luck because even with reasonable accommodation he would still be unable to do the job. A doctor's opinion as to an employee's condition or requirements could

---

[6]Llewellyn Rockwell, Jr., "Disabilities Act Suits Proliferate," *Human Events*, June 5, 1993.

[7]Tamar Lewin, "Court Supports Aid to Disabled For Bar Exams," *New York Times*, Sept. 16, 1998, p. A1.

[8]David Tuller, "Disabled Student Sues Marin College for Bias," *San Francisco Chronicle*, Jan. 27, 1996.

[9]Ken Hoover, "Government Files Job Discrimination Suit Against UPS," *San Francisco Chronicle*, March 21, 1997.

[10]Geanne Rosenberg, "When the Mind Is the Matter," *New York Times*, Nov. 7, 1998, p. B1.

have the unintended effect of scuttling his lawsuit opportunities, leading some doctors to ask lawyers to draft their medical notes.[11]

That it should sometimes be difficult for employees to win discrimination lawsuits against their employers strikes some as an outrageous situation. "It's a horrific Catch-22," declared Chai Feldblum, a Georgetown Law Center professor who had been instrumental in drafting the ADA. The EEOC sought to ride to the rescue with new guidelines, in 1997, to the effect that a mental problem could be labeled a disability even if it did not hurt a person's job performance.[12]

And watch out for that "being regarded as having an impairment" language. A salesman was fired because he couldn't follow verbal directions. This problem is not considered an ADA-covered disability, but the salesman claimed his employer had acted as though it had been, and he won a settlement.[13]

Even more ridiculous was the case of a supermarket chain manager. Numerous employee complaints charged that he had manhandled, berated and threatened them. He denied everything, and the obliging chain transferred him to another store where there had been no history of personnel problems. Within three months, 51 complaints came to the district manager: the transferred manager had, they said, thrown food off shelves and ordered employees to clean it up, and threatened to fire everybody for no valid reason.

Executives met with the manager, and it was agreed that he would take a three months' leave of absence. Then he requested another month. And then two more months. And more. And more. Finally the chain fired him.

Unbeknownst to the chain, their man had not been just resting and meditating all this time. He had prepared to open a sign-painting business and had also obtained a real estate license and begun selling real estate, working up to 80 hours a week at these new pursuits.

When unsuccessful, he reapplied to the supermarket chain for employment. Unbelievably, they offered him a job; but it was as a clerk, because no manager's positions were then open: he could apply for one when one became open.

---

[11]Ilana DeBare, "What is a Disability?" *San Francisco Chronicle*, Oct. 5, 1998, p. E1.
[12]Geanne Rosenberg, "When the Mind Is the Matter," *New York Times*, Nov. 7, 1998, p. B1.
[13]Editorial, "Bill Clinton and the ADA," *Wall Street Journal*, May 20, 1994.

No way, said he, and sued in federal court. His employer had been told that he had, among other things, "organic mental syndrome, not otherwise specified." The trial court threw out his suit, since his business activities clearly demonstrated that he did not have an impairment that substantially limited one or more of his life activities. But a higher court reversed this ruling. The employer might have *thought* he had such an impairment; he must have his day in court.[14]

Complaints of discrimination on the basis of emotional or psychiatric impairment are soaring. The EEOC recorded 91 in 1992, but in 1997 there were 2,789.[15] Employers have found that it is not a very good idea to try to help employees who show signs of such problems by referring them for counseling or treatment, because if they do, an employee who would have been out of luck with a discrimination lawsuit because his problems did not rise to the level of a disability will now be able to argue that the referral proves that he was *regarded* as having a disability and thus has the green light.

All in all, to say the least, it is far from obvious that the new regime is an improvement on the former practice of allowing the employers who are directly involved to cope with employees' strengths and weaknesses, great and small, perceived and unperceived, according to their best judgment, with the marketplace and the "bottom line" as judge and jury.

DEFECTS OF CHARACTER, RESPONSIBILITY, AND SELF-CONTROL
It would be bad enough if the only defects that had to be accommodated were those it was beyond the power of the individual to correct. But so mindless is the lunatic egalitarian ideology – and, perhaps in part, so cynical the legal profession in promoting litigation – that lack of self-control, obnoxiousness, and insufferability can give someone the basis for demanding special consideration and bringing a lawsuit. Contemptibility can amount to a protected disability.

What transforms impossible and outrageous conduct into a protected disability? If someone walks like a jerk, talks like a jerk, and acts like a jerk, as in the case of the supermarket manager, why should his employer not simply be able to treat him like a jerk? There are fancy names for all sorts of obnoxious and insufferable behavior patterns, providing a ratio-

---

[14]*Holihan v. Lucky Stores, Inc.*, 87 F.3d 362 (9th Cir. 1996).
[15]Geanne Rosenberg, *Ibid.*

nale for claiming they are "mental impairments" covered by ADA. The Diagnostic and Statistical Manual of Mental Disorders published by the American Psychiatric Association lists, for example, "narcissistic personality disorder," "anti-social personality disorder" and "oppositional defiant disorder." Manifestations of the last-mentioned are "negativistic, defiant, disobedient and hostile behavior toward authority figures." Among its diagnostic criteria are "often deliberately annoys people" and "spiteful and vindictive."[16] Not only the unfit but also the character-deficient and the out-and-out despicable have been endowed with special legal rights.

This is not a fanciful or alarmist interpretation. No less an authority than the Equal Employment Opportunity Commission has weighed in with a stern pronouncement that employers must take "reasonable steps" to "accommodate employees with psychiatric or emotional problems." New guidelines "say employers should be alert to the possibility that traits normally regarded as undesirable – chronic lateness, poor judgment, hostility to co-workers or supervisors – 'may be linked to mental impairments.' "[17] Indeed, claims of discrimination based on emotional or psychological impairment are rising rapidly.[18] Lunatic egalitarianism sees its mission as raising up the impaired at the expense of the rest of society, whether the deficiencies are of qualifications or experience, physical strength, mental strength, emotional stability, character, or decency.

(This lunacy is not restricted to the workplace. In schools, out-of-control brats urgently in need of discipline are now considered to be suffering from "attention deficit disorder." Fully 13% of public school children are considered "disabled." And Congress in its wisdom passed the Disabilities in Education Act in 1995, forbidding any disciplining of these young darlings beyond sending them home a maximum of 10 days per school year.[19] A California boy sold cigarettes on campus, swore at his teacher, and threatened to kill classmates; a federal appeals court

---

[16]George Will, "How You Can Be An Obnoxious Jerk and More," *San Francisco Chronicle*, April 4, 1996, p. A19.

[17]"Mental Disabilities Have to Be Accommodated, Employers Told," *San Francisco Chronicle*, April 30, 1997, p. A9.

[18]"Filing a discrimination suit?" *Wall Street Journal*, Jan. 5, 1999, p. 1.

[19]June Kronholz, "Educators Say Proposed Law Boosting Ability To Punish Disabled Kids Doesn't Go Far Enough," *Wall Street Journal*, May 14, 1997, p. A24.

ordered the school district to pay $20,000 a year for a private tutor for the young terror suffering from "attention deficit disorder."[20])

The reader may have a feeling of *deja vu*. Indeed, the natural response to unsatisfactory conduct that here is called "discrimination against those with disabilities" is often called "racism" when the conduct is that of minority-group members, as noted in an earlier chapter.

There is, of course, a hierarchy in these matters. It can safely be assumed that accommodation to "racial hostility syndrome" and "sexual offensiveness syndrome," manifested respectively by racial slurs directed at minority-group members and by obscene and suggestive remarks and gestures toward women, will not be required of employers. Hitler gets no sympathy as a sufferer from "ethnic-obsessive personality disorder," nor industrial polluters as victims of "profit-preoccupation syndrome."

A 400-pound man claimed that his weight was the reason he was terminated from his job with an auto parts store chain (which the company denied), and further that his obesity was genetic in origin and thus covered by the ADA. An Alameda County, Calif. jury awarded him $1 million.[21] Does obesity even need to be "genetic" to be covered? Maybe not. The Equal Employment Opportunity Commission, in the Clinton Administration vigilant on behalf of the victims of America, argued that it did not in a Rhode Island case in which a 300-pound woman sought damages because she was not hired as an attendant at a state school for the feeble-minded, and a federal appeals court upheld a jury's award of $100,000 to the woman. This was only fair, the court reasoned, because other conditions stemming from voluntary conduct, such as alcoholism, are covered under federal disability laws.[22]

In Tennessee, a 5'4", 360-pound woman sued a theatre chain because she could not fit in the theatre seats.[23] (The Act applies to public accommodations as well as to employment.)

A Florida district appeals judge was caught shoplifting and was removed from the bench; he claimed that he was depressed because his

---

[20] "Free Education for 'Anti-Social' Boy," *San Francisco Chronicle*, July 25, 1995.

[21] Michael Liedtke, "$1 million awarded in obesity bias case," *Contra Costa Times*, Sept. 7, 1995.

[22] Wade Lambert, "U.S. Court Ruling Bars Hiring Bias Against the Obese," *Wall Street Journal*, Nov. 23, 1993.

[23] Joe Edwards, "Obese woman sues theaters for bigger seats," *Contra Costa Times*, Feb. 25, 1994.

215

daughter had failed to be admitted to law school and his son was getting poor grades in school and that his depression was a disability under ADA.

A former Northwestern University professor was fired after he pleaded guilty to collecting his mother's Social Security checks for five years after she died. He sued, saying he suffered from "severe depression and procrastination behavior."[24]

A guidance counselor at a Connecticut high school lost his job after being arrested for cocaine possession; he argued that he was the victim of illegal discrimination since his cocaine addiction was a disability.

After the Valdez disaster, Exxon Corp. adopted a policy of excluding employees with histories of drug or alcohol problems from safety-sensitive jobs. Not so fast! The ever-vigilant EEOC sued the company for violating the ADA. And a Coca-Cola Co. executive, dismissed after he allegedly made threatening remarks at a party and engaged in dangerous behavior, was awarded over $7 million by a Dallas jury on the grounds that the company had failed to make reasonable accommodation for his alcoholism.[25]

For those with defects of character or attitude as well as those with defects of mind or body, then, ADA has created essentially the same sort of lawsuit racket as laws against sex and race discrimination. The number of ADA-related complaints to the EEOC has grown rapidly from year to year; in 1994, for example, 18,859 were filed, up 23.5% from the previous year. According to Michael Casey, a lawyer specializing in defending employers from such suits, only 2-4 out of hundreds are legitimate. Yet the cost of defense is such – $50,000 to $75,000 a case – that most employers settle them. "Legalized extortion" is Mr. Casey's term for this activity.[26]

The lawsuit racket is of course only one of the costs of this absurd law. Another and very major one is represented by the diminished ability of employers to hire the best-qualified people and set appropriate standards for performance and conduct. It would be bad enough if this came into play only with respect to disabilities beyond people's control, but, as was made clear above, the problem goes much further.

---

[24]Edward Felsenthal, "Disabilities Act Is Being Invoked In Diverse Cases," *Wall Street Journal*, March 31, 1993, p. B1.

[25]Robert Frank and Alex Markels, "Coca-Cola Loses ADA Alcoholism Case," *Wall Street Journal*, July 3, 1995, p. B3.

[26]"Disability Act Is a Failure," *Human Events*, April 28, 1995, p. 4.

At least applying the term "disabled" to obnoxious employees is not likely to produce the misery that resulted some years back when it was decided to use housing designed for the elderly to house "disabled people" as well. Since these turned out to be, under the bureaucrats' expansive definition, "younger disabled people, most of them mentally ill or drug or alcohol abusers," the old people were soon cowering behind the locked doors of their apartments as their new "disabled" neighbors would "panhandle, litter, have loud late-night parties and . . . urinate in the elevator or appear naked in the hallways."[27]

Is all the workplace turmoil and cost actually helping avert genuine discrimination against the disabled? According to a study by Vocational Econometrics Inc., based on census data, employment of the disabled actually *fell* between 1992 and 1993 by 3%.[28] A more extensive study, based on six years' experience, was conducted by the highly respected National Bureau of Economic Research and released in late 1998. It showed that before the ADA took effect in 1992, disabled workers received wages an average of 40% less than the non-disabled and that after six years the difference was still 40%, but that employment rates for all groups of the disabled except women 40 and over *had fallen sharply,* "a clear break from past trends."

"The reason: The law increased the cost of hiring disabled workers, including exposing employers who hire them to litigation."[29]

The study suggests that the idea of bigotry against the handicapped was always a myth; that employers were perfectly willing, all along, to hire the disabled at appropriate wages (and make *truly* reasonable accommodations as needed: indeed, might not a candidate wanting a job have been happy to pay for them himself?) but are not eager to bring on board people specially empowered to cause trouble and sue them.

One can certainly see why employers might be considerably more reluctant to give someone who seems to have a disability a chance under today's laws. And they dare not even ask such an applicant questions whose answers might reassure them as to his ability to do the job. Once again, government meddling has done more harm than good.

---

[27]Tamar Levin, "Frightening New Era In Public Housing," *San Francisco Chronicle*, Aug. 16, 1992.

[28] "Disability Act Is a Failure," *Human Events*, April 28, 1995, p. 4.

[29]Carolyn Lochhead, "How Law to Help Disabled Now Works Against Them," *San Francisco Chronicle*, Jan. 3, 1999.

CHAPTER XI

HOMOSEXUALS

It should be obvious by now that anti-discrimination legislation, in the real world, has the practical effect of bringing about preferential treatment for the groups it covers, and that it also brings in its train a growing discrimination lawsuit industry which industriously shifts wealth from business firms, and ultimately the public as a whole, to ad hoc partnerships, or joint ventures, of lawyers and complainers. The number of federal lawsuits alleging race, sex, disability or age discrimination more than doubled between 1992 and 1996, from 10,771 to 23,000.[1]

It should therefore also be obvious that if discrimination "based on sexual orientation" – which as a practical matter means discrimination against active homosexuals – were prohibited, as has been proposed by the Clinton Administration and recently less than overwhelmingly rejected by Congress (and it has recently been proposed again), results would similarly go far, far beyond prohibiting real discrimination.

Those who seek such legislation can be presumed to be well aware of that fact. If it were to be illegal to discriminate against homosexuals in employment, only the most naive can fail to foresee constant complaints of discrimination, effective preferential treatment for homosexuals in employment, and proliferating litigation. Indeed, when it looked as though California's governor was going to sign such legislation, the "co-chair" of the San Francisco Bar Association's Committee on Gay and Lesbian Issues looked forward optimistically to "affirmative action": to "remedies that make up for past discrimination." (Minority leaders, he felt, were

---

[1] "Job Bias Cases Flooding Courts," San Francisco Chronicle, May 12, 1997.

219

less than enthusiastic about such legislation for fear that homosexuals would become "serious competitors for affirmative action.")[2] In localities where discrimination based on sexual orientation has been made illegal, the predictable results in terms of lawsuits have occurred. Dissatisfied with his performance, the board of trustees of San Francisco's opera house fired an executive; according to the board's chairman, only when he sued, claiming he had been fired because he was a homosexual, did the board members realize that he was one.

Based on what has been held to constitute sex discrimination in the form of a "hostile work environment," including nudes on workers' calendars in the case of women employees and jokes about race in the case of minority-group members, it can safely be assumed that in no time any expressed disapproval of homosexuality or homosexual practices, or looking askance at the mannerisms of a flamboyantly homosexual fellow-employee, would constitute the basis for a big-bucks discrimination lawsuit against the employer: and just as employers now are desperately censoring their employees' speech and conduct and policing their workplaces to prevent the existence of anything women might take offense at, or claim they took offense at, they would be vigilantly suppressing anything indicative of less than wholehearted approval of homosexuality. And every homosexual who was dissatisfied with his career progress would be tempted to file a suit charging discrimination.

In a sex-discrimination case that reached the U.S. Supreme Court, a woman sued Price Waterhouse because she had not been made a partner. All the evidence, from her supporters as well as her opponents, was to the effect that she tended to be aggressive to the point of abrasiveness and that sometimes she was unduly harsh and difficult to work with: certainly an understandable reason for her non-promotion. The case arose before the Americans With Disabilities Act was passed, so she could not sue on the basis of a "disability" such as "abrasive personality disorder." But she had evidence of sex discrimination: a partner had advised her to "dress more femininely, wear makeup, have her hair styled, and wear jewelry." This was "sex stereotyping."[3] It is not hard to see what would happen if the employer of a homosexual employee made suggestions about his lavender shirts or her crew cut.

---

[2]*San Francisco Chronicle*, June 1991.
[3]*Price Waterhouse v. Hopkins*, 490 U.S. 228 (1989).

There is wide variation among characteristics said to occasion dis-crimination in terms of whether they are voluntary, whether they are relevant to job qualifications, and whether they reflect on a person's character or psychological health.

Race is entirely involuntary, totally irrelevant to job qualifications,[4] and in no way reflects on character or psychological health.

The same is true of sex, except that within certain ages the potential for pregnancy and what it entails is absent in all males and present in nearly all females.

Age is also involuntary and has no character or psychological-health connotations. As such it is irrelevant to ability to do a job, but it is relevant to length of availability for work. This is most obviously true where there is a mandatory retirement age. Otherwise, this comes into play only where many years are involved. A robust septuagenarian deter-mined to reject inducements to retirement can have more likely years of service ahead of him than a 50-year old with a bad heart. But thirty years of potential effective service are as a practical matter not in the cards for a person of 75.

Disability by definition affects qualification: although a disability may not be relevant to a particular job, it does affect versatility and limit the employer's staffing flexibility. Some disabilities, e.g., being blind from birth, are totally involuntary and do not reflect on the individual at all; some, such as being crippled from falling while drunk, reflect at least on his past; others, such as being obese or given to abusive conduct, on him here and now.

What about homosexuality?

The waters are sometimes muddied by talk about "sexual orientation," as though the basis for discrimination in this area was something as inherent, beyond the individual's control, and morally neutral as skin color. This is not really quite the way it is. When homosexuals encounter discrimination it is not because of inclinations known only to themselves and not acted upon but because one way or another it seems clear that they are acting upon such an orientation. There is a passage in the Bible to the effect that someone who looks on a woman to lust after her has already committed adultery with her in his heart – Jimmy Carter was much laughed at for his confession along this line – but in normal usage

---

[4]Except in rare cases such as undercover work; a white would have trouble passing as an "inner-city" drug dealer.

it is understood that there needs to be action before we think of someone as an adulterer.

How would anyone know that someone was sexually attracted to members of the same sex? If he has chosen to abstain from acting on that attraction, whether because he believes it would be morally wrong or out of concern for his career or marriage, he is hardly likely to broadcast his secret attraction.

And why would anyone want to discriminate against him? Rejecting temptation for religious or moral reasons indicates admirable character. I would be more inclined to discriminate in favor of than against such a person.

It is far from clear that even the orientation is beyond the power of the will. An article in the *Wall Street Journal* by four psychiatrists and clinicians described the success of many therapists in reorienting men experiencing unwanted homosexual desires.[5] It prompted letters to the editor from former homosexuals who had redirected themselves. One wrote, "I . . . found far greater joy in marriage and fatherhood than . . . in years of a fruitless search to meet my needs in other ways."[6] Still, it certainly seems clear that having homosexual desires in the first place is generally no more voluntary than being a member of a particular race.

But that really doesn't matter, because it is voluntary actions rather than inclinations that are the basis of disapproval of what typically is called simply "homosexuality." People are accused of "discriminating against" those who engage in conduct which is generally regarded as morally objectionable and also suggestive of other deficiencies.

Outlawing such discrimination would go beyond making being difficult and disagreeable a protected "disability," idiotic enough though that is. Obnoxiousness, at least, is not considered one of the grave moral evils by any major religion. Nowhere in Dante's *Inferno* are to be found persons damned on the grounds "often deliberately annoys people" or other manifestations of the "oppositional defiant disorder" discussed in the previous chapter. Yet homosexual acts are severely condemned by all the major religions. Laws forbidding discrimination against homosexuals, in effect, would declare that the teachings of Judaism, Christianity and Islam are invalid and are not entitled to respect in this area.

---

[5]Charles Socarides, Benjamin Kaufman, Joseph Nicolosi, Jeffrey Satinover and Richard Fitzgibbons, "Don't Forsake Homosexuals Who Want Help," *Wall Street Journal*, Jan. 9, 1997.
[6]Letter, *Wall Street Journal*, Feb. 4, 1997.

To be sure, offensive behavior in the workplace is unwelcome to all, not just to some, and it is by definition *in the workplace* and not something done elsewhere, so it is arguably not as much of an imposition to require people to hire and work with open homosexuals as to require them to hire and work with jerks.

And yet in another way it would go much further, to tell Americans that their religious and moral convictions about homosexuality cannot properly have any force or effect in their personnel policies. This would be, you will note, a rather selective rejection. An employer could indulge his religious or moral beliefs or his sense of right and wrong by refusing to hire those who cheat at cards or on their spouses, those guilty of drunken brawling, wife-beaters, etc.; but the state is, in effect, to pronounce its authoritative determination that religious teachings against homosexuality are false and deserving of no weight. This would seem rather much for a state, or the federal government, to take upon itself.

Americans are far from agreed that active homosexuality is as neutral and irreproachable a thing as having a dark skin or being a female. The 1993 General Social Survey by the National Opinion Research Center at the University of Chicago found that 71% of those questioned believed homosexual sex was "always wrong," up from 67% in 1977, and that only 40% felt it should be legal.[7] Is it really appropriate for government to forbid treating homosexuality as a negative factor in employment decisions in the first place, let alone guarantee homosexuals the preferential treatment and lawsuit opportunities that anti-discrimination laws create?

According to Karlyn Bowman of the American Enterprise Institute, polls show that 80% of Americans oppose workplace discrimination against homosexuals.[8] Certainly, except in unusual cases, being an active homosexual, as such, is as irrelevant to job qualification as skin color. Hardly any employers would list "irreproachable personal life pursuant to traditional sexual morality" as a job requirement or concern themselves with their employees' sex lives. And only at the highest corporate levels, where the company's head represents it to the public, shareholders, employees, and government, and might be expected to participate with top execu-

---

[7]"Public Opinion Of Homosexuals Stays Negative," *San Francisco Chronicle*, Feb. 16, 1993, p. A5.
[8]Roger Clegg, "The Enda Big Government?" *The Weekly Standard*, Sept. 22, 1997, p. 16.

tives and their spouses at social events, would homosexuality be a negative qualification.

The situation is different in sensitive areas. The Boy Scouts are an example of one. Because of basic common sense and the principle of erring on the side of caution, parents are no more inclined to have their teenage sons led on camping trips by male homosexuals than their teenage daughters by heterosexual bachelors. There is also the matter of role models. For an open homosexual to be a Scoutmaster or to occupy other positions which may be taken as indicating that the person holding them is worthy of emulation and of irreproachable character and morals is objectionable to those who do not consider active homosexuals in that category.

A 1994 University of Maryland study found that male homosexuals earned 11-17% less than heterosexual men of similar age, occupation, marital status and residence and that the corresponding difference for lesbians was 5-14%.[9] This may or may not be due to discrimination on account of their homosexuality.

On the other hand, there is a strong counterbalance to such employment discrimination as exists in the form of preferential treatment at present voluntarily accorded homosexuals in a variety of ways.

This is particularly noticeable in the case of AIDS, which in the vast majority of cases in this country is spread by homosexual activity. In terms of publicity, funding, priorities as to public health measures, and approved public attitudes, this disease has been placed in a class by itself, on a different plane entirely from ordinary diseases that afflict Americans in general.

From publicity in the media, one might think AIDS was virtually the only disease in town, cutting a devastating swath across the country. But, in a recent year, heart disease killed 750,000 Americans and AIDS only 34,000. Yet federal spending on AIDS is about equal to that on all other diseases combined – it went over $2.5 billion in 1993, vs. $743,000 for heart diseases[10] – helping fund a multi-billion-dollar AIDS industry.

State laws typically require notification of the sex partners of those diagnosed with traditional sexually-transmitted diseases, such as syphilis. But in the case of people with AIDS, their interest in privacy trumps

---

[9]"The 'Gay Elite' is a myth," *Wall Street Journal*, Aug. 16, 1994, p. 1.
[10]Carolyn Lochhead, "House OKs $2.5 Billion To Fight AIDS," *San Francisco Chronicle*, Oct. 8, 1993, p. 1.

others' right to their health: mandated confidentiality, rather than notification of those put at risk, is usual. Similarly, the fact that a doctor or dentist had AIDS was long deemed not something the patient had a right to know. Thus the well-known case of the unfortunate Florida woman who contracted a fatal case of AIDS from her dentist. His condition was kept confidential by Florida law, and he continued to practice after learning of his condition.

In this Scare of the Week era, Americans are generally encouraged to go into hysterics about the most remote and far-fetched potential threat to health. Electromagnetic fields from kitchen appliances or power lines; microscopic residues of pesticides on vegetables and fruits (remember the Alar scare?); "second-hand smoke" in the air; lead paint on the walls; asbestos in the ceiling. People fled their homes in a development near San Francisco because some old auto batteries had been buried in the ground. Even the potential threat posed by the lead in lead crystal receives serious attention. Health threats, even remote and implausible, are a serious matter. No one scoffs or ridicules the fearful as "chemophobes."

But, you're afraid you might get AIDS from a homosexual waiter, or fellow-worker? Are you some kind of homophobic nut? In 1993 a federal judge ordered California prison officials to place HIV-infected inmates in food service jobs or be guilty of discrimination against the disabled[11] (he was subsequently overruled by a higher court.)[12]

Consider the dramatic difference in status between cigarette smokers with lung cancer and homosexuals with AIDS. To be sure, there is some effort, spearheaded by the lawsuit industry, to make smokers into innocent victims of powerful tobacco-industry advertising, but basically the unfortunates with lung cancer are regarded as people who gambled with their health and lost.

Not so with those with AIDS. They are the focus of a barrage of sympathetic publicity and an unending series of gala and other fund-raising events; theirs is a cause embraced by an array of prominent people with a wholeheartedness and fervor that would be appropriate in the case of dying war heroes (*dulce et decorum est pro perversione mori?*) or missionary

---

[11]"Ban on Food Jobs For Inmates With HIV Ruled Discrimination," *San Francisco Chronicle*, May 7, 1993.

[12]Barbara Ertegun, "Inmates With AIDS Told Not To Serve Food," *San Francisco Chronicle*, Nov. 8, 1994.

priests whose selfless work with lepers had afflicted them with a dread disease. Recently there was a nearly full-page ad in a San Francisco paper promoting the latest "AIDS WALK." Can you conceive of a LUNG CANCER WALK, "to raise money to fight lung cancer and support the people with lung cancer," benefitting "the following lung cancer service organizations": Lung Cancer Emergency Fund, Asian Pacific Lung Cancer Coalition, Mobilization Against Lung Cancer, San Francisco Black Coalition on Lung Cancer, American Indian Lung Cancer Institute, and Instituto Familiar de la Raza-Latino Lung Cancer Project, with a high percentage of those actively involved in the organizations being cigarette smokers?

Why are people with AIDS so much more deserving of sympathy than people with lung cancer? We know that if you are worried about getting lung cancer, you ought not to smoke cigarettes; but it is equally obvious how you can virtually eliminate your risk of getting AIDS. Certainly, the sex drive is powerful, but nicotine is notoriously addictive.

The current canonization of homosexuals is perhaps even more striking, and the relatively recent rejection of Judeo-Christian moral teachings particularly demonstrated, by contrasting the current treatment of AIDS with that of another sexually-transmitted disease, syphilis, in the days when there was no known cure.

Before penicillin, syphilis too was a deadly disease, also frequently striking those in the prime of life and killing them unpleasantly. Lord Randolph Churchill, according to the 1967 Encyclopaedia Brittanica, "suffered from a crippling disease which killed him by inches," and Donizetti, creator of such beautiful music, experienced "melancholia, presaging the final stages of general paralysis" and "degeneration into helpless insanity."

Significantly, the encyclopaedia didn't even mention the disease's name. It was too shameful. Recall that classic example of invective and repartee attributed to two members of a long-ago Parliament: "I am convinced that my opponent will die either on the gallows or of a loathsome disease." "That will depend, my Lord, on whether I embrace my opponent's principles or his mistresses." Syphilis was shameful because everyone knew it almost always was transmitted by illicit sexual relations: and just garden-variety heterosexual philandering or fornicating, not by committing what have long been considered particularly objectionable "unnatural acts" or "the crime against nature."

Can anyone imagine a "syphilis march" in the 20s or 30s, prominently including prostitutes and their customers, with thousands of enthusiastic sympathizers, demanding finding a cure as a top national priority? Al Capone becoming a virtual national hero for announcing that he had it? "Syphilis vigils" with candles? A lovingly-made "Syphilis Quilt" taken around the country to be reverently displayed like the Shroud of Turin or some other holy relic?

The special treatment of AIDS and of people with AIDS reflects the strong sympathy of America's media and intellectual community for homosexuals – a sympathy which can also be discerned in the almost unfailingly favorable portrayal of homosexuals on television. The fundamental reason for this sympathetic, almost adulatory, attitude on the part of the discussion-shaping class is simply that most Americans – along with their religions – look askance at homosexuality. To those alienated from the American mainstream, the fact that the mainstream looks askance at homosexuals is a badge of honor for the homosexuals and one more manifestation of the mainstream's impossibly ignorant, bigoted condition. Wholehearted support for homosexual causes is thus as mandatory as was support for the civil-rights movement in the 1960s.

Most Americans, however, do not share the intellectual and media community's reverent attitude toward homosexuals. One reason is that they have some respect for their religions' teachings on the subject.

RELIGIOUS TEACHINGS

The great majority of Americans are Christians and many are Jews, and in the Judeo-Christian tradition, going back to the Old Testament, homosexual acts have been considered morally objectionable, to put it mildly. "Thou shalt not lie with mankind, as with womankind; it is abomination" (Leviticus XVIII: 22). "If a man lie with mankind, as he lieth with a woman, both of them have committed an abomination; they shall surely be put to death; their blood shall be upon them" (Leviticus XX: 13)."[13]

St. Paul had a similar view, writing, in his Epistle to the Romans, "And likewise the men, leaving the natural use of the woman, burned in their lust one toward another; men with men working that which is unseemly, and receiving in themselves that recompense of their error which was meet (I:27)."

---

[13]King James version.

This is pretty unambiguous. Is there some reason it should not be taken seriously by those who believe the Bible expresses God's view of the matter? Have times changed in some significant and relevant way?

Religious leaders differ as to the extent to which Biblical injunctions ought to be considered "inoperative" because of changed conditions. Orthodox Jews continue to avoid pork and shellfish despite modern developments in refrigeration and understanding of how to avoid trichinosis. Reform Jews take a different view.

But so far as I know no religion has adopted the position that because of penicillin, modern contraceptives, and modern knowledge of human sexuality, adultery is no longer morally objectionable. For that matter, syphilis didn't come to the Old World until Columbus' men brought it back.

And as far as homosexual activity is concerned, there was no AIDS in ancient Israel. So "changed conditions" since Biblical times would seem, if anything, to reinforce, rather than invalidate, its prohibition.

Furthermore, religious leaders, including those of the largest Christian body, Catholicism, continue to take the position that is clear in their scriptures, that homosexual acts are morally wrong. (The Catholic Church has been at pains to make the point that merely having homosexual desires, while constituting a disorder, is not a sin, whereas acting upon them is.) There are certainly those in the Protestant clergy whose personal insight, or whose *real* religion, readily trumps the scriptures of their nominal religion. The Episcopal bishop of Newark, New Jersey, dismissed St. Paul's injunctions against homosexuality as no doubt the words of a "repressed homosexual." But they do not represent the Christian mainstream. Indeed, at its 1998 Lambeth Conference, the bishops of the Anglican Communion, of which the American Episcopal Church is a part, voted 526-70 that homosexual acts were incompatible with Scripture.

While there are relatively few Mohammedans or Hindus in the United States, it may also be observed that both these major world religions condemn homosexual acts. In Hindu India, "any carnal intercourse against the order of nature" is punishable by ten years' imprisonment, often under rigorous conditions.[14]

---

[14]"Gays Demand Repeal of Harsh Indian Law," *San Francisco Chronicle*, Jan. 1, 1995, p. A10.

OTHER PROBLEMS WITH HOMOSEXUALITY

Religious convictions are not the only reason for a negative view of homosexuality. To be sure, to judge from television, homosexuals are almost without exception the salt of the earth: well-adjusted, honorable, responsible, often wise, witty and talented individuals. But the reality as to homosexuals in general is not quite the same.

For example, in 1991, the results of a study commissioned by the Lesbian and Gay Substance Abuse Planning Group and financed by the city of San Francisco were reported in the local press. According to it, one-third of homosexual men in the area who were infected with the AIDS virus reported having had "unsafe sex" during the past year "while drunk or high." The study also found that 31% of *all* male homosexuals surveyed reported using drugs and alcohol "at levels deemed to be dangerous or addictive." For lesbians, the figure was 18%.[15]

As the *Chronicle* article noted, one would think unnecessarily, 31% was a "much higher rate" and 18% "substantially higher" than that of the general population. Homosexual sympathizers have attributed these drug and alcohol problems to the stresses that go with being homosexual, but this seems unconvincing in the case of San Francisco, the national homosexual capital. On the other hand, in fairness, perhaps the homosexuals attracted to that mecca are unrepresentative of homosexuals as a whole. Still, the extent of the problem is not suggestive of a high level of psychological health.

Nor is the incidence of "unsafe sex" so long after AIDS became widely recognized. A 1996 study presented to an international conference on AIDS in Vancouver, British Columbia, indicated that "40 percent of young gay men admit to having had unprotected anal intercourse within the past six months."[16] A 1994 study in San Francisco had shown a figure of one-third – "often with men they had met in bars, dance clubs, parks and on the streets."[17]

Other aspects of the "gay lifestyle" typically go uncriticized, apparently on the principle that homosexuals are *sui generis* and normal stan-

---

[15]"High Rate of Lesbian, Gay Drug Abuse," *San Francisco Chronicle*, Oct. 30, 1991, p. A18. All such statistics presumably relate to active homosexuals.

[16]Laurie Garrett, "More young gay men are engaging in unsafe sex," *Contra Costa Times*, Oct., 1996, p. 1.

[17]David Perlman, "Unsafe Sex Common Among Bay Area Gays," *San Francisco Chronicle*, Aug. 8, 1994.

dards and judgment must be suspended in their case. Why this should be so is not clear, if homosexuals are normal people like everybody else except that they are attracted to the same rather than the opposite sex.

With respect to humans in general, psychiatrists say that stable, mutually-respecting long-term relationships are a sign of emotional health and maturity. Homosexuals of course cannot get legally married, but, in this era of the "significant other," such relationships, without benefit of clergy, are common among heterosexuals. A heterosexual man whose sex life consisted of a long series of one-night stands, many with prostitutes, would probably be considered to be suffering from arrested development or to be lacking in maturity and the ability to relate constructively to others at an adult level. Yet studies indicate that hundreds of sex partners are typical in the case of homosexuals. "Need someone new? So do our 3,300 other weekly callers," reads an advertisement for "Sexconnect" in a San Francisco homosexual newspaper.

Other practices relatively common among homosexuals would also be unlikely to be considered indicative of good emotional health if practiced by heterosexuals. Do many heterosexuals enjoy urinating on each other, or being urinated on? Yet "golden showers," "water sports," is a popular homosexual activity. Sadism and masochism are also big in the "gay" community. At a 1997 birthday party for a homosexual political consultant attended by 500 guests, including many of San Francisco's political leaders, the high point of the entertainment on stage occurred when a man had a Satanic symbol carved into his back and was then urinated on and sodomized with a bottle of Jack Daniels.[18]

There would seem to be a link between this popularity of sadism and masochism and the violence rather noticeable among homosexuals. Because of the media's sympathy for this supposedly oppressed group, careful reading of stories is necessary to discern what they are really saying. "Anti-Gay Killings Are Grislier, Study Finds" at first glance suggested one more example of the oppression of these poor people. "A study released . . . by a San Francisco human rights group says the majority of anti-gay slayings involve a higher degree of violence than most homicides and a frightening number are the result of serial killers."

---

[18]Phil Matier and Andy Ross, "Jack Davis Offers To Quit In Party Flap," *San Francisco Chronicle,* May 7, 1997, p. 1.

Ah, but it turns out that "in more than three-quarters of the cases, the victim picked up or was picked up by the killer in a park, gay bar or similar setting." In other words, the unusual violence is basically that of homosexuals killing each other. The "human rights group"'s executive director admits that this is true in "many" cases, but insists that nevertheless "such crimes can still be considered acts of anti-gay bias," because they are caused by "internalized self-hatred" brought on by uncertainty over the perpetrator's own sexuality.[19] This is worthy of a Jimmy Carter federal judge.

A common feature, at least of San Francisco's homosexual world, was the sex club or "bathhouse." Men went there and engaged in sex with strangers. (They were subsequently closed by the health authorities, but in 1999 an effort to reopen them began.) A *San Francisco Examiner* reporter described a visit. Prominent were "glory holes," holes in the wall at, well, waist height. The ultimate in anonymous sex. If there are any equivalent establishments in the heterosexual world, where men and women have intercourse through holes in the wall, I at least, in my sheltered life, have not heard of them. Would not any heterosexual who engaged in such conduct be regarded as sick? This sort of thing makes the traditional homosexual encounter in a public rest room, itself repugnant enough by normal standards, seem almost romantic by comparison.

If these things were aberrations, far out of the mainstream of homosexual life, one would expect to find responsible members of the homosexual community denouncing them and protesting that they are totally unrepresentative of their community. One is reminded of Sherlock Holmes' famous "curious incident of the dog in the night-time."[20]

In fact, homosexuality was on the American Psychiatric Association's list of disorders (in its Diagnostic and Statistical Manual II) until 1973, and it is not easy to present a convincing case to the effect that its removal was due primarily to new scientific discoveries and insights rather than to a determined campaign by homosexuals and their sympathizers.[21]

Now of course even if lack of emotional health is relatively common among homosexuals, that doesn't mean that it affects a given individual,

---

[19]Ken Hoover, *San Francisco Chronicle*, Dec. 20, 1994.

[20]But "the dog did nothing in the night-time," Inspector Lestrade responded in *Silver Blaze*. That, replied Holmes, was the curious incident.

[21]See Charles W. Socarides, M.D., *A Freedom Too Far*, Adam Margrave Books, 1995, pp. 157 ff.

which is why homosexuality – active homosexuality – as such is generally irrelevant to a person's qualification. But these indications do make reluctance to validate the homosexual way of life for reasons other than religious ones understandable.

In summary, the case of homosexuals, unlike the other groups discussed, involves both conduct and a distinct religious and moral dimension. While in this area discrimination is far from nonexistent, it is not without a substantive basis.

CONCLUSION

It is clear from the preceding chapters that reports of wide-spread mistreatment of Americans on the basis of race, sex, age, and disability are, as Mark Twain said of reports of his death, greatly exaggerated.

In the light of elementary and widely-understood economic principles applicable to profit-seeking enterprises, it would be very surprising if it were common for groups of people to be systematically underpaid and under-utilized because of personal characteristics irrelevant to their qualifications, let alone so common that it made sense to, of all things, give bureaucrats and the courts supervisory authority over workplace fairness in a free-enterprise economy. It's obviously bad for profits either to hire less-qualified people for the same pay or to pay more for the same qualifications. And any problem of this sort ought to be self-correcting, as with any practice that puts a company at a disadvantage relative to its more-efficient competitors.

The same, of course, applies in the case of a company foolish enough to choose its suppliers, its borrowers or other customers, its location, or whatever, on the basis of irrelevant characteristics.

(Governments, funded by taxpayers instead of customers, do not face competition or work on the profit motive, and it has long been recognized that cronyism and favoritism of various types are a particular problem there. Hence statutory requirements for competitive bidding and civil-service examinations; and, hence, discrimination complaints aimed at the *procedures*.)

Only dogged hostility toward the groups involved could explain businesses' insistence on such self-defeating policies, and it would be hard to believe that so many Americans harbor such attitudes, and moreover keep them so well hidden.

It is part of human nature to wonder why things happen. In the absence of scientific knowledge, among primitive peoples today as in ancient times, mysterious forces are often held responsible. It does not rain because the rain god is angry. An epidemic is caused by witches, or their helpers the cats. The baby is sick because someone put a curse on it.

As civilization and human knowledge have progressed, and as understanding of how things work, of the natural forces and natural laws that govern the world and its component parts, has steadily grown, the sphere of supposed malevolent (or benevolent) intervention has shrunk correspondingly. In an advanced society, as the causes of events affecting humans are understood and analyzed, it is typically only the ignorant who attribute them to sinister forces.

Still, if there were patterns of differing success from one group to another that couldn't be explained except as the result of malevolent discrimination, one would have no choice but to accept that explanation and its consequences in terms of public policy.

But that is not the case. In every case studied, whether in employment or in areas such as the obtaining of loans or contracts or insurance, innocent and straightforward explanations for differing results among groups were readily apparent upon analysis. Not only that, studies allowing for relevant variables were seen to show no "gaps."

All of which is exactly what one would expect to find, in a rational economic world self-regulated by Adam Smith's "invisible hand." It is hard to see how in the free American economy water should consistently flow uphill, or cream remain helplessly trapped at the bottom rather than rise to the top. There is indeed a great deal to be said for common sense and for accepted wisdom and long-standing understanding based on observation.

Of course people treat each other unfairly for innumerable reasons. Occasional acts of unfairness relating to race or to sex, like occasional acts of unfairness with other origins, are simply a part of life. The solution is to seek a better employment situation, lender, landlord, or whatever. If the businessman is a jerk, his loss is likely to be another businessman's, or a businesswoman's, gain.

The fact that pervasive discrimination against certain groups is a myth, of course, means that it is totally inappropriate to favor one group at the expense of another to "compensate" it for non-existent mistreatment by the other.

It also means that from a practical standpoint as well as from a philosophical standpoint there is no more reason for government and the courts to be second-guessing decisions for possible unfairness related to race, age, sex, or disability than for possible unfairness in general. Unfairness involves lots of individual cases, each with its own facts, and unfairness for reasons other than those addressed by bias laws can be every bit as outrageous as the most egregious race- or sex-discrimination case.

The real problem with the anti-discrimination laws, as real-world laboratory testing of up to 35 years has made clear, is not a logical or a philosophical one, but the practical one of their effect. Individual cases of real discrimination are not dealt with with surgical precision, as if a sharpshooter skillfully brought down a dangerous criminal in a field. It is rather as if a cannon were fired at him in a crowd. He is brought down, all right, but at a tremendous cost to innocent people.

The resulting situation in the workplace, with a more than twenty-fold increase in federal bias actions from 1970 to 1989, is described in devastating detail in Walter Olson's fine 1997 book *The Excuse Factory: How Employment Law is Paralyzing the American Workplace.*[1] Not only is the dollar cost huge, the resulting state of affairs particularly favors the paranoid, the hypersensitive, and the unscrupulous. Whining and accusing others of reprehensible behavior are rewarded, as is willingness to make a mockery or a racket of the law. Results in other business contexts subjected to governmental "anti-discrimination" efforts are similar.

As has been seen, the effect of anti-discrimination laws – and, indeed, for many who understand this, those laws' very purpose – is not so much to protect members of a specified group from discrimination, from being treated less favorably than others because of their status (which nearly everybody already agrees would be wrong and foolish), as to exempt them from the reasonable standards and requirements that apply to others.

Thus their heavy burdens and costs cannot be justified on the principle *fiat justitia, ruat calelum* (let justice be done though the heavens fall); for the *de facto* system of preferences that anti-discrimination laws have brought about means that the very same sort of discrimination sought to be suppressed is visited upon *more* people. They may be people of a different race or sex, but they are still innocent people, equally undeserving of being discriminated against.

---

[1] Free Press; review, Tim W. Ferguson, "The New Shakedown Artists," *Wall Street Journal*, May 20, 1997.

And reverberating far beyond the business world is the effect the obsession with groups and beating the drums about discrimination has on society, in terms of divisiveness, disharmony, Balkanization, and poisoning and embittering those who are continually told that they are victims. Overall, the present situation is a disaster.

The fight against "discrimination" is now largely a lunatic levelling crusade, a political payoff scheme, and a racket. It has created a system of *de facto* preferential treatment or "affirmative action" for members of groups with below-average qualifications in one area or another and a bonus program for the shameless. With relatively little benefit, it has taken away longstanding individual rights, slandered the American people, imposed hundreds of billions of dollars in burdens, unfairly penalized millions of innocent people, and spread inter-group disharmony and ill-will on a massive scale. This is a price that obsessive levellers or money-smelling opportunists may be happy to see the country pay, but not one that it should continue to accept.

It's tempting to try to "have it both ways" – that is, unstack the deck in favor of discrimination lawsuits that result in *de facto* preferences, while still providing a remedy for the deliberate discrimination that practically everybody finds reprehensible. Laws could be passed prohibiting class-action discrimination lawsuits, providing that no inference of discrimination might be drawn from statistics as to group representation in a work force or in positions in it, and requiring that actual purposeful discrimination be demonstrated by a preponderance of the evidence in every case, with no *Griggs* "disparate impact" allowed: a convincing pattern of different treatment of identically-situated persons correlating to their race or sex (or other characteristic involved) would have to be demonstrated.

On the basis of decades of experience, it is highly doubtful that even the most carefully drawn amendments along this line would achieve their desired purpose. Consider the following language:

> Notwithstanding any other provision of this subchapter, it shall
> not be an unlawful employment practice for an employer to
> apply different standards of compensation, or different terms,
> conditions, or privileges of employment pursuant to a bona
> fide seniority or merit system, or a system which measures
> earnings by quantity or quality of production or to employees
> who work in different locations, provided that such differ-

ences are not the result of an intention to discriminate because of race, color, religion, sex, or national origin, nor shall
it be an unlawful employment practice for an employer to give
and to act upon any professionally developed ability test provided that such test, its administration or action upon the
results in not designed, intended or used to discriminate because of race, color, religion, sex or national origin.

That sweeping language, which in fact is part of the Civil Rights Act
of 1964,[2] would seem clearly to rule out any requirement that, say, the
employer prove that any test used accurately measures qualities essential
in a particular job. No matter. An official of the EEOC had an agenda
including making it difficult for employers to use criteria which adversely
affected minority eligibility, the EEOC accordingly promulgated a regulation providing that such a test was permissible only if it "fairly measures the knowledge and skills required by the particular job or class of
jobs," and the Supreme Court, ignoring the clear language of the statute,
stated that the EEOC was "entitled to great deference" and that only
"business necessity" could permit the use of tests that were flunked by a
higher percentage of blacks than whites.[3]

In the light of how judicial activism has transformed government and
society in so many ways since the New Deal days and the amazing ways
in which legal minds have liberated themselves from the plain meaning
of words, having laws on the books forbidding "discrimination," no matter how carefully qualified, is an invitation to – God knows what: it is
like having a loose cannon on deck. Over 20 years after the Civil Rights
Act outlawed sex discrimination, the Supreme Court found that its definition included sexual hanky-panky of which the employer was unaware.[4]
In early 1999, a federal judge found that excluding college athletes with
SAT scores below a certain level from athletic scholarships violated the
section forbidding racial discrimination by educational institutions.

The law against discrimination served as the basis for making a federal
case out of the Los Angeles transit authority's allocation of funds between buses and subways (the argument was that a higher percentage of

---

[2]42 U.S.C. 2000e-2(h).
[3]*Griggs v. Duke Power Co.*, 401 U.S. 424 (1971).
[4]*Meritor Savings Bank v. Vinson*, 477 U.S. 57 (1986).

the bus riders were minority-group members); in May 1999, the Clinton Administration, ludicrously, used it to attack colleges' use of the SAT or "any educational test which has a significant disparate impact on members of any particular race, national origin, or sex" in admissions, unless they could prove that it was "educationally necessary and that a practical alternative to the test doesn't exist."[5]

It is not just a quota economy (see p. 116) that the law is being used to promote, but in fact a quota society. For with average qualifications varying from group to group, any rational selection criteria whatsoever will have a "disparate impact" on those with less ability to meet them. The idea is to impose burdensome and costly requirements of "validation" (akin to the burdens on employers under the *Griggs* decision and the 1991 civil Rights Act) in the hope that quotas will replace qualifications as the basis for selection in one area of American life after another.

(This of course only applies on behalf of anointed victim groups. No crusades are in sight to have the police stop and search more women motorists, or to get more whites and Asians onto professional basketball and football teams.)

Even without an effort to broaden the scope of such laws, they inevitably generate enough how-many-angels-can-dance-on-the-head-of-a-pin legal analysis to boggle the mind. Does equal treatment for men and woman mean that a woman gets the same amount of pregnancy leave as a man? Well, no; that wouldn't make sense; women get pregnant and men don't. Then does it follow that if women are out sick, on average, more than men, this too must be accommodated, even if it means women are then less cost-effective than men? Would it constitute discrimination to pay women less accordingly? If they are paid the same, are men, who are out for medical reasons less, being discriminated against? How much less can a disabled worker be paid because he is less productive before the differential constitutes illegal discrimination? *None* of this should be a matter for bureaucrats and the courts; conditions of employment should be settled among consenting adults in the free market.

The best solution would be to repeal the anti-discrimination laws altogether. As was noted in Chap. VII, this was proposed by Richard A.

---

[5]Amy Docker Marcus, "Standardized Test Guides Could Lead to Lawsuits," *Wall Street Journal*, May 26, 1999, p. A2.

Epstein, James Parker Hall Distinguished Service Professor of Law at the University of Chicago, in his 1992 book, *Forbidden Grounds: The Case Against Employment Discrimination Laws* (Harvard University Press). But for all intents and purposes these laws have long been taken as a given. It is, therefore, quite encouraging that such a sizeable minority as 27% were willing to tell the December, 1997 New York Times/CBS News Poll that they believed laws to protect minorities – the group commonly believed most in need of protection – against employment discrimination were "not necessary."[6]

Returning to a system of free individual choice, with the employer as free from second-guessing as to the propriety of his motives as the actual or potential employee has always been in choosing to accept or reject, or quit, employment as he sees fit, and with comparable freedom in other business decisions, would instantly lift a tremendous burden from the economy. Hundreds of thousands, perhaps millions, of diversity managers, sexual harassment consultants, bureaucrats, and lawyers, etc., would become available for productive work, and business managers would be spared a major distraction and impediment to sound business decisions, including hiring the most suitable people. All this would boost productivity, living standards, profits, and stock prices.

As the renowned economist Walter E. Williams has pointed out, citing a 1997 study, there is, worldwide, a close correlation between economic freedom and both prosperity and growth rates.[7] The attenuation of private property through interference with its owners' freedom to manage it is costly. When it is severe enough, as in Western Europe, the result is stagnation: Germany, whose economy was buoyant not long ago, now has a 10% rate of unemployment and has created virtually no additional private-sector jobs in ten years. We, with much more economic freedom, are, by comparison, enjoying a boom. But that is no reason not to make things better.

And much more than money is involved. With group membership no longer conferring special rights, people would no longer have an incentive to be constantly on the watch for signs of possible group-based mis-

---

[6]Sam Howe Verhovek, "In Poll, Americans Reject Means But Not Ends of Racial Diversity," *New York Times*, Dec. 14, 1997, p. 1.

[7]*More Liberty Means Less Government*, Hoover Institution Press, 1999, p. 173.

treatment. And the law would no longer encourage a national preoccupation with race, sex, disability, and age, a preoccupation which divides rather than unites Americans.

And we would be spared a great deal of the constant whining and accusations about "discrimination" of one sort or another that have become such a prominent feature of the news.

Repeal would of course not affect the prohibition on discrimination by government that derives from the Equal Protection Clause of the Constitution rather than from legislation. But it would return the private sector to where it had been prior to 1964's departure.

And those who felt like giving women or minorities preferential treatment would no longer need to fear the lawsuits that would be encouraged if Title VII remained on the books and the Supreme Court overruled its *Weber* and *Johnson* decisions (see Chap. VII). A member of a minority group who felt kinship with others of his ancestry, whether African or Korean, and wanted to help them get ahead, could freely give them a break in employment. Such favoring of others from the "old country," after all, perfectly legal at the time, helped numerous immigrant groups throughout American history. And any private businesses desirous of using preferences would be assured that there would be no legal obstacle to their doing so.

The American people have been willing to make tremendous sacrifices in the name of what they understand to be right. Americans as a whole thought Prohibition was at least worth trying, as a "noble experiment," although a significant minority knew better. By 1933, when the 18th Amendment was repealed, the national consensus was, not that greater vigor was needed to crush Americans' inclination to drink alcoholic beverages, but that the experiment was doing more harm than good and it was time to put an end to it.

This experiment has also failed. The voters are indicating that they want to put an end to the divisiveness and injustice of open race and sex preferences by government. Recognition of how similar in practical effect antidiscrimination laws are – as well as of their other baleful effects – ought to build support for their repeal. Government control of personnel management or of loan approvals makes no more sense than socialism generally. It is time to stop the meddling and restore self-government and individual rights to the American people.

240

PUBLISHER'S
APPENDIXES

APPENDIX A

NEGROES SEEK RESPECT IN A COLOR-BLIND SOCIETY, NOT PRIVILEGE IN A RACIST SOCIETY

Due to my reputation as a theologically conservative religious leader in the Negro community who is dedicated to church and human rights, I was sent an advance galley of M. Lester O'Shea's book by the publisher and asked to comment upon it. And, I am glad to have this opportunity because I believe O'Shea makes a clear-cut case for the elimination of government control as a "cure" for the many misdiagnosed claims of racism alleged by members of "privileged" classes or groups. He presents a perfectly logical argument as to why the claims of members of these "protected" groups of widespread discrimination are not only false but frivolous allegations supported only by an ill-founded theory of ageism, ethnicism, sexism, ableism and racism.

It is ironic that the proponents of "affirmative action" have chosen to ignore the fact that this very philosophy and the implementation thereof, greatly compromise our long-standing, free-market approach to economics and as a consequence erode one of the very pillars of personal freedom that could aid the Negro in his quest for upward mobility.

Free-market capitalism is based on the idea that the greatest degree of economic, social and political advantage is accorded those who earn them in free competition with others seeking to provide similar goods or services. As a Negro male (or more correctly an "other" since I am the progeny of more than one race, who like O'Shea, have not adopted the transitional nomenclature, e.g. Afro or African American), I am not so troubled by the possibility that affirmative action will discriminate against qualified White males in favor of a member of a "privileged" class, as I am that conclusions, such as those reached in books as *The Bell Curve* and other studies suggesting that the American Negro's intelligence quotient is below that of American Whites and Asians not be addressed. As the writings of the eminent historian, Dr. Thomas Sowell have shown, cognitive ability (IQ), is a result developed over many generations of one's culture, not race. To further examine this statement compare the average IQ of middle-eastern Arabs with the average IQ of their Israeli neighbors, both of which are of the same Semitic race. Or, take a community of scientists such as at Los Alamos, NM and compare the cognitive and motor abilities of their children with children in an average community. You will find that those from the scientific community score much higher on cognitive ability and lower on motor ability than average.

Nobel laureate and geneticist Francis Crick estimated that the amount of information contained in the chromosomes of a single fertilized human egg is equivalent to a thousand printed volumes of the Encyclopedia Britannica. These are the coded instructions which transmit information from parent to child for the development of body and mind. If in a culture survival depends upon motor ability, it is that ability which is most developed and passed along genetically. If survival depends upon cognitive ability it is this ability which becomes most highly developed and passed along. Currently Negroes, due to their ancient culture, excel in motor ability. For Negroes living in a technical society requiring cognitive ability, the improvement of cognitive ability must be a priority. To be given a "handicap" by do-gooders will thwart the effort required to excel in cognitive ability and relegate Negroes to an inferior status.

If protected groups and their advocates believe that discrimination is widespread, they need only address the voluntary segment of society, not government for its remediation. Continued claims of racism, sexism, ageism, etc. fly in the face of our existential reality. However, it is not to the advantage of the various "rights" advocates or segments of these advantaged classes to admit that their claims are spurious or that the former laws were adequate.

If there were no racism, sexism, etc., in order for organizations of the various group rights advocates to continue, they would have to create such situations to continue to raise money. It is an insult to the Negro to imply that Negroes would not be educated or upwardly mobile without being board certified members of a "privileged" group.

There are Negroes in this country who have succeeded in spite of obstacles just as there are Whites. There have been Negroes in every field of endeavor who have distinguished themselves. Long before Colin Powell, there were the father and son, Benjamin Davis, Junior and Senior who were generals in our military services. Charles Drew is hailed as one of the great men of medical science and is so recognized across the globe.

For the Negro to buy into such an insidious idea that race alone impedes us is a cruel hoax, the perpetrators of which, cannot possibly be concerned with the total integration of the Negro into all of American life. Let me suggest, for reasons that become apparent to any rational human being, Negro or White, that inherent in the philosophy that the skin color of the Negro is repugnant to White admissions officers, CEO's, etc. is in itself, racist thinking. One cannot help but ponder whether or not the White liberal establishment and the Negro proponents of affirmative action are not consciously or unconsciously relegating the Negro to a permanent status of inferiority on the American landscape as the last resort in an attempt to advance a political agenda that will destroy the principles, morals, values and ethics subscribed to by the majority of our citizens regardless of skin color, gender, physical or emotional handicaps.

It is telling that in the past, the traditional Negro civil rights organizations have vehemently opposed any assessment of the Negro based on race, that they now embrace affirmative action.

Even a cursory study of the beginning of this particular application of affirmative action (Affirmative Action actually began with legislation in the 1930's to give advantage to another class, namely members of the labor unions) reveals its potential for promoting inter-group conflict and an image of Negro inferiority.

With Lincoln's Emancipation Proclamation, in theory at least, the Negro became an active participant in this republican form of government. Legislation should not regulate personal choice unless that personal choice is extra or illegal. Negroes and other Americans cannot help but be struck by the ill-fatedness of those presently in the vanguard of social planning. Native Americans who are besieged by problems of alcoholism, low self-esteem, etc., have been accorded the "right" to own and operate tax free casinos almost with impunity in order to make restitution for the breaking of treaties by people whose descendants are few if any at this time of our history. It is outrageous to think that American social policy would introduce still another vice to this group in order to remediate their condition. That the liberal establishment is boldly and openly participating in the distortion and destruction of individual freedoms in the name of remediating past and present evils, real or perceived, is somewhat naive. That Negroes and other members of advantaged or privileged classes do not see that this kind of social engineering cannot but result in a degree of racism and classism the likes of which has never been experienced in America before is tragic.

Never before in our history has a perceived notion of oppression resulted in activist judges contributing to the perversion of the constitutionally mandated separation of powers and the loss of personal freedoms. It is most unfortunate that Negroes, women, the handicapped, those with Hispanic surnames, as well as all of the other groups of protected classes, have seemingly failed to recognize that their very participation in affirmative action greatly enhances their potential to fall victim to the whims of social architects.

Again, we are the victims of the insidious social engineering of White liberals and their Negro colleagues. Can there be any doubt in anyone's mind, whether Negro, White, Asian or "other," that few will question why it is that a handicapped person occupies a position for which they are competent or why a competent female attorney is a partner in a Wall Street firm? Neither eyebrows nor questions will be raised, but the Negro sitting in the executive suite or who is the dean of the law school will always be looked upon with suspicion not only by Whites but by fellow Negroes, who will have lingering in the back of their minds the question, "Did this guy make it on his merit or is he a by-product of affirmative action?" While Justice Clarence Thomas has impressive credentials, there will always be those who will question whether or not affirmative action was the vehicle that admitted him to Yale Law School, not to mention General Colin Powell and other outstanding Americans who happen to be Negro. Of course, those of us who are convinced that in order to succeed we must be guided by the same rules of competence as all others harbor no such thoughts; but obviously we represent a small minority who have chosen to bypass membership in the advantaged or privileged class. It is still true that many Negroes welcome the challenge of the free-market and work for achievements that transcend any of the "isms" protected by affirmative action.

The fact that women, the handicapped, aged, and members of other "disadvantaged" groups were afterthoughts of the proponents of affirmative action has not been lost on either Negroes who receive advantage or the White males who are disadvantaged by this vehicle. I have heard of more than a few cases of Negroes who ostensibly were beneficiaries of affirmative action who are now convinced that it serves as a perpetual albatross of inferiority around their necks.

O'Shea's experience as an early enlistee in the civil rights movement, his training as a lawyer and his position as a senior corporate executive places him in a unique situation to render a thorough going analysis of the complexities of affirmative action. The fact the he has undertaken this task at this juncture of his busy life, reflects his very strong conviction that the issue has not disappeared with the defeat of proposition 209 in California and similar legislation in other states. O'Shea convincingly argues that racism, sexism, ageism, ethnism, ableism do not loom as large on the American horizon as liberals and members of the advantaged classes would have us to believe.

That having been stated, I believe that underlying O'Shea's thesis is a far more compelling issue than that of the cure being worse than the disease. The myriad of lawsuits brought by persons on either side of the issue and the volumes of complaints received by governmental civil rights agencies as well as government's passion for filing amicus briefs on behalf of the aggrieved members of protected classes not to mention the rash of agencies whose sole function it is to oversee and enforce affirmative action now referred to as "goals" suggest one idea above all others and that is that as our ethical and moral standards have declined, and we have become more and more obsessed with the idea of race. While many factors have come into play in human history to divide people, the use of race is relatively recent and is probably not as rampant elsewhere as it is in the United States.

The state's obsession with race has only served to obscure the reality that America is being "demonized" by a liberal political agenda which promotes the genocide of unborn infants, child and adult pornography, immorality in media and a pervasive irreverence for our Judeo-Christian heritage.

Considering the conclusions reached by O'Shea, one cannot help but recognize the disingenuous activism of government in its encroachment on personal freedoms; therefore, it is our government's obsession with race that has resulted in this and other ludicrous programs ostensibly intended to redress this "problem."

Every government application form raises the question of race, which in and of itself, is divisive. Racism, by O'Shea's or any other rational account, is certainly not anything that Negroes should be preoccupied with. Our concern must be that of recognizing that affirmative action simply serves as a mechanism for the control and debasement of individual freedoms by the state. The creation of advantaged classes is antithetical to the principles upon which this country was founded. No group should be more convinced of that, and opposed to its premises, than the Negro. Not only is it antithetical to the principles upon which this country was founded, but it demeans long held ideas of human worth and dignity.

Lester O'Shea has developed his thesis with precision. In fact, he has pointed out so many absurdities and inconsistencies in our social policy via affirmative action I am hard put to understand how White liberals and their Negro collaborators can logically continue their support of affirmative action without doing violence and ultimately destroying those institutions which have well served the Negro since reconstruction.

In light of the philosophy of affirmative action, how do White liberals and their Negro cohorts justify soliciting funds to perpetuate Negro colleges under the banner of the United Negro College Fund? How is it possible to continue funding and financing to rebuild Negro communities, establish Negro owned banks and businesses and at the same time participate in affirmative action? Is not the underlying philosophy of supporting culturally and racially restrictive institutions antithetical to the interest of affirmative action? Will there come a time when Negro churches who worship in the context of their own unique theological as well as a cultural milieu, be denied their right to choose leaders in their cultural context and be forced to choose a member of a new advantaged class whatever that class may be?

Since affirmative action is readily available and millions of dollars have been allocated to various agencies to both investigate and enforce its propositions, why is it necessary to have Negro colleges or any other Negro institutions? Certainly if "Big Brother" can impose on institutions that have been largely White, they can invade those that are predominantly Negro.

In conclusion, to accept the concept of the right of government to interfere in the freedom of the marketplace and to compromise the right of private property, is to deny the Declaration of Independence and the principles upon which the United States was founded; the benefits of which were extended to women and Negroes many, many generations ago.

DR. R. THOMAS COLEMAN

Dr. Coleman, the recipient of many awards and honors, studied at Columbia University (New York City), The Urban Theological Education Program (St. John's University and New Brunswick Theological Seminary), The College of New Rochelle (B.A.), Princeton Theological Seminary (M.Div.), and United Theological Seminary (D.Min.).

He has successfully completed a number of continuing education credits at various institutions including Auburn, General and Union Theological Seminaries in New York and Virginia Union University's Dr. Samuel DeWitt Proctor School of Theology.

Dr. Coleman is a founding member of the African American Institute for Racial Harmony and Social Justice.

Appendix B

College Sociology

(Publisher's note): Prior to the beginning of her senior year in high school, Nannette Coleman took a sociology course at Muskegon Community College for extra credit. The paper she wrote for this course, "Affirmative Action" together with her teacher's comments (in italics), follow.

Affirmative Action

The phrase "affirmative action" first appeared as part of the 1935 National Labor Relations Act. Here, it meant that an employer who was found to be discriminating against union members or union organizers would have to stop discriminating, and also take affirmative action to place those victims where they would have been without the discrimination. In civil rights, the term "affirmative action" first appeared in President John F. Kennedy's Executive Order 10925, wedded to this color-blind view of the world. The term was repeated in President Lyndon Johnson's Executive Order 11246. Firms under contract with the federal government were not to discriminate, and were also to "take affirmative action to ensure that employees are treated during employment without regard to their race, creed, color or national origin." Section 706(g) of the Civil Rights Act of 1964 also permitted courts to order "affirmative action" in cases where an employer was "intentionally engaged in" an unlawful practice (the denial of opportunity on the basis of race).

I have taken a position in opposition to Affirmative Action; I believe affirmative action: (1) unfairly discriminates against whites because of their race; (2) compromises many good meritocratic standards; (3) stigmatizes its purported beneficiaries; and (4) using race to distribute benefits deepens racial ways of thinking; instead of moving toward a more colorblind unified society.

[You need to look at how things use to be.]

First, Affirmative Action suggests that equal opportunity in American society is not possible without special advantages or disadvantages to certain groups. This program aimed at achieving a colorblind society is based strictly on ethnicity which is contradictory in itself. African-Americans and females who were at one time victims of discrimination, now inadvertently place Caucasian males in the same disadvantaged position.

[White males are still first hired – last fired – promoted faster and have more net worth than any group in the country – don't worry about them!]

Second, affirmative action suggests that minorities, as a group, are less capable, less hard working, and less committed and therefore need special privileges to succeed. Stephen L. Carter's "Reflections of an Affirmative Action Baby" illustrates his personal experience . . .

"As a senior at Stanford University back in the mid-1970's, I applied to about half a dozen law schools. Yale, where I would ultimately enroll, came through fairly early with an acceptance. So did all but one of the others. The last school, Harvard, dawdled and dawdled. Finally, toward the end of the admission season, I received a letter of rejection. Then, within days, two different Harvard officials and a professor contacted me by telephone to apologize. They were quite frank in their explanation for the 'error.' I was told by one official that the school had initially rejected me because 'we assumed from your record that you were white.' (The words have always stuck in my mind, a tantalizing reminder of what is expected of me.) Suddenly coy, he went on to say that the school had obtained 'additional information that should have been counted in your favor' – that is, Harvard had discovered the color of my skin. And if I had already made a deposit to go elsewhere, well, that, I was told, would 'not be allowed' to stand in my way should I enroll at Harvard. Naturally, I was insulted by this miracle. Stephen Carter, the white male, was not good enough for the Harvard Law School; Stephen Carter, the black male, not only was good enough but rated agonized telephone calls urging him to attend. And Stephen Carter, color unknown, must have been white: How else could he have achieved what he did in college? Except that my college achievements were obviously not sufficiently spectacular to merit acceptance had I been white. In other words, my academic record was too good for a black Stanford University undergraduate, but not good enough for a white Harvard law student. Because I turned out to be black, however, Harvard was quite happy to scrape me from the bottom of the barrel."

Statistics show that women account for fifty-two percent of the population, eighty percent of whom work, but less than ten percent occupy positions in the executive suites. The solution is not to pass laws requiring that fifty percent of these positions be filled by women, but to implement programs that encourage, train, and promote women and other minorities to executive position.

[This is what affirmative action is!]

Thirdly, Affirmative Action suggests that every successful African-American or woman attained their positions through Affirmative Action and similar advantaged programs. This leads to the perception that their success is unearned, but merely given to them on a "silver platter."

Fourthly, using race to distribute benefits deepens racial division. The white male is subject to feelings of hostility toward minorities due to his regression caused by their progression. Discrimination can't possibly end when Affirmative Action can cause an employer to look at two different protected classes and be forced to make a decision on who will be chosen for that job position. An alternative would be basing preexisting affirmative action programs on socioeconomic disadvantages rather than ethnicity.

In conclusion, Affirmative Action has many flawed dimensions. In considering this policy in the future, what is a black female like myself to do when she no longer is considered the minority, and another group becomes the protected class and begins to receive the benefits she feels should also be available to herself? Where are the hopes for future generations in such a society? These factors should have been considered before the policy of Affirmative Action was introduced to society.

[Good argument – I couldn't disagree more.]

M. Lester O'Shea – Personal Background

Education

Harvard Business School, M.B.A. 1963

Oxford University, Fulbright Scholar in politics, philosophy, and economics

Stanford University, B.A. 1959 in economics; Phi Beta Kappa, highest honors

Golden Gate University School of Law, J.D. 1995, highest honors

Governmental, Political and Community

J. William Fulbright Foreign Scholarship Board, Washington, 1987-1980

National Advisory Council on Adult Education, Washington, 1983-1987

Commission on California State Government Organization and Economy, 1984-1988

Presidential elector 1980; Chairman San Francisco Republican County Central Committee; executive committee, California Republican Party; board of governors and executive committee, Commonwealth Club of California

Published Works

Tampering with the Machinery, McGraw-Hill, New York, 1980. Foreword by William E. Simon.

Are the Courts Handcuffing the Police? Commonwealth Club of California study, 1973.

Articles in Human Events, California Political Review, St. Croix Review, Los Angeles Times, San Francisco Chronicle.

Business and Social

Real estate investor and developer, Associated with Pacific Legal Foundation, Sacramento, 1996. Investment banker, New York and San Francisco, 1963-1970. Founder and managing partner, General Western Co., San Francisco, 1967-1988. Member Philadelphia Society, Federalist Society, National Association of Scholars, State Bar of California.

INDEX

BOOKS OF INTEREST

ON

SIMILAR SUBJECTS

Available through all bookstores
or directly from the publisher,

HALLBERG PUBLISHING CORPORATION

P.O. Box 23985 • Tampa, Florida 33623
Phone 1-800-633-7627 • Fax 1-800-253-7323

The following is quoted from one of the seventeen thought provoking essays contained in our new collection of Nock's essays (many of which have never before appeared in book form) entitled, *The Disadvantages of Being Educated.*

───────────── ❧ ─────────────

"When the State has granted one privilege, its character as a purveyor of privilege is permanently established, and natural law does not permit it to stop with the creation of one privilege, but forces it to go on creating others. Once admit a single positive intervention 'to help business,' as our euphemism goes, and one class or group after another will accumulate political power in order to command further interventions; and these interventions will persist in force and frequency until they culminate in a policy of pure Statism – a policy which in turn culminates in the decay and disappearance of the society that invokes it.
"Such is the grim testimony borne by the history of six civilizations, now vanished, to the validity of the law that man tends always to satisfy his needs and desires with the least possible exertion."

– ALBERT J. NOCK
THE GOD'S LOOKOUT, 1934

───────────── ❧ ─────────────

Albert J. Nock (1870-1945) was a radical, in the venerable
sense of the word: one whose ideas cut to the root and make
you think again about things previously taken for granted.

— Edmund A. Opitz

ISBN 0-87319-041-6
224 pages, Trade Paper, $14.95

memoirs of a superfluous man

Albert Jay Nock

"This is the kind of book that gets under a person's skin,
performing catalytically to persuade the reader into
becoming what he has it in him to be."

— Edmund A. Opitz

ISBN 0-87319-038-6
352 pages, Trade Paper, $16.95

An essential history of Colonial America and must reading for students of government and advocates of man's right to Life, Liberty and Property.

ISBN 0-87319-023-8
112 pages, Trade Paper, $9.95

"Albert Jay Nock's Mr. Jefferson, is a superb biographical essay, beautifully written and penetrating in analysis; Mr. Nock understands Jefferson so well that one despairs of going at all beyond him."

Richard Hofstadter
Columbia University

ISBN 0-87319-024-6
224 pages, Trade Paper, $14.95

THE LIBERTARIAN THEOLOGY OF FREEDOM

"Beginning with the 'Great Debate' between Reverend Opitz and the Dean of Faculty at Union Theological Seminary, John Bennett, this is a sterling book of powerful arguments. Ed Opitz could never stomach the one-sided political biases of the seminaries and publications of the mainline churches; yet he retained his civility and his gift for reasoning based on evidence . . . The history of how 'the Social Gospel' captured the mainline churches presented in the Preface is also a gem. If you love to explore alternative views, this book is a wonderful invigorating read."
— MICHAEL NOVAK
   AMERICAN ENTERPRISE INSTITUTE

"Ed Opitz is the dean of a growing school of thought working to reconsider the claims of religious faith and economic freedom . . . this book makes available to a new generation his penetrating insights and passionate commitment to the principle that human dignity is best advanced within a social framework of freedom."
— JEFFREY O. NELSON
   INTERCOLLEGIATE STUDIES INSTITUTE

"No one has done more than Edmund Opitz to show that our political-economic freedoms are not simply compatible with, but thoroughly dependent on, our faith."
— M. STANTON EVANS
   NATIONAL JOURNALISM CENTER

"A must read to better comprehend the important linkage between religious principals and individual liberty."

— RON PAUL

THE
LIBERTARIAN
THEOLOGY
OF
FREEDOM

by

The Reverend

Edmund
A. Opitz

"This book by Rev. Opitz will go a long way to help those in mainline churches appreciate the critical importance of liberty in the construction of a just society. It will disabuse all readers of the notion that to be a libertarian, one must be a libertine."

— FR. ROBERT A. SIRICO
ACTON INSTITUTE FOR THE STUDY OF RELIGION AND LIBERTY

ISBN 0-87319-046-7
160 pages, hardcover, $18.95